MW01029472

ALSO BY CLAIRE HOFFMAN

Greetings from Utopia Park: Surviving a Transcendent Childhood

SISTER, SINNER

SISTER, SINNER

The Miraculous Life and Mysterious Disappearance of Aimee Semple McPherson

CLAIRE HOFFMAN

FARRAR, STRAUS AND GIROUX
NEW YORK

Farrar, Straus and Giroux
120 Broadway, New York 10271

Printed in the United States of America
First edition, 2025

Library of Congress Cataloging-in-Publication Data
Names: Hoffman, Claire (Journalist), author.
Title: Sister, sinner : the miraculous life and mysterious disappearance of Aimee Semple McPherson / Claire Hoffman.
Description: First edition. | New York : Farrar, Straus and Giroux, 2025. | Includes bibliographical references and index.
Identifiers: LCCN 2024035161 | ISBN 9780374601713 (hardcover)
Subjects: LCSH: McPherson, Aimee Semple, 1890–1944. | International Church of the Foursquare Gospel—Biography. | Evangelists—Canada—Biography. | Evangelists—United States—Biography. | LCGFT: Biographies.
Classification: LCC BX7990.I68 H64 2025 | DDC 269/.2092 [B]—dc23/eng/20241026
LC record available at https://lccn.loc.gov/2024035161

Designed by Gretchen Achilles

1 3 5 7 9 10 8 6 4 2

To my husband, from whom I learned unconditional love

To my daughters, whom I strive to teach that they can be powerful women, even in the face of mistakes

And to Aimee, who has taught me the power of belief

CONTENTS

SISTER, SINNER

PROLOGUE: "AND SHE DID NOT COME BACK"

Thirty-five years old and wildly famous, Aimee Semple McPherson greeted her reverent admirers as she escaped her Temple. After just seven years in Los Angeles, Aimee had become the most recognizable woman in a city that was already specializing in fame. Just after lunch on that warm afternoon in May 1926, Aimee was headed for the beach, her sensible heels clicking along the sidewalk toward the parking garage. "God bless you, Sister!" called the devoted chorus of voices that had become a constant in her life.

Behind her, Angelus Temple rose from the sidewalk like the Roman Colosseum—circular, pillared, and vast. Known by locals as "the Million Dollar Temple," it was one of the largest churches built in the history of the world, constructed with the same lavish splendor as the new movie palaces being erected around the city.

Seating almost six thousand people, the groundbreaking megachurch hosted what the papers called the greatest show in town. Aimee regularly hired the most talented set and costume designers from Hollywood to help her make the gospel live and breathe for her followers. Camels, lions, and even a motorcycle had made their way across the planks of her stage. Aimee had built the church through force of will and a supernatural sense of destiny, raising the funds during years of itinerant tent revivals around the nation, each dollar given to her in what she called "love offerings." The building stood as a monument to her: the pioneer of a new global religion.

That morning, Aimee drove to Bullock's, a swanky downtown department store where she bought a dress for her fifteen-year-old daughter and put another on hold for herself. After shopping and a quick meeting at the Temple, Aimee went to pick up her brand-new black Kissel sedan, which some whispered was too splashy an extravagance for a woman of faith. There was a lot of talk in Los Angeles about Aimee and all the money she was making.

The dark side of fame had beset the lady evangelist. As her congregation and fortunes had grown, so too had ominous incidents: obsessed fans showing up in the middle of the night, a madwoman arrested for trying to murder her, and even a botched kidnapping plot.

But earlier that spring something even more frightening had happened to Aimee: widespread whispers of a scandal. A woman had appeared at the Temple and accused Aimee of sleeping with her husband, Kenneth Ormiston, Aimee's chief radio engineer. The woman threatened to go public with her accusations of infidelity if Aimee didn't stop the affair. Aimee had been married twice, but she was a born-again fundamentalist Christian, a pioneering figure of Pentecostalism. To her thousands of followers, she preached a strict moral code—no drinking, no smoking, no swearing, no dancing, no movies, and most certainly no out-of-wedlock sex. For her working-class audience, she conjured a nostalgia for the old-time religion, often costuming herself in a nurse's uniform when she preached. To those who adored her, she was the embodiment of virtue, a living saint: Sister Aimee. The idea of her committing adultery was blasphemous.

As Aimee cruised down the smooth asphalt of Venice Boulevard toward the Pacific, she passed orange groves and fields of flowers. The afternoon light was breaking through the fog that hung over the city in late spring, and Aimee could smell summer coming in the air. As she turned onto Pico Boulevard, construction sent her in the wrong direction. For a few minutes, the evangelist was lost. But she'd been down to Venice Beach three times that week, and she soon found her way to the Ocean View Hotel. She was accompanied by her dutiful, perpetually anxious secretary, Emma Schaeffer.

At approximately one o'clock in the afternoon, the women entered the beachfront hotel at the corner of Rose Avenue and Ocean Front Walk. They were escorted upstairs by the manager, to room 202. In recent weeks, Aimee had become a bit of a regular there, trying to take more time for herself. She would reserve a room for the day, then head to the beach to work on her sermons under an umbrella, taking breaks to swim in the bay.

Once in room 202, Aimee changed into an emerald-green bathing suit and cap, put on a robe, and padded downstairs in her bare feet. Her secretary remained fully clothed, in a dark, floor-length dress, complete with corset and collar. Emma couldn't swim. With a sweet, mousy face, she revered Aimee and would do anything for her, but she herself wasn't the sort to walk around in public in a suit and robe.

The two women walked a few blocks to the oceanfront Lick Pier, where the Giant Dipper roller coaster rattled along metal rails. There they ate their favorite treat—a single waffle, served on wax paper from a hot fryer. At two o'clock in the afternoon, they rented an umbrella and pitched it in front of the hotel.

The day was pleasant, calm, sunny, sixty-eight degrees. As the sun blazed down, Aimee focused on her Bible, working on her sermon for the next Sunday. She scrawled down the title, "Light and Darkness," in her notebook and sat with the words. She let their meaning—the ancient duality and symbiosis of the two elements—suffuse her. She felt the waves themselves were delivering her a sermon—on the world and all its contradictions. "It had been that way since the beginning," she wrote. "The glint of the sun, gleaming light, on the tops, and shadow, darkness in the troughs. Ah, light and darkness all over the earth, everywhere."[1] Wasn't the world made of opposites and contradictions? Wasn't she?

Aimee flipped the Bible's worn pages to the first chapter of Genesis. "And God said, Let there be light; and there was light . . . And God divided the light from the darkness." The sea was glassy smooth, the waves gentle. Aimee spent the next hour scratching out ideas about good and evil in the Bible, in the world, and in one's self.

At three o'clock, Aimee announced to Emma: "I'm going to take a little dip."

Bible in hand, Emma watched her boss swim back and forth in the surf for ten minutes or so. In the 1920s, a woman swimming alone was an odd sight and likely seemed dangerous to onlookers. "The horizon beckons me," Aimee had once told a concerned lifeguard. Although Emma was used to Aimee's fearlessness, she kept an eye on her. When Aimee finished, she trotted up from the water and playfully dripped on her secretary.

"Was the water cold?" Emma asked.

"Not a bit," Aimee said. "Feel me."

Emma felt her boss's arm and found it "just as warm as could be."

Wrapped in her robe, Aimee briefly went back to work on her sermon. Her mood was dreamy. Amid the beauty and hushed reverie of the beach, her mind rested on all that was happening back at the Temple. On the page, she drew a small sun.

Around 3:30 p.m., Aimee asked her secretary to call the Temple and tell them she would be late. She gave instructions for that evening's sermon: a slideshow depicting her recent trip to Palestine, with accompanying music. Emma went to the drugstore to call the church.[2]

Aimee set down her notes on the towel and made her way back to the water. She left behind her Bible and a purse containing $200 in neatly rolled bills (more than $3,500 today). She began to swim again, this time away from the shore, toward the horizon. Emma made the call, fetched the juice and box of candy that Aimee had requested, and returned to the baking sand to wait.

Fifteen minutes passed before Emma started to worry that something was wrong—she was sure she had seen Aimee gesturing to her from the water when she'd returned to their towels. She had assumed her boss was teasing her, suggesting Emma bring the cold juice into the depths that Aimee knew Emma couldn't navigate. Had she imagined that? She anxiously watched the ocean as other swimmers returned to shore. Emma's view of the water was unobstructed.

As the sun lowered, Emma paced the shoreline. She still couldn't spot Aimee. Anxiously, she asked two boys coming out of the water if they'd seen the evangelist, describing the bright green of her suit, the brown shade of her bathing cap. She found a lifeguard and told him that the most important woman in the world was missing. The guard responded, "Well, it doesn't make any difference to us, the name of a person; one life is just as precious to us as another." Still, he quickly gathered a group of lifeguards, and they made their way into the ocean. Someone set out in a small rowboat. Emma began to cry. She begged the hotel manager to help her. The waves pounded the shore. All the swimmers had left the ocean.

At 4:20 p.m., the manager called the police.

From the hotel, Emma called Angelus Temple, demanding that Aimee's mother, Minnie Kennedy, come to the phone immediately. Emma couldn't get the words out at first, she wept so hard. "She has disappeared in the water, and I can't find her," she stammered. The manager of the hotel took the phone to speak to Mother Kennedy, as Aimee's mother was known in the press—an established, locally famous power broker and show mother. "I believe you know that Sister McPherson came down with Miss Schaeffer this afternoon to take a swim. It is now nearly five o'clock and we have not been able to find her." Mother Kennedy's response was curt. "She is drowned," she responded.

"Oh, no," protested the manager, surprised at the fatalistic conclusion. "No, no she is not drowned, as far as I know. But up to this time we have not been able to find her," he said. "You'd better come down."

"Do all you can," Aimee's mother said firmly. "I don't think it would do any good to come down. Have the car sent in and get her belongings."[3]

In the cool of the May evening, word spread as if by magic that one of the city's most famous residents had vanished. Curiosity seekers and the faithful swarmed the Venice sand. Emma was in a daze, completely distraught. A temple member was deputized to retrieve the secretary and the car and bring them back downtown. At dusk, Emma searched the parsonage apartment for Minnie, to comfort her and share in her grief. But Minnie was gone: she was already onstage.

Inside Angelus Temple, the pews were packed, the sacred space hushed and dark. At the rostrum, Minnie and her granddaughter, Roberta, stood with their hands clasped tightly. They presented Aimee's planned lantern slideshow of her recent trip to Palestine. On the screen, tinted photographs of biblical landscapes were interspersed with images of Aimee touring the Holy Land. The evangelist was the slow-motion star as the images showed her visiting the River Jordan where Christ was baptized, the mount upon which he was crucified. It was a commingling of past and present, Aimee inserted seamlessly into the procession of Christian history. For her audience this was logical: Aimee was a modern-day saint.

The newspaper reporters who had tiptoed into the front row to take notes on the tragedy were transfixed by the scene, by young Roberta, who wore a "flowing biblical dress" as she kept her voice "strong and without an outward taint of sorrow." From beyond the thick walls of the Temple, the shrieks of newsboys on the sidewalk could be heard: "Aimee McPherson believed drowned!" When the song ended, sharp cries and stifled sobs echoed through the audience.

The slideshow finished. Minnie led Roberta to the front of the podium. She took her hand and turned to the people who filled the audience. "This is Roberta, children," she said. "She will carry on the work of her mother for God." Roberta smiled sadly as her grandmother continued. "The body may sleep at the bottom of the sea—but the soul goes marching on," she told them. She recounted Aimee's life, filled with miraculous healings, the hard work of converting the unbelieving, of her travel to heathen lands, all her singular achievements, and above all, the connection to God's love that she'd given to so many.

"Never was there a touch of intimacy in her references of her daughter," reported the *Los Angeles Examiner* the next day. "Always, it was a eulogy for one whom she believed walked in the footsteps of the Savior and whom she believed at that moment was in his ministering embrace."

Minnie described the last few hours of that day: Aimee's swim, her disappearance, and then the terrible phone call. Finally, with the first tremble in her voice, raising Roberta's hand up, Minnie shouted: "It is God's work. And she did not come back."

Cries and shrieks reverberated among the thousands congregated, their voices transported out into the night via the in-house radio station, KFSG, which was broadcasting the service across Southern California. Minnie shouted from the stage: "She is with Jesus—pray for her!"[4]

By dawn the next day, five thousand people crowded the sands of Venice Beach. Two airplanes flew overhead, scanning the coast. A dozen rowboats bobbed in the waves, with divers probing the depths. Farther out, motorboats used grappling hooks to rake the deeper reaches of the ocean. Police boats cast seine nets through the waves. There was speculation that Aimee's body could have been pushed by the currents under Lick Pier, where a roller coaster had fallen into the ocean two years before, creating a gnarled metal trap for swimmers. A squadron of police and U.S. Coast Guard members scoured the ocean from Venice to Topanga Canyon.

The waves grew larger as the day wore on. Each time a boat returned to the shore, a horde of Aimee's followers mobbed the vessel, demanding news. When a floating object was mistaken for the evangelist's body, officers rushed to quell the frenzied crowds. Riot police were called to stand guard in front of the Ocean View Hotel. The devoted formed prayer circles, sang hymns, and passed around binoculars.

The chaos intensified; a twenty-six-year-old diver died of hypothermia after his equipment failed him in the cold ocean depths. A woman, a disciple, floundered into the ocean, saying she wanted to meet the evangelist in death. She quickly did. The crowds grew during the week, and by the weekend, according to some newspaper counts, twenty thousand people had amassed on the shoreline, praying for a miracle.

In the weeks that followed, the search for Aimee's body continued, with Los Angeles's burgeoning newspapers covering the story constantly. The city and the world were caught up in the incredible story of the vanished lady evangelist. Each day, the front pages printed new photos of the search teams and Aimee's children looking brave, her followers weeping. They even ran an odd photo of Minnie photographed down by the shore with a half smile, standing next to Ormiston, Aimee's rumored lover. He was away when she disappeared and rushed back into town to put to rest the rumors that he had run away with her. The papers were happy to print every fresh theory of a kidnapping or an affair and even daily testimonials of sightings, as people up and down the California coast reported catching a glimpse of Sister Aimee.

Inside the thick walls of Angelus Temple, Aimee's mother tried to ignore the buzz of madness in the pews, out on the sidewalks, in the newspapers. As May became June, she tried to put aside the deluge of mail and telegrams, filled with detailed and conflicting accounts of her daughter's whereabouts. She half-heartedly met with police officers and detectives, and she smiled sadly for the cameras.

Her attempts to move forward were stymied when she received a ransom letter from a group of kidnappers who said they had taken her daughter. They described alarmingly accurate and intimate details about Aimee. Calling themselves "the Avengers," they said they had taken the evangelist in retribution for her fight against the LA underworld, and they demanded a half-million-dollar payout. Included in the envelope was a greasy hank of auburn hair. Minnie rolled the hair through her hands but told investigators she was sure the claim was a fraud. "I would look at the letter and the hair and pray for light," Minnie would later recall.[5] "None came."

By mid-June Minnie spent her days planning Aimee's funeral, a massive commemoration of the most important woman in the world. During those long nights, Minnie slept uneasily, the hank of hair under her pillow.

But in her wildest dreams, Minnie could not have conjured what would come next—the dark and demented frenzy of scandal that would soon consume her, her famous daughter, and their legacy. How could she have imagined that their story, starting in the cool shade of their little Canadian farm, with its soft grass, its fresh milk, and the simple clarity of the gospel, would somehow intersect with the sinister forces of the Los Angeles underworld, with the frenzied powers of the media, with the corrosive shine of fame, and with the rabid public that was desperate for the truth? For Aimee Semple McPherson would not rest in peace.

PART I

RISE

How marvelous that our God shrouds the future with an impenetrable cloud, drops a veil over all the to-morrows of our lives that not one of us may know what a day nor an hour will bring forth! Marvelous, and infinitely kind; for if we knew all that the future held, we might not always have the stamina to march on. Resolution might falter, courage might swoon at the fantastic monsters and the hooded goblins that lay just ahead.

—Aimee Semple McPherson,
In the Service of the King

1

PROPHETIC BEGINNING

Just weeks after her baby was born, Mildred "Minnie" Kennedy bundled up little Aimee and marched through the wilderness of southwestern Ontario, ignoring her in-laws, who screamed at the nineteen-year-old mother that she'd lost her mind. "You'll kill that baby! You don't know anything about a baby!" Undeterred, Minnie headed to her beloved Salvation Army Barracks, where she brought the squalling infant to the altar and promised the heavens that this being would be an exemplary soldier who would "spend all its life in Salvation War."[1] On that late fall day in 1890, the church filled with shouts and victory cries. Outside, the Christian soldiers fired three volleys into the air. Minnie glowed with purpose and joy. She had given Aimee "fully for the Salvation of the world."

Minnie had found meaning in her own life when she joined the Salvation Army at the age of twelve, just seven years before. With the motto of "soup, soap and salvation," the Army preached a gospel that emphasized tending to the earthly needs of people, offering them the chance to accept Jesus and find salvation wherever they were at that moment in life. The Army brought an immense energy and theatricality to its evangelism. With its loud and catchy songs, the Army's pageantry and conviction gave Minnie the promise of an empowered life; she dropped out of school and spent her days surrounded by Salvationists, cleaning the group's barracks in the city of London, Ontario. Within a few months of her conversion, Minnie's mother died.[2] Minnie begged for the Salvation Army soldiers to let her stay with them. They agreed, making a miniature uniform for the tiny little girl and teaching her to play the trombone in their parades.[3]

At the age of fourteen, money pressures necessitated that Minnie find a paying job. She went to work for James Kennedy, a farmer and bridge builder who lived with his adult son and his sickly wife. In less than a month, his wife was dead. Scandalously, Minnie quickly became her widower boss's very young bride. His children were not pleased to have the teenage maid become their stepmother: Minnie was fifteen and James was fifty, although they both lied about their age on the marriage certificate. Alienated inside her new family, Minnie mourned the loss of meaning she'd had with the Army and prayed to the heavens that she would have a daughter who would fulfill her own thwarted ambition to do divine work.[4] Aimee's published recollections of her childhood frequently hint at some unsaid darkness between her own father and mother, but she never explains it. She describes her mother's feelings about married life on a farm as a "grind in the prison house." When mentioned at all, her father is depicted as akin to the biblical Joseph: old, tired, and not as important as Jesus.

Minnie relied on the Salvation Army as the main source of community and excitement for herself and her daughter. They attended weekly meetings and sang hymns together each night. Minnie worked as "Junior-Sergeant-Major" for the Army, running the local Sunday school for children. The Kennedy farm was five miles from the Army headquarters. Minnie would walk through rain and snow on a series of country roads to do the lessons, or, on sunny days, plunk young Aimee on her handlebars and ride her bicycle to work.

Aimee wrote with sentimental warmth of her childhood home in Salford, in a two-story gabled Victorian farmhouse covered in vines next to an apple orchard. Nicknamed "Kozy-Kot," their farm was a place where Christian values were lived in earnest—even though

James was a Methodist and Minnie was a Salvationist, they agreed on the basics of a virtuous life. There was no drinking or smoking, no dancing or secular music. Aimee, though, was a whimsical child, and her father indulged her with music and books. Minnie bottled cider from their orchard and sold it in town, always stashing away a little money to buy her daughter pretty clothes. Economically, they did well and were regarded locally as an "up and coming family."[5] In Aimee's telling, her childhood was almost like a parable, filled with the word of God and hard work. On the farm, she gathered water from the well, carried wood for the stove, and helped care for the animals. By all accounts, Aimee's father left the parenting to his intense young wife.

Largely isolated on the farm, Aimee spent her days playing church, arranging her playthings into a congregation as she preached and sang to them. She admired her mother and always took on Minnie's official-sounding title, demanding her imaginary congregants call her "Sergeant-Major." By the time she was five years old, Aimee knew much of the Bible by heart. When she entered "the little white school-house," Aimee was intent on being at the top of the class. As an only child, she was deeply competitive and a bit of a know-it-all, according to her own recollections. But she was also a natural leader, organizing group activities and debates. When her classmates mocked her for being a part of the Salvation Army, she made a drum set from a metal cheese box and a ruler, and soon, according to Aimee, she had her detractors following her around the schoolyard as she banged the drum, pantomiming the very thing they'd mocked.

Aimee sought out opportunities for performance. By the time she was in high school, she became an elocutionist, reciting verse in school and performing skits at her father's Methodist church. She later wrote that she and several friends considered taking to the stage, "so turned were our silly heads by the applause of the people."[6] As a teenager, Aimee was thriving: pretty and popular. She flourished socially—attending church oyster specials, strawberry festivals, and sewing circles.

Caught up in the social whirlwind, teenage Aimee worried that she had lost her connection to God and that she'd become too worldly, too caught up in hedonistic entertainment and ideas. "Ah sin," she would later lament. "With what dazzling beauty, with what refinement and velvet dost thou cover thy claws! How alluring are the fair promises with which thou enticest the feet of youth! How cunning are the devices of the enemy!"[7]

For Aimee, that enemy was partially hiding in the guise of her public-school education, where she learned new ideas that led her to question the literal truth of the Bible—like the theory of evolution. *On the Origin of Species* was published in 1859 in Canada, and four decades later, as Aimee was enrolled in high school, it was taught as a textbook across North America. Aimee wrote later of her conversation with her science teacher, who insisted that Charles Darwin was correct, and that mankind had evolved from the muck and mire of the ocean through thousands of years of evolution, from fish to primates—not in a matter of days, as described in Genesis:

> "Tell me," I pleaded, "which is right; my schoolbook or my Bible?"
>
> "Little girl," the high school teacher answered as he looked down from his superior height, "your Bible is a wonderful book, as a classic of English literature it has no rival, but . . ."
>
> "Yes," I was all eagerness, "tell me."
>
> "But as for Genesis, the story of creation, and like passages, I'm sorry to say they are not only untrue but ridiculous."
>
> "The story of creation not true?"
>
> "It is merely a myth."[8]

Aimee was shaken. The notion that the Bible did not contain a true account of the beginning of the world was a radical undermining of all she had been taught. In sermons later, she would recall the searing pain of the doubt caused by Darwin's teachings, a moment when she saw the possibility of her worldview shifting—of moving away from God. "I had a feeling that the ground had opened up and swallowed me. I was falling down, down, down, down into a black coal chute where leering specters jeered, 'There is no God! There is no heaven! There is no hell! If the Scriptures tell one lie, they must leak like a sieve! Now where's your faith? Now where's your faith?'"[9]

By the time she had turned seventeen, she had even developed a skepticism about religion that shamed her in front of her parents. "I was overwhelmed by disturbing doubts,"[10] she wrote. At home, she kept those doubts largely hidden from her mother, even as her own state of mind became increasingly tempestuous and confused.

All that doubt vanished one night in December 1907, when James Kennedy took his seventeen-year-old daughter to theater rehearsal in their horse-drawn sleigh. She was in high spirits, admiring the town's store windows decorated in green and red tinsel. She planned to practice a holiday skit she had written, casting herself in the lead role. She was giddy as they passed a small white church. She had read in the town newspaper about the "Holy Ghost" revival that had come to town, and she asked her father to stop. James worried that Minnie would disapprove of attending the services of a fringe faith that catered to the lower class, but he had trouble saying no to his daughter. The idea, she pleaded with him, would be just to have a laugh as they watched some hokey itinerant preacher and the ragtag locals act out a weird religious practice. She'd heard of Holy Rollers—Christians so named because they writhed on the floor, their bodies overtaken by the Holy Spirit. Aimee wanted to see the spectacle for herself.

"Daddy, I'd like to go in there tomorrow night. I believe that's the place I have heard about where they jump and dance and fall under the power and do such strange things. It would be loads of fun to go and see them," she begged.[11]

Her father relented, and the following night, they stepped inside and slid into the last pew. Aimee looked about with delight, observing the farmers and dairy workers shouting out a chorus of "Amen" and "Hallelujah" from the pews. She smiled with a sense of superiority, her fashionable hat bedecked with flowers and a golden locket hanging from her neck. "None of the wealthy or well-known citizens of the town were there. Dressed as I was in worldly attire with my foolish little heart filled with unbelief and egotism, I felt just a little bit above the status of those round about me and looked on with an amused air as they sang, shouted, testified and prayed."

Then the preacher stepped to the front of the church, a six-foot-two-inch-tall Irishman, with long, delicate hands, Aimee noticed as he pushed a forelock of dark hair out of the way to reveal bright blue eyes. Aimee felt a physical jolt. She was spellbound as, at the pulpit, the preacher drew a harsh line with his words, shouting out that the world was made up of two kinds of people—saints and sinners. The easy slide into sin that he described included everyday Christians who went to church on Sunday and then spent the rest of the week embracing worldly pleasures such as dancing, singing, ice-skating, going to the motion pictures, and listening to "rag time" music. This sinful life he painted was exactly Aimee's—her everyday vanities and pleasures were cast in the sharp relief of this handsome man's words. "Why, it just looked as if somebody had told him I was there, so vividly did he picture my own life and walk."

She felt a shock of recognition and guilt as he shouted out "Repent! Repent! Repent!" from the small wooden platform. "You must be born again!"

Those words, Aimee would recall, were like arrows into her heart. "He really spoke as though he believed there was a Jesus and a Holy Spirit, not some vague, mythical, intangible shadow, something away off yonder in the clouds, but a real, living, vital, tangible, moving reality dwelling in our hearts and lives . . ."

Aimee had been raised in a Christian home, with biblical truth as an explanation for every experience. Every challenge that presented itself in the teenage girl's short life had been viewed through the lens of the New Testament. But this man was doing something different: he seemed to collapse time and space with his words—forming a new reality before her eyes. As he told it, Jesus was alive and present—so close Aimee could feel him on her skin.

Aimee watched, riveted, as the young man at the front of the room closed his eyes. She felt he stretched his arms out right in her direction. He began to speak in another voice, deep and uncanny, with sounds and syntax that Aimee could not recognize. She knew in that instant that his voice had become the voice of God, a voice speaking directly to her, saying "YOU are a poor, lost, miserable, hell-deserving sinner!"

She watched as people fell to the floor and made wild sounds she didn't understand, their bodies seemingly electrocuted by the preacher's words. Aimee felt as if a light were shining on her. The Irishman's condemnation of her sinful state, the description of herself as adrift and damned—it all rang true. "No one had ever spoken to me like this before. I had been petted, loved and perhaps a little spoiled: told how smart and good I was." For Aimee, the preacher had held up an enchanted mirror, and she had seen herself for the first time.

"Oh, how could I have looked down upon these dear people and felt that I was better than they? Why, I was not even worthy to black their shoes. They were saints and I was a sinner," she later wrote.[12]

Historians have described the spread of Pentecostalism in America as a cyclone, with an eye that formed in Topeka, Kansas, on January 1, 1901. On that day, in a rented Victorian mansion, a group of believers full of hope for the new century gathered around a young woman and shouted out for God to enter her body. The believers were led by Charles Fox Parham, a mustachioed Iowan with a taste for the mystical. Parham had spent the previous decade traveling around the United States, seeking experiences in Holiness camps—a nineteenth-century phenomenon that emerged out of the Methodist tradition. The Holiness movement emphasized salvation through a personal connection to Jesus, and as the century drew to a close there were many Christians who eagerly awaited the biblical Second Coming.

Parham ran into a missionary at a commune in Maine who told him a story that would change his life forever: evangelists in far-flung outposts around the globe had witnessed newly baptized Christians falling into a sudden trance and speaking in strange, unknown languages. Parham was jubilant—he knew immediately that these trances were a sign of the Second Coming. He recognized the behavior as glossolalia, or speaking in tongues, depicted in a single passage in the Bible in Chapter Two of Acts. Parham recalled the description of the Pentecost, the dinner that took place after the death of Jesus, when the apostles and Jesus's mother, Mary, gathered to share a meal in the room where the Last Supper may have taken place. It read:

And when the day of Pentecost was fully come, they were all with one accord in one place
And suddenly there came a sound from heaven as of a rushing mighty wind, and it filled all the house where they were sitting
And there appeared unto them cloven tongues like as of fire, and it sat upon each of them
And they were all filled with the Holy Ghost, and began to speak with other tongues, as the Spirit gave them utterance.[13]

For Parham, these stories of people speaking in tongues confirmed a deep spiritual suspicion: he was living in the apostolic age, a time when the divine was active and alive in the world and special gifts were bestowed upon chosen true believers. Parham returned to his home in Topeka and set up a Bible school in an abandoned eighteen-room Victorian mansion, where he immersed his three dozen students in Holiness teaching, faith healing, and the belief that they were chosen to usher in a new millennium. They called this new sect Pentecostalism. In these early days, the four gifts of Pentecostalism were defined as glossolalia, prophecy, the interpretation of tongues, and the power to heal.

For many evangelical Christians, the turn of the calendar page to the new century was infused with anxious foreboding and a sense of biblical import. Parham's congregants believed that Jesus's return to the earth was imminent, and the signs of his arrival were everywhere. This gave his movement an urgency, and the sense that all the chaos and change in the world had been foretold in Scripture.

On that New Year's Day, Parham laid his hands on a thirty-one-year-old woman named Agnes Ozman. The small crowd of believers gathered around. The woman begged Parham to bring forth a baptism of "the Holy Spirit." Her words were echoed by those around her, soft prayers in unison for a divine sign. According to those gathered, Ozman began to spontaneously speak a language she had never heard or studied—she would later say it was "bohemian," but Parham insisted it was "Chinese," although there was no one present who spoke Mandarin or Cantonese. But Ozman's experience was transformative, and soon Parham and the others were also struck with the same gift, crying out and speaking in the unknown tongue. Word spread quickly about the strange behavior. Neighbors complained, telling the newspapers that "they sing and shout and yell and moan until life is a burden to those living in that part of town."[14] Locals dubbed Parham's school the Tower of Babel.

Many saw this as blasphemous behavior, but Parham began to travel around the United States, leading revivals and teaching about these miraculous gifts. For these early believers, there was a radical supernatural importance to the experiences they were having in church. These gifts were seen not just as a vital and personal experience with God but as a sign of the end-times and the coming restoration of Christ's kingdom on earth. For those who were there, it elevated their sense of themselves as divinely chosen actors at a pivotal moment in history. As born-again apostles, they avoided the modern world—fashionable dress, dancing, card playing, secular music, movies, drugs or alcohol. Parham preached that the connection between the individual and the divine was direct and personal. Still, few of his congregants experienced the gifts of glossolalia. Around the world, including at a mission for girls in India, there were accounts of spontaneous baptisms of the spirit. But the experiences were scattered, rare.

All that changed with William J. Seymour. In the fall of 1905, Parham set up a free Bible school in Houston. Parham, who had a complicated and conflicted relationship with race, invited a few African American men to hear him lecture—but he made them sit outside, in accordance with the Jim Crow laws of the time.[15] One of those students listening through the doorway was Seymour, a short, stocky, charismatic man who was blind in one eye. Born in Centerville,

Louisiana, to parents who had been emancipated from slavery, he had worked as a train porter. But since boyhood, he had been subject to divine visions. As an adult, he joined a Holiness church, which taught that along with conversion, sanctification through a physical experience was required for entry to heaven. Seymour, according to his later writings, listened through the doorway and was energized by the preacher's concept of sanctification of the spirit through a personal and physical experience with the Holy Spirit. Soon, Seymour began to preach this doctrine of Holy Ghost baptism. He was not a fire and brimstone preacher but rather made an impact with his profound devotion. A white woman from California heard him preach and was so moved that she invited him to come to her Holiness church. "It was the divine call that brought me from Houston, Texas, to Los Angeles," Seymour would later write. "The Lord sent the means."[16]

The following year, in the spring of 1906, Seymour traveled to a tumbledown old stable house on Azusa Street in downtown Los Angeles. Soon after Seymour began preaching about the gifts of the Holy Spirit, attendees began to speak in this strange manner, falling to the ground, wailing in ecstasy, and laying hands on one another to heal broken bodies and disease.

Seymour preached night after night for weeks. The crowd that filled the building and the streets outside was interracial, interdenominational, and exuberant. One participant observed that the color line had been "washed away in blood." Ten days into the revival, on April 18, 1906, a massive earthquake struck San Francisco. Newspaper headlines detailed the horrors: thousands dead, devastating fires, the city reduced to rubble. At the Azusa Street mission, all this was seen as evidence of an extraordinary moment of global transformation—the earth moved under their feet as powerful aftershocks roiled the state.

The *Los Angeles Times* would report that "the devotees of the weird doctrine practice the most fanatical rites, preach the wildest theories and work themselves into a state of mad excitement in their peculiar zeal. Colored people and a sprinkling of whites compose the congregation, and night is made hideous in the neighborhood by the howlings of the worshippers, who spend hours swaying forth and back in a nerve-racking attitude of prayer and supplication."[17]

The history of global religion changed with the Azusa Street revivals. Established Protestant leaders and the newspapers of the day pushed back against the boisterous form of worship, opining about the lack of decorum and the interracial crowds. All the major religious institutions dismissed the new sect as a singular and vanishing oddity. They couldn't have been more wrong. After steady incremental growth in the first half of the twentieth century, Pentecostalism then exploded in the 1970s. By the twenty-first century, it became the fastest-growing sect of Christianity with an estimated 650 million practitioners around the globe, a quarter of the world's Christians.

But in 1907, just six years after that cyclone in Kansas and one year after Azusa, word had spread around the United States that the power of God was being felt and seen in downtown Los Angeles. A man named William H. Durham, a thirty-three-year-old pastor from Chicago, heard about the Azusa revivals and soon took a train to California. On March 2, Durham spoke in tongues as Seymour stood over him and prophesied that he would be a leader in ushering in the Holy Spirit's return to earth. Durham returned to Chicago and transformed his North Avenue Mission into a hub for midwestern Pentecostalism. One day, a young Irishman showed up in his church.

Robert James Semple was an intense man who had left the family farm in a small village in northern Ireland in 1898 and sailed to New York, in search of adventure at the age of seventeen. After living in America for a decade, he'd made his way to Illinois and worked his way up to a position as a salesclerk at the Marshall Field's department store. Living in Chicago, he visited Durham's North Avenue Mission, and it was then that Semple received the gift of the tongues. He vowed to spend his life as an evangelist, spreading the message that the Holy Spirit was immediately accessible to all. He began to preach while working odd jobs as he traveled north to Canada, where on that snowy night at the end of 1907, he shouted out about the gifts of the Pentecost to the wide-eyed seventeen-year-old Aimee Kennedy.

From the last pew, her eyes on the handsome preacher, Aimee

experienced a religious rebirth. And she fell madly in love. Semple seemed an embodiment of everything true to this "little country girl" whose memories of that fateful night would be always of girlhood vanished, and salvation found. "I had never heard such a sermon," Aimee later wrote. "Using his Bible as a sword, he cleft the whole world in two." Aimee understood that she could no longer toy around with Christmas plays and oyster suppers at church. There was no time or space for a trivial life. For Aimee, Robert's words pierced the fog of her teenage mind. It was like someone had at last turned the lights on. "That man certainly believed and meant what he said. It was as though he drew a straight line down the center of the universe, placing God on one side and the devil on the other, lining everybody up—sinners on the one side and saints on the other."[18]

2

THIS IS THAT

"Come on, Daddy, let's go," she said to her father, overwhelmed and unable to handle the intensity of her feelings. They tiptoed out, leaving the chaos of the church behind. In the days afterward Aimee threw away her ragtime music, her dancing pumps, her novels. She tossed them all into the iron stove in the dining room and lit a match to burn away the trappings of sin. "Invisible hands had reached out and were shaking my soul," she recalled.[1] Her parents ran inside from the barn where they'd been working, thinking there was a fire, but Aimee calmly announced that she had been converted. She saw everything in a fresh light: God was alive right here, right now, all around. She had been a frivolous and sinful creature, but no longer. "No more putting glue in teacher's chair or helping to lock him in the gymnasium or practicing dance steps in the corridors at noon hour. A wonderful change had taken place—all old things had passed away and all things had become new. I had been born again and was a new creature in Christ Jesus."[2]

Aimee began to pray constantly. She craved the mystical power of the unknown, the sense that she was like those early Christians. She willed the Holy Spirit to come down into her, to infuse her and lead her to speak in tongues. She also began to have ideas of preaching—just like Robert Semple.

"Mother, do women ever preach the gospel?" Aimee recalled asking Minnie one night as she did the ironing.

"No, dear."

"Why?"

"Oh you and your whys! Well, Eve, the mother of all living, was the first transgressor."

"But if a woman was the first to bring sin into the world, why should she not be the first to take it out again?" Aimee responded smartly.

Minnie ran the iron over the pillowcases in silence.

Finally, she responded: "I don't know."[3]

Minnie watched Aimee's fervor with growing concern. She did not like her daughter's manic enthusiasm, the overzealous way she began to speak about Jesus, the questions about the way they lived their lives. While Minnie saw herself as an enthusiastic Salvation Army soldier, the physical wildness of the Pentecostals frightened her. She forbade her daughter to return to the church. But Aimee began to leave school early, sneaking out to attend Robert's prayer service.

Aimee became entirely focused on speaking in tongues. If she received the gift of glossolalia, then it would mean that Jesus was alive inside of her. She wanted this desperately, an intense longing that she wrote of later as heartfelt and extreme. "Oh, Lord, I am so hungry for your Holy Spirit," she pled. "I am so hungry for Him I can't wait another day. I will not eat another meal until you baptize me."[4]

One morning, Aimee awoke early after being stranded at another Pentecostal woman's house during a snowstorm. She had been unable to return home, nor contact her mother. She went to the window, frosted over with ice, and looked out on the farmland coated in snow. Shivering, she began to pray again. "Lord, fill me!" she begged. "Fill me that I may serve Thee." Her voice, her entire being, was an urgent plea. Then she felt a quietness come over her body and envelop her.

She heard a voice inside her head speak to her with exquisite tenderness. "Child, cease your strivings and your begging; just begin to praise Me, and in simple, child-like faith, receive ye the Holy Ghost."[5]

Aimee felt a force enter her. She knew she was being overtaken. Her mouth began to form sounds and words she did not know. She was speaking in tongues! "Joy like the billows of the sea swept over me," she wrote two decades later. "The fountains of the deep were broken up, my soul was flooded with an indescribable joy." She wrote that she felt physically charged, "until my whole body was atremble with the holy spirit. I did not consider this at all strange as I knew how the batteries we experimented with in the laboratory at college hummed and shook and trembled under the power of electricity." During this ecstatic awakening she vowed to be an evangelist, to serve as an agent of this mysterious and living force. She wanted everyone to experience and know this rapturous state of love, and the incredible assurance of God living inside of you. "The Lord filled me full that day—full to overflowing—and at last took my tongue and spoke through me in a language I have never learned."[6]

Aimee described the feeling of her body being physically transformed. "The cords of my throat began to twitch, my chin began to quiver, and then to shake violently, but oh, so sweetly! My tongue began to move up and down and sideways in my mouth. Unintelligible sounds as of stammering lips and another tongue, spoken of in Isaiah 28:11, began to issue from my lips."[7]

From that moment on, Aimee saw herself as a figure whose fate was part of a larger Christian epic. As the strange sounds and motion took over her, her sense of herself shifted. While she'd always been told she was the fulfillment of her mother's wish, and that she had been dedicated to Christian service at a young age, Aimee now had physical evidence that God was choosing her. From then on, she lived with a voice inside her head, the voice of God that spoke directly to her and guided her actions, large and small.

Aimee was exhilarated as she made her way home in the melting snow. She regaled her parents with her vivid experience of the divine. She was giddy, elated, a teenager whose world had been lit on fire. "How happy I was, oh, how happy! Happy just to feel His wonderful power taking control of my being," she recalled.[8]

But Aimee's encounter moved her mother from concern to fury. Aimee and Minnie had butted heads over small things such as Aimee's clothes or her love of theater, but religion was the center of their home and their connection; their view of the world was tightly intertwined. Minnie disapproved of this unseemly new form of Christianity. To make things worse, Minnie had received a note that week from the high school saying her daughter was suddenly falling behind, often not even showing up to school, skipping classes to go pray at the Pentecostal mission. Probably even more embarrassing, Minnie was visited by a church officer and told that her daughter, the girl who had been celebrated as prophesied, was behaving in a manner unbecoming to a Salvation Army warrior. "Mother scolded and cried and almost broke her heart over her daughter," Aimee wrote later, "who had, as she supposed, been cast under some dire spell by those 'awful' people."

Minnie forbade Aimee to go back to the church, telling her that if she returned to the Pentecostal mission, she would not be allowed to attend high school. "Those things were only for the Apostolic days. I will look up the scriptures and prove it to you when you get home tonight."[9]

Clever and filled with conviction, she told her mother that she would drop her new faith—but only if her mother could show Aimee that the Bible said these divine gifts were false. That January morning, with the breakfast dishes around her, Minnie pulled out her pencil, a sheet of paper, and her Bible. As Aimee walked out the door for school, Minnie went to work, searching for evidence to prove her daughter wrong.

When Aimee returned at five-thirty that afternoon, she found her mother seated at the table, the dishes still dirty. Minnie looked up at Aimee, stunned, her eyes red. Aimee was right, she said. As Minnie had returned to the well-worn pages, she had been shocked to discover an abundance of Scripture that supported her daughter's newfound idea of miraculous divine gifts coming amid the last days.

Minnie had spent her day reading of how before Jesus returned to earth, the world would be filled with decadence and a loss of spiritual integrity—a description of the world that sounded shockingly familiar to her in 1907. This worldview, called premillennialism, was a foundational concept for Pentecostals, asserting that they were living in the time just before Jesus would return to earth for a thousand-year reign. Those who understood this timeline and accepted the spiritual awakening and divine gifts would be tasked with ushering in a new millennium.

Minnie looked up at her daughter, the enormity of this new knowledge weighing on her. This was the moment. This moment now—with Robert Semple and Aimee's experience of the Holy Spirit inhabiting her body—this was the moment that had been foretold.

"I must admit that of a truth," she said with a trembling voice to her daughter. "This is that which was spoken of by the prophet Joel, which should come to pass in the last days!" Finally, Minnie understood: Aimee's gift of tongues was a sign of the times. From that moment on, "This is that" was a phrase that held great meaning for Aimee, so much so that she would use it as the title of her first memoir a decade later.

"This is that" was their rallying cry—Scripture was history. Exceptional things were happening in an exceptional time: *this* which they were experiencing was *that* which had been prophesied. Aimee was overjoyed, throwing her arms around her mother's neck and dancing her around the kitchen. Together they sang a favorite gospel song, "'Tis the old-time religion! And it's good enough for me!"[10] They were united again in a shared vision of divine guidance.

3

FALLING IN LOVE WITH DESTINY

Over the cold winter, Aimee did everything she could to stay in touch with Robert Semple. One evening, at a fellow convert's home, Robert described to Aimee how he wanted to bring his message to "idol-ridden" China. The world was full of souls that would be harvested like "great fields of golden grain." He needed to save them, he told Aimee. And he wanted her as his partner.

"Aimee, dear, will you become my wife and enter the work with me? I love you with all my heart," she recalled him saying, still gushing two decades later in her memoir. "I closed my eyes very, very tight. The room seem filled with angels who lined either side of a golden, sunlit path of life that stretched away into the vista of coming days of glorious love and joyful service." She knew her answer. Romantic and spiritual love explosively intertwined. "My lips whispered 'yes' to Robert and my heart sang 'yes' to the Lord."[1]

Meanwhile, Minnie was heartbroken when her seventeen-year-old daughter announced that she had agreed to marry the young Irish pastor. Minnie wanted to stop her, but James counseled that there was no point in arguing with their headstrong child. Aimee did what she wanted; her parents knew that.

Robert and Aimee were married on August 12, 1908, nine months after they first met. The wedding took place on the lawn of the family farm, beneath the apple trees, and just a few weeks before Aimee would have started her senior year of high school, a few months before her eighteenth birthday. The surreality of her sudden adulthood felt almost hallucinatory to Aimee. She wrote in her memoir of the night before her wedding, and her fanciful state of mind. "In my dreams wedding presents became mixed with wedding cakes and pies, a cutglass and silver cruet chased salt and pepper holders around in endless circles. The horn-handled carving set chased the roast chickens around the festive board, wedding dress and veil floated up, up, up on a mountain of presents to reach the orange wreath which rested on top, then with the slip of a foot on a jelly-roll. A harmless dreamland fall. Down, down, down into a marsh-mallow whipped cream cake with icing three feet deep."[2]

A local paper described Aimee as a "very popular" bride who was "a gold medalist in elocution" and who had "always been a cheerful contributor at local entertainments." Aimee wore a white silk gown as she marched with her father from her childhood bedroom to the yard, where she and Robert exchanged vows under a canopy of cedar and pine. A local Chinese man who credited his conversion to Christianity to Robert delivered the wedding cake. As the guests feasted, the sky darkened, and rain began to pour. Aimee gazed at her groom and did her best to ignore her mother's gloomy mood. Aimee had been the center of Minnie's world since the day she was born, and her daughter's marriage to Robert stole away all that sense of velocity and excitement that Aimee had provided her. With a thunderstorm gathering, the newlyweds escaped by train.

They moved to the neighboring city of Stratford, thirty miles away. The air was thick with soot from the local foundry, where Robert took a day job, manufacturing boilers for train cars. They lived in a tiny walk-up apartment, with grimy curtains, a fold-out bed, and a cracked mirror. Aimee, still months away from her eighteenth birthday, tried to be brave in the face of her newfound poverty. Robert was unworried by their material situation, focused solely on his mission to evangelize. "We're in the field now, darling," he told her. "Nothing matters but the cause of Christ."

Despite their hardship, euphoric love and purpose pervaded the couple's new life. Robert eagerly preached in the homes of newfound converts. Aimee did her best to keep house by day and at night played the piano and sang at the revival meetings. They thrilled with the knowledge that they were on a path to bring salvation to the heathens who had not yet heard the good news of the gospel. But their ambition was greater than Stratford. They dreamed and prayed for the means to move to Chicago. As would so often be the case, the answer to Aimee's prayers came from Minnie. God "laid it upon my Mother's heart to provide for the fare and other necessary expenses."[3] They made their way to Chicago, where they spent the next year working with the burgeoning Pentecostal community.

In early 1909, Robert and Aimee were both ordained by William Durham himself, becoming pastors of his Full Gospel Assembly. Ordination in this grassroots evangelical faith was determined by group consensus, a decision made when the group felt that a person had been divinely called.[4] It was with Durham that Aimee first experienced divine healing. One day, she fell down a flight of stairs, painfully injuring her foot. She was diagnosed by a doctor with torn ligaments and had to use crutches. A week after the accident, Aimee received a message to pray for healing with Durham. "In the name of Jesus, receive your healing," Durham called out. Aimee wrote that she "suddenly felt as if a shock of electricity had struck my foot. It flowed through my whole body, causing me to shake and tremble under the power of God. Instantaneously my foot was perfectly healed, the blackness was gone, the parted ligaments were knitted together, the bone was made whole."[5] From then on, the gifts of divine healing felt as integral to Aimee as the gift of tongues.

The intense physical and visceral nature of the Pentecostal charismatic gifts marked a pivotal moment in the history of religion. Church historians at the time would call it a new element in the religious life of the world. The visible manifestation of the divine into the bodies of the individual as an act of grace became a radical act of egalitarianism that would change the shape of global Christianity in the century to come. Whereas Martin Luther and the early Protestant faith emphasized Jesus as a model to live with, this new experience of Pentecostal gifts put the individual in conversation with the Holy Spirit. It was less about text and more about experience. Jesus had become personal and palpable.

With this individual experience, suddenly anyone could be given divine powers, including women. While divine power had once been bestowed only upon kings and clergy, Pentecostalism allowed people from the margins—women, minorities, the poor—to be empowered by a divine act. There had been other moments like this in American history—such as the First and Second Great Awakenings—when ecstatic religious movements briefly leveled the field and allowed female preachers to rise to power. But these openings were short-lived.

At the turn of the century, Aimee was unusual as a female evangelist, but not alone. Over the previous three centuries of American history, women had been the foundation of church life—in almost every Christian congregation, women filled up at least two-thirds of the pews. Women performed the essential—and often invisible—work of raising money, cooking food, playing music, and, most important, sending their children to church, ensuring the future congregants. But, almost always, men stood at the front; men made the decisions; men delivered the sermons and provided the structural leadership to the flock.[6]

There were of course wonderful exceptions: Ann Lee, whose visions became foundational in creating the Shaker religion; Mary Baker Eddy, who used her own experience of divine healing to found the Church of Christ, Scientist; and Helena Blavatsky, an esoteric mystic, who co-founded the Theosophical Society. And in the nineteenth century, women such as Sojourner Truth and Harriet Livermore were powerful and popular preachers with national reputations.

But to walk into an American church over the centuries and find a woman at the front, preaching, would be fairly extraordinary. Pentecostalism shook that ground—a little. In early Pentecostal missions, women could participate in several ways. They could experience the Holy Ghost and speak in tongues. They could interpret the experience of others—a subset of gifts, wherein they could translate the words and sounds that another person was making. And they were allowed the space to stand up and testify, or speak about their experience. Divine healing was also a space where women had been allotted some autonomy—especially when it came to "female disorders." And a rare few—just a handful during this era—had been ordained to preach.

Robert Semple supported Aimee's enthusiasm for her burgeoning abilities, and he encouraged Aimee to evangelize alongside him. Besides her mother, he was the first to see and really encourage her gifts. And from her writings, it's clear that Aimee, in this time, felt an increasing sense that she was destined to be an evangelist. After seeing her preach to a large group for the first time, he wrapped her in his arms and congratulated her. "I say! How did you ever do it? I didn't know we had a second preacher in the family!"[7]

Robert's goals were global. They set sail for Europe in February 1910. There, in Ireland, they visited Magherafelt, Robert's hometown, where Aimee met Robert's parents, who were delighted with their son's young bride. But as Robert's mother heard the couple's plans to sail to China, she felt a strong foreboding that she would never see him again. Aimee wrote letters to her mother, filled with excitement for the near future where she would transform the world.

Back home, reading her daughter's starry-eyed accounts of Europe, Minnie felt adrift. James was seventy-three years old to her thirty-nine, and more than ever she chafed at their age difference and the dullness of farmwork. In central Canada, endurance was the way of life. Residents made their living cheese-making and pork-packing, and days were often spent in agricultural toil and nights tending to family. Religious faith was observed quietly inside the tidy brick buildings of the Congregational and Presbyterian churches. While the town had an evangelical community, belief was often channeled into discreet devotion, performed for a distant and judgmental God. An energetic woman like Minnie, with her only child married and gone, had little to look forward to beyond long years of housework and prayer. The quiet of her home, the absence of her vivacious daughter, and the dull rigor of farmwork made Minnie frustrated. Her vitality, and her divine ambitions, demanded that she change her circumstances.

In the fall of 1908, Minnie had bought the family farm from her seventy-one-year-old husband, bequeathing him the right to reside there until his death. The purpose given was to avoid an inheritance tax, but tongues wagged in Salford about how she'd steamrolled the quiet, well-regarded James to pursue her own sense of ambition. Minnie was not a popular figure in town—scarred from her impoverished childhood, she argued over every penny with local merchants, and hoarded a small nest egg of money. Aimee was gone, and with her home empty, and cash in hand, Minnie packed up her suitcases and said the lord was calling her. Her sense of destiny was too strong, and there was too much work to be done for her to be handcuffed to Kozy-Kot and their insignificant little existence. Minnie used her savings to buy a ticket to New York City, where she rented a walk-through apartment on Fourteenth Street. With her daughter and her newfound Pentecostalism far away, Minnie returned to the faith she knew best: the Salvation Army. She lived near its headquarters on Seventh Avenue and joined a boisterous group of fellow soldiers. She was pursuing her divine ambition.[8]

On June 1, 1910, Aimee and Robert stepped ashore in Hong Kong, where they were met by two fellow Pentecostal missionaries. Just two years before, Aimee had been a high school girl on a farm in central Canada. But the woman who walked off the boat was six months pregnant, a missionary's wife, and doing what felt like urgent global work. Her community in Hong Kong was limited—a small group of Pentecostal missionaries had arrived just three years prior to establish their mission in the fall of 1907. The Chinese had been of particular fascination to the Pentecostal movement ever since Agnes Ozman first spoke in tongues. Since that moment their mission to evangelize to the Asian continent felt preordained.

First among the Pentecostal missionaries to arrive in Hong Kong was a North Carolina man named T. J. McIntosh who had experienced the gifts of the Holy Spirit and believed that the sounds he made were the Chinese language. Although he had never studied Mandarin or Cantonese, McIntosh believed when he arrived that he would be fluent. He was disappointed when he landed in October 1907 to find that no one understood him. Soon he modified his understanding of the gifts of the Holy Spirit to be meant solely for personal edification, not international communication.

Protestant missionaries had been in China for one hundred years, and while they offered some touchstone to the newly arrived Pentecostals, there was also judgment and division from the more established missions, who weren't thrilled to have what they saw as a fanatical sect arriving on their missionary shores. At the time of Aimee and Robert's arrival, there were approximately 1,300 Protestant missionaries in China, with just a small group in Hong Kong.[9]

Aimee's recollection of that time is one of an increasing division. There was a fervor in their home as Robert delighted at the opportunity to enact large-scale salvation. "Just think," he told his wife after a long day of evangelizing in the streets. "Every third baby that is born in the world is Chinese. One-third of the people in the world are Chinese, every third funeral is that of a Chinese. What a mighty task lies before Christianity!"[10] Her description of Robert at that time is of a man who is lost in a dream. Robert would cheerfully sing the old-time church song "Bringing in the Sheaves," changing it to "Bringing in Chinese." Their imperialistic view of their new home was transactional: they were there to change the locals. But for Aimee that separation grew into a heightened state of isolation and horror.

Aimee's writings from Asia read as feverish and alienated. With Robert out preaching, Aimee hid inside during the blaze of the day and wandered the streets at night. She described Hong Kong as frighteningly uncivilized. She watched as a horse died in the road and then was devoured by dogs, the bones left in the sun to bleach. She was terrified when she witnessed a Hindu funeral, with a body burned on a pyre, and was rattled by the "awful rhythm" of the call to prayer at a nearby mosque. She was overwhelmed by the smell, convinced that "the air was filled with demons and the hosts of hell, in this wicked, benighted country, where for many centuries devil worship has been an open custom."[11] Repulsed by the "peculiar" local food, Aimee and Robert subsisted on tinned milk and potatoes.

Their sense of alienation cut into their own union. Aimee wrote that her husband seemed to be drawn nearer to God, but more distant from her. Robert spent hours alone in prayer. He was filled with premonitions. He and Aimee would sometimes go down together to the beach at sunset. But Aimee wrote that, sitting there, absorbed in watching the people, she'd suddenly realize her husband was missing. She'd find him hidden away behind beach boulders, praying passionately. Later, he would disappear for long hours to the nearby missionary graveyard, named "Happy Valley." Robert and Aimee had been so wedded to each other in their mission, but after just a few weeks in the field, she clearly felt that her soulmate was slipping away from her.

Then, just two months after their arrival, Aimee and Robert both came down with malaria, and they were taken to a hospital that served missionaries. She was eight months pregnant, and her room in the ladies' ward was on the opposite side of the hospital from Robert. His health started to decline rapidly. She was allowed to see him only on visiting days. One night, sitting by his bed, she felt overwhelmed with fear. She was alone, pregnant, and impoverished in a place where she felt estranged. As she sat by Robert's bed, she willed herself to stay tethered to him and the intense hope and purpose they had once shared. "I gazed at the thin, pale face, so changed in these few days, but feeling that I must be brave and encouraging." Robert awoke briefly and smiled wanly at her and said: "Good night, dear; I'll see you in the morning."

Aimee returned to the women's ward. She listened to the sound of the bodies around her, heaving and sighing. An uneasy sense kept her from sleep. Robert died in the night.

"I was never permitted to look upon the face of my dear one again," she wrote, "as the doctor was anxious to spare me all suffering possible, but Oh, how could I have borne it when I saw them pulling down the shades in hopes that I would not see, and heard the heavy tread of feet as they carried their burden past our windows and down the steps, if it had not been for this precious Holy Spirit?"[12] Robert was buried in Happy Valley, the graveyard where he had spent so much time praying for lost souls.

On September 17, less than a month later, Roberta Star Semple was born, named for her father. Her middle name, Aimee said, signified the hope she placed in her daughter and her belief that she would change the world. At four and a half pounds, the baby was "a tiny mite of a thing." Doctors, Aimee later wrote, told her that her sickly infant had a one in thirty chance of surviving. Aimee received money from a missionary in Chicago, who wrote to her that she had awoken in the night with an urgent divine message: "Little Sister Semple is in trouble! Rise immediately and send her sixty dollars!"[13] The woman sent sixty dollars, which paid for Robert's funeral expenses. Aimee wrote to her mother, and word of her situation spread back across the Pacific to the evangelical community. A collection was assembled by her mother and sent to Hong Kong to bring Aimee and Roberta home.

At the end of October, Aimee boarded the *Empress of China*, carrying her baby in a basket, along with less than fifty dollars. The ship sailed from Shanghai to Japan to Honolulu and finally to California. Despite her circumstances, Aimee managed to see providence and blessings everywhere she looked—the fellow passengers who slipped her blankets and spare change, the opening of a cloudy sky to rays of sunshine. But she strained to hear the divine voice in her head, to find some sense of direction. She had seen Robert as her destiny, believed that together they would change the world.

She preached to a small group in the ship's saloon every Sunday of the monthlong sail. They were captivated by the sweet-faced, heartbroken young widow and her emotional readings from Scripture.

Aimee wrote that she became a sort of pet to those on board, as "ladies in glittering evening dresses came tapping along on jeweled heels to mother me and offer advice about the baby." When she disembarked, the ship's purser gave her an envelope—the passengers had taken a collection for her that totaled sixty-seven dollars. This paid for her journey from San Francisco to Chicago and then on to New York City. "My thoughts began to keep time to the ceaseless tattoo of the clicking car wheels. What'll you do? What'll you do? What'll you do? Now, what'll you do?"[14] Aimee arrived in New York City in November 1910. As she would time and again, Minnie scooped her up and saved her.

4

FLAMINGO IN A CHICKEN COOP

In 1910, as Aimee arrived to reunite with her mother, New York City was experiencing a tidal wave of immigration: more than 40 percent of its residents were foreign-born. People in search of a new life were seen as ripe for religious conversion. Salvation Army warriors stationed themselves at the docks and the immigrant neighborhoods of downtown to evangelize to the freshly landed. Institutional power—in the city government and the media—saw the Salvation Army as a radical scourge on the city, something wild and bizarre that needed to be checked. Twenty-five years earlier, in 1885, *The New York Times* published an editorial that complained, "The Salvation Army appears to be organized for the purpose of applying the methods of the variety show to Christianity. It undertakes to minister to the same craving for vulgar modes of excitement . . . [T]he Salvation Army holds that a man need not be civilized in order to be Christianized."[1]

The Salvation Army was one of the most successful of the new evangelical Protestant sects that had exploded in the nineteenth century in Europe and America. William Booth, a minister who found his start as a pawnbroker in the gritty back alleys of London, had seen the destitution of the urban factory workers he served and knew that empty pews and dusty dogma were not the answer to transforming lives. Instead, Booth used the language of battle for bringing Jesus into people's hearts. Using the urgent imagery of warfare to unify a newly urban population, Booth's soldiers attracted do-gooders who liked the militaristic rhetoric and tiered system of achievements for good works. Their uniforms and their songs created an instantly recognizable cohesion. The Army also appealed to the down-and-out—beggars, alcoholics, and prostitutes; with the motto of "soup, soap and salvation," it preached a gospel that emphasized tending to the earthly needs of people, offering them the chance to accept Jesus and find divine salvation wherever they were at that moment in life. The Army intended to make everything that was secular sacred. Theirs was "the cathedral of open air." It was a world-changing concept.

At thirty-nine years old, Minnie gloried in her return to work. She helped the Army run a boardinghouse and put on parades and pageants. She rang bells on street corners, organized charitable efforts, sold copies of their magazine, *The War Cry*, and shouted out Jesus's name for all to hear. Like Minnie, the earliest Sallies were women who were drawn from small towns, and who flourished with the Army's egalitarian outlook on gender. The sense of purpose and ambition granted to female members was something not generally available to women in their work at the turn of the century. Evangeline Booth, the glamorous and determined daughter of the Army's founder, served as their leader in New York City.

When Aimee arrived in New York after a long month of travel, across ten thousand miles, she was exhausted and limp, Roberta sickly and underweight. Minnie had rented an apartment on Fourteenth Street, in a fashionable area that was then the theater district. But Aimee spent days sleeping and nursing her baby, rarely leaving her mother's apartment. "The loom of life seemed then to be but a tangled maze," Aimee wrote, "whose colorings had suddenly plunged from mountain-tops of sunlit glory to the depths of a seemingly endless valley of bewildering gloom." When she did venture outside the apartment, she felt Robert's absence everywhere as she watched couples laugh, walk hand in hand in the streets, coo over their children. "Everywhere, the world was one big ache for Robert."[2] Worse, when she saw people who had known her as a newlywed, she was often questioned about the foolhardiness of their mission to China. Her heart, she wrote, was "constantly pierced" by these questions. Aimee began to have a nagging sense that she had made mistakes, and to have doubts that her future was cosmically ordained after all. She had no response to questions about the decisions that led to her current circumstances. "I could not answer them, not being able to see the will of God in all this yet myself."[3]

Minnie finally jostled Aimee out of her despair, telling her she needed once again to sing the good news of the gospel—true happiness and a relief from her sadness would come only from reconnecting to God. Minnie told Aimee that if she went out to work for the Army, Minnie would stay home with Roberta. Minnie borrowed a uniform for Aimee and sent her out to the streets. Aimee was assigned the job of collecting money in the grand lobbies of Broadway theaters. She stood and rang a large brass bell and asked passersby, "Are you saved?" On one hand, the work restored in Aimee some sense of purpose. But standing amid the elegant theatergoers in their silk gowns and furs, Aimee was taken back to her glory days in high school theater productions. With sophisticated temptations surrounding her, intoxicating and glittering, she felt an urge to return to those worldly things that had delighted her before her conversion to Pentecostalism with Robert.

One night, a few weeks after she started working for the Army, Aimee met Harold McPherson, a man neither worldly nor divine. Harold glimpsed Aimee outside a Broadway theater. Aimee was no longer the blinking teenager—grief and hardship had aged her, defined her features, sharpened her eyes. She wore her long auburn hair in a braid, her face broad with an angelic softness. Her voice as she called out was forceful and clear and a little bit sultry. Harold was enchanted.

Harold McPherson's Christian faith—like most things about him—was mild and reliable. There had been a brief moment, at the age of seventeen, when he had considered becoming a preacher after attending a revival meeting held by a traveling British evangelist named Gipsy Smith. That dream had led him to enroll in a Baptist college in Missouri, but when the cost of caring for his mother and sister mounted, Harold put off his own ambitions and went to work. He moved to New York in 1910, when his sister was seeking specialists for an undefined medical condition that rendered her homebound. He found a job at a restaurant to support his sister's treatments, and after his mother and sister returned home to Providence, he found an apartment to share with a few other men and made a small life for himself in the city, while sending money back home.

After Harold first glimpsed Aimee, he made a point of passing by the theater where she shook her tambourine, and he would even secretly follow her home and keep an eye on her from around the corner as she let herself into her tenement building. After a few weeks, he worked up the courage to introduce himself and offered to accompany her home. They were both twenty years old.

During this time Aimee described herself as profoundly lonely, the emotion coming over her in those days like a "terrifying grip."[4] Harold's steadfast sweetness and stoic nature must have felt like a balm—but in her various memoirs she never described their marriage in more than a sentence or two, and she does not even mention him by name: he was a life chapter she would prefer to have erased. But according to a series of interviews conducted by Roberta with Harold at the end of his life, Harold really did fall madly in love with the young widow, who seemed to him deeply sad and terribly innocent. He took her often that winter of 1911 to the ice pond in Central Park near Sixtieth Street—likely a joyous reprieve for Aimee, who had loved skating in Canada. While he was too embarrassed to sweet-talk Aimee, he relied on songs of the day to speak his mind. As they glided across the ice together, he hummed in her ear: "Let Me Call You Sweetheart" and "I'm Falling in Love with Someone."

As the months wore on, Harold slowly romanced Aimee. He

enjoyed squiring her around the city on his days off, taking her to the Broadway Automat, where the actors dined, or a fashionable new Hungarian restaurant. On their most memorable date, he took her to the New York Hippodrome, where they watched "Around the World," one of the most spectacular productions in the city's history. From their seats, the couple watched as live camels marched across the stage, amid real blowing sand. The set of a house on fire burned down in actual flames. Most enchanting to Aimee was a group of women in spangled costumes who dove into a giant tank in front of the audience and vanished. Miraculously, they emerged from the water as mermaids. It was the first major production she'd seen, and the memory of it would stay with her for a long time.

Harold had a dangerous desire for anyone entering marriage: he wanted to change the girl he was in love with. "He vowed," Roberta later wrote, "to devote himself to making her forget her sad past."[5]

One Sunday afternoon—less than a year after they met—the young couple walked along Fifth Avenue, watching well-to-do New Yorkers out for a stroll. Harold stopped and asked Aimee if she would marry him. He told her that he would raise Roberta as his own and that they could build a good and simple life for themselves.

She gave a hesitant yes—she was desperate, she would write later, for a home and economic stability for her daughter. But the divine voice in Aimee's head had returned in full force, pushing her to spread the gospel. That voice would always be louder than any others. From the beginning, her reaction to Harold's ardor was lukewarm. Aimee told him that she would marry him only with the understanding that God would always come first. No matter what, she told Harold, if God "should call me to go to Africa or India, or to the Island of the Sea, no matter where or when, I must obey God first of all." Harold accepted Aimee's stipulation. "He agreed and we were married under these conditions, and settled down in a furnished apartment,"[6] Aimee wrote later with rare economy.

At the age of twenty-one, Aimee had a second husband.

Harold would have agreed to anything Aimee asked, Roberta later wrote. "Even to letting her join a circus or become an aviatrix.

He was confident that he could make her happy; that once they were settled in their own home, she would promptly forget her peculiar obsession."

What did intimidate Harold was Minnie, who didn't think this milquetoast fellow was good—or godly—enough for her daughter and granddaughter. To Minnie, Harold was a city slicker, a worldly interloper who had interfered with her plan to get Aimee back to her—and God. But when Minnie laid out her concerns for Aimee, she pushed back to defend him. Minnie's doubts only strengthened headstrong Aimee's decision to marry.[7]

Harold told Aimee her mother would come around on their relationship once she saw how happy they were. Until that time, he said, it would be better if they built their own life, far away from Minnie's stern gaze. Aimee saw this as an opportunity to get Roberta, who was perpetually unwell, into a healthier environment. They left New York and moved to Chicago. Harold encouraged Aimee to stay at home with the baby. Decades later, he recalled how he bought a white wicker stroller for Roberta in the hope that Aimee would enjoy pushing her baby. This gift showed a lack of insight into his wife. As time went on, he began to resent how they had to hurry through their meals so Aimee could go back out on the streets to shout the gospel with other Salvation Army soldiers. In the summer of 1912, Aimee became pregnant again and they moved to Providence, to be near his mother and sister. Harold was sure the new baby would settle his spirited wife.

Relations between Aimee and her in-laws soured quickly, and living next door to Harold's family, she found the apartment unbearable. She left often to visit her mother in New York, ringing bells with Minnie for the Salvation Army, until she became too pregnant to travel. Back in Providence, inside the cramped apartment building, tensions grew. Harold's mother found her daughter-in-law high-strung and self-centered. According to Aimee, her mother-in-law took every opportunity to make her feel foolish.

"Well, Aimee, I don't see what more you want. I don't believe anything could make you happy. It must be your disposition,"[8] she said. Aimee's friends at that time described her in ways that were at odds with how she wanted to be seen. "A blonde with a very fascinating smile," said one. "A nice little housekeeper," who was a "little on the happy go lucky side,"[9] said another. The misery of being trapped in the small apartment with hostile in-laws next door thickened into a depression once Aimee gave birth to her son, Rolf McPherson, in March 1913. For months, she would shut herself away in her bedroom and cry out Jesus's name from the darkest corner, unable to face her mundane life. She was, as a contemporary biographer punned, "a flamingo in a chicken coop."

Her mother-in-law told her flailing son that what his "high-strung" wife needed was hard work. Annie McPherson would later accuse Aimee of being wretched to her son, of beating him, abusing him, pulling his hair, tearing his clothes, threatening to take his life, and her own.[10] She told Harold they needed to move out and that Aimee would then naturally funnel all her restlessness into homemaking. Annie McPherson said housekeeping would occupy Aimee's mind and keep her from thinking so much about herself. Harold obeyed.

In their new apartment, things got worse. Harold left each day to work at a nearby grocery store, and Aimee was left to tend to her young children and the home. By her own description, she seemed to be losing her tether to the world around her—to her children, to her husband, even to her faith. She makes no mention of going to church during this time. The whistle of the teakettle and the sound of voices were unbearable. "I hated the sunshine and wanted to keep the shutters closed and the window-shades drawn tightly," she later wrote.

> Time after time I tried to shake myself from my lethargy and depression and busy myself with household duties. Such a fever of restlessness came upon me that it seemed as though I must wear the polish off the furniture and the floors by dusting them so often. A dozen times a day I would take myself to task as I would catch sight of my tearful face in the looking-glass, saying: "Now, see here, my lady, this will never do! What right

> have you to fret and pine like this? Just see those shining, polished floors, covered with soft Axminister and Wilton rugs. Just look at that mahogany parlor furniture and the big brass beds in yonder, the fine bathroom done in blue and white, the steam heat, the softly-shaded electric lights, the pretty baby's crib with its fluff and ribbons, the high-chair and the rocking horse. Why aren't you glad to have a home like this for the babies, as any other mother would be?"[11]

"Was this all?" Aimee wondered. She had been born as a prophecy, her mother had always told her. And with Robert, she'd felt that her fate was guided toward great things, a life that would change the world around her. Cooped up in the little Rhode Island apartment, with her young children, Aimee saw only her own failure. There were days on end when she couldn't even get out of bed. Minnie came to visit a few times, and, when she couldn't come, she sent money to the struggling young couple. Aimee seemed keenly aware of her mother's disappointment, painting herself as a glorious promise that had been broken. "She thought of the day she had prayed for the little girl who should go out in the world to preach the Word," Aimee wrote of Minnie, "the day of the dedication under the banners of blood and fire, the golden future of joyful service, and here was the wreck!"

The wreck grew worse. Soon the floors were dirty, the linens stained, the dishes in a pile in the sink. Her infant son squalled from his crib, while her three-year-old daughter was frail and perpetually underweight. It was a life of unending routine and domestic failures. All of Aimee's promise—all the ambition she had embodied since her mother held her up in the Salvation Army church service—had come to nothing.

In 1913, at the age of twenty-three, Aimee was hospitalized. What began that year with bouts of vomiting, internal bleeding, and heart tremors would result in two nervous breakdowns, appendicitis, and, finally, a hysterectomy. In her memoirs, Aimee described the surgeries, which led to hemorrhaging, as brutal and barbaric. When the surgeries finished, the doctors diagnosed her with "intense nervousness." Within months, Aimee was hospitalized again. "The poor, unconscious 'what-there-was left-of-me' was put back in the bed and I opened my eyes on the white walls of the hospital—quivering with pain from head to foot, which, instead of growing better grew worse and worse."[12] Stitched up and sedated, Aimee gazed blankly out the hospital window, watery-eyed and dazed.

The nurses who attended to her could not have seen any trace of the once headstrong, bright young girl who had mastered her high school dėbates, the girl who had cowed the boys of the schoolyard and made the bullies her underlings. The doctors would not have known that this was a woman who, as a teenager, had sailed across oceans to bring the word of God to others. Aimee had once been outspoken, precocious, and driven, but now she was lost.

"Twice my mother had been called by a telegram to see me die," Aimee would later write dramatically. According to Aimee, her mother wept at her daughter's bedside, "renewing and redoubling her vows to God to help in every way to get me back into the work."[13]

Aimee was losing her mind, losing her will to live. But on a winter's day, the higher power returned to her life with a command. A voice of authority and divinity came into the hospital room, a voice that matched her dormant sense of destiny: "GO! Do the work of an evangelist: Preach the Word 'The time is short; I am coming soon.'"[14]

Aimee had no choice but to follow this divine call and let go of all earthly expectations of who she should be. When she told this news to Harold and her mother-in-law, they dismissed her, belittling her as "hysterical" and a malcontent. Take care of your babies, take care of your family, they told her. But something had changed inside of her. The voice that she had heard was a command.

She returned home from the hospital with a secret plan: to escape. She wired her mother and asked for money. Minnie responded immediately—as she always would. On the night of June 29, 1915, while Harold was out with friends, Aimee slipped from the house, piled her children and suitcases into a taxi bound for the depot.

"I knew that tongues would wag and heads shake. I knew there would be much talk and little understanding," she later wrote. "Yet knowing all this, I went."[15] She caught a midnight train to Canada, where her mother awaited her, once again.

5

ESCAPE FROM PROVIDENCE

With my little baby clasped in one arm and Roberta sleeping in the other, I held them tightly to me as the immensity of what I was doing swept over me. The streets were dark and almost deserted as we rolled along toward the depot."[1]

It was noon on the last day of June 1915 as their train rolled into the Ingersoll station. Minnie and James came together, even bringing Aimee's childhood pony to welcome her. As they passed the small white schoolhouse of her childhood, Aimee felt struck by the physical memory of the past—of the way her heart had exploded when she saw Robert for the first time, how he had altered her world so radically. She felt empty and ashamed—she had strayed so far away from her purpose.

Inside her childhood home, Aimee felt the unease and depression from Providence begin to dissipate. Minnie took charge of her grandchildren and instructed Aimee to rest. She knew what would bring her daughter back to life: Jesus. A ten-day tent revival was taking place in the town of Kitchener, some thirty-five miles away. Minnie gave Aimee a ticket, which bought a seat at the revival and a cot in a sleeping tent. She helped Aimee pack her bag. Caring for two young grandchildren was a small price to pay "to see you get back to God and back to the place where He wants you," Minnie told Aimee.

Aimee obeyed her mother but stopped impulsively at the post office on her way to the train station. She scrawled out a telegram to Harold. "I have tried to walk your way and have failed," she wrote. "Won't you come now and walk my way? I am sure we will be happy."

As she stared out the train window, Aimee felt "leaked out,"[2] embarrassed in anticipation of seeing those who had known her only as the rosy-cheeked and vivacious young wife of the handsome Robert Semple. The demands of the everyday had worn her down, and her soul felt stained both by misfortune and by the commonplace circumstances she had found herself in. By choosing an ordinary life with Harold, she had ignored her divine calling to spread the gospel.

In Kitchener, Aimee climbed into a wagon with a group of other revivalists, and they made their way to the outskirts of town to a forest clearing known as Poorhouse Bush. The setting, the excitement of the crowd—about a hundred Pentecostal converts—buoyed Aimee. On the first evening, she joined others when the minister gave the call to prayer, an invitation to all in need of rebirth. With her head bowed on the rough wooden planks, her skin pressed against the heat of bodies around her, Aimee began to weep. Memories of the past flooded in. She felt lost, broken. She would later recall an intensely personal conversation between her and God as she begged for forgiveness.

"The next thing I knew the Spirit was speaking in tongues through me, giving me the interpretation . . . I was laughing and weeping and shaking." All Aimee's sadness left her, replaced with an intense surge of God's love. "Such love," she would remember, "was more than my heart could bear. Before I knew it, I was on my back in the straw, under the power."[3]

There, on the ground, surrounded by other bodies jerking and convulsing, she surrendered. Had she been a bad mother and a bad wife? Had she not done enough to save Robert from death? Had she chosen a secular path with Harold? Had she lost her way?

None of it mattered. Only this mattered. She was a vessel of divine power. Aimee began to crawl amid the bodies around her, kneeling, then walking, reaching out and laying hands on those around her. She tried to direct the energy coursing through her into others. At her touch, one man shrieked and fell back. He hit the ground hard and began speaking in tongues. She felt her mind illuminate, and she gave an interpretation of the foreign sounds he was shouting. A force beyond imagination had taken over her body, and she felt as if a dam burst, her heart broke, and she was overwhelmed with love. The absolute surrender of the experience made her feel giddy and wild and hopeful. She was, as she put it, returned once again to God's grace, slain under the power. "I was laughing and weeping and shaking. A little knot of people gathered round to rejoice with me. The Spirit lifted me to my feet and I walked up and down praising the lamb for sinners slain."[4]

Aimee stayed up late into the night. Her soul throbbed, awash in the beauty of it all, her voice joining in the din of those around her as their cries filled the air of the waxed canvas tent and went out into the dark summer sky. She awoke the next day with the absolute conviction that her experience of glossolalia had legitimized her decision to leave Providence. Over the next few days, she worked and prayed around the clock. Never had she labored harder. She stayed up till two in the morning, washing dishes and serving food with the other volunteers. She harmonized with the crowd of believers, humming with happiness. She was born again. Her excitement contagious, Aimee found herself shouting out revelations that were given to her.

On the periphery, a woman watched her, impressed with the potential and capacity of Aimee to direct the presence of the Holy Spirit. Sister Elizabeth, as she was known, invited Aimee to come to the nearby town of Mount Forest in the coming weeks and preach to her own small congregation of Pentecostals. Aimee accepted and returned home to her family filled with excitement and purpose: all she wanted in the world was to evangelize. According to Aimee, the children seemed to be happily enjoying life with their grandparents. Sitting on the kitchen table were letters from Harold, who demanded that she return "to wash dishes" and "take care of the house" and, above all, "act like other women." There was no chance of Aimee acting like other women again. "Oh, don't you ever tell me that a woman cannot be called to preach the gospel!" she exclaimed in her first memoir. "If any man ever went through one hundredth part of the hell on earth that I lived in, those months when out of God's will and work, they would never say that again!"[5]

6

SLAIN UNDER THE POWER

Mount Forest, Ontario, a bucolic town of four thousand residents, had a firmly established community of Anglican, Methodist, Presbyterian, and Baptist churches. Sister Elizabeth had ushered in Pentecostalism, stirring up this quiet Christian town, but it hadn't gained much hold. A small storefront had been transformed into a fifty-seat meeting hall, and often, she told Aimee, the seats were filled only by her own inner circle of friends and family. But on August 15, 1915, a young widow with an unbridled enthusiasm for the Holy Spirit arrived in town, and Sister Elizabeth had high hopes she might change the fate of their mission.

This time Aimee was going to be the main attraction, not the sideshow, as when she'd been Robert's pretty teenage wife, occasionally taking the pulpit to give testimony. Aimee brought her children with her, and as she walked down Mount Forest's narrow streets, feeling nervous anticipation, she held their hands tightly. Sister Elizabeth welcomed Aimee into her home, and their families prayed together. Quickly the gifts of the Spirit descended into the room, and many began to speak in tongues. Sister Elizabeth knew God had sanctified her choice.

But hours later, when Aimee went to preach in the meeting hall, she was struck by how small it was, with its narrow chairs and its tiny platform. "A doll's church," she observed. Aimee looked at all the empty seats and told her host that she feared the locals might have been "preached up"—weary of too much church service. Aimee made a decision that would soon become part of her mythology. She employed a theatrical tactic called the hallelujah run, which she'd learned from the Salvation Army. Grabbing a chair, she said, "I'm going out to get a crowd," and ran onto Main Street. She stepped on the chair and silently raised her hands toward the sky. Curious bystanders stopped and gathered around this woman in a long skirt and a ruffled blouse and stared. They wanted to see what she would do. Aimee joyfully recalled their confusion:

> "What's the matter with her?
> "Dunno."
> "What ya' reckon it is?"
> "Maybe a cataleptic state."
> "What kind of a state?"
> "Cataleptic; sorta' unconscious-like."
> "Think so?"
> "Sure."

Her eyes shut, Aimee had to keep from smiling. The minutes passed and the crowd grew until finally, Aimee hopped off the chair and ran through the street, carrying it above her head and shouting, "Quick! Come with me!" There were fifty or more following Aimee through the streets.

She raced through the front doors of the Victory Mission with the crowd surging behind her. "Shut the doors," she shouted to the lone usher after the last person entered. "Don't let anyone out."[1] Aimee preached for forty minutes, using her own adventures and tragedies to illustrate the power of God's grace. She knew that a woman preacher was an oddity to them, that she was a curiosity and a stunt. But she did not care.

"Oh Lord, send Thy mighty power today. Lord, send the power. Send the power, Lord," she shouted. By the end of the service, attendees shouted their praises, and by the next night, the meeting hall was filled with a standing-room-only crowd. By the third night, the services had to be moved outside as the crowds swelled. Shouts of "Glory to Jesus" and "Hallelujah" were heard from blocks away. By the end of the week, Aimee was preaching to five hundred people who, by her account, wept and "gave their hearts to the Lord." Whatever the words were that Aimee spoke on those late-summer nights of 1915, she connected her message profoundly for the gathering of rural Canadians, on the cusp of monumental societal change.

Aimee had harnessed the wildness of Pentecostal spirit and used her charisma to draw people in. The services in Mount Forest soon became unruly, the crowds raucous. The local town crier, who Aimee wrote was "the football of everyone in his drunkenness," was known mockingly as "Monkey Abe," for his oddly proportioned body. When the lady evangelist respectfully called him "Mr. Connor," he became the first to fall under her power. He was good advertising—he was soon striding up and down the streets, crying out, "Hear ye, hear ye! I have given my heart to Christ. Come down to the revival tonight and hear Sister McPherson preach about the Christ who saved even me." The town turned out to see her. On one of her last nights in town, a young boy named Jim fell to the ground during Aimee's sermon. His limbs began to vibrate, and his eyes rolled back in his head. Aimee stood over him, chanting "Hallelujah" over and over and over. People ran outside the church, and someone tried to find his parents. On the streets someone screamed that Jim had been hypnotized by a witch. At last, the boy began to speak, frothing at the mouth as he shouted "Glory! Glory! Glory" repeatedly. A police officer arrived and insisted that Aimee and Elizabeth come down to the police station. But they weren't detained long—they shouted and danced until the exasperated officers let them go.

The next night, back in front of a packed church, Aimee became a delighted ringmaster. She fed off the excitement and fervor of the crowd, who looked up at her and screamed, their bodies losing control. As she laughed and cried out for the Holy Spirit, she caught sight of a familiar face at the back of the church: Harold.

He stood against the wall, watching mutely. His young wife who had been so sick for over a year was transformed, fully alive, the most beautiful woman in the world. He was overcome. He too surrendered to the higher power. He stepped forward and, in Aimee's words, "received the baptism of the Holy Spirit, spoke in tongues and glorified God."[2] On his knees, before Aimee, Harold accepted his wife and the demands of her urgent God. Every fiber of her being expanded, ballooning up with purpose and conviction. "He told me that he recognized that God had called me into this work and would not have me leave it for anything in the world,"[3] Aimee wrote triumphantly.

That night, Harold agreed to give up their home in Rhode Island and to travel as evangelists, bringing the Holy Spirit to the world. Aimee told the crowd of her dreams of itinerant preaching. She raised sixty-five dollars in the collection plate. With that money, she said, she would start her journey as an evangelist.

Aimee and Harold returned to Kozy-Kot and told Minnie of their intentions. She was annoyed that Harold had resurfaced. The conversation, by Aimee's account, was tense.[4]

"But what are you going to do?" Minnie demanded. "Where will you preach? Has any other church invited you?"

"Well, no," Aimee said, "but we are going to buy a tent. Harold will pitch it and make the benches and I'll do the preaching."

"But how are you going to live? Don't forget, you have two small children."

"Oh, we'll have little sleeping tents to pitch on the campgrounds. We'll be fine."

"Never!" said Minnie. "You can do what you want to with Rolf. He's your son, Harold. I can't stop you. But little Roberta stays with me. She is much too frail for that kind of gypsy life. I'll keep her under my wing for a while, and then we'll see."

Minnie was furious that Aimee was leaving her—again for another man and without a plan. She had repeatedly put her daughter at the center of her world, only to be pushed to the side. Minnie had believed in their shared divine destiny, but Aimee kept choosing a different path.

"What will you do for money?" Minnie said angrily.

"Oh, mother! God will provide. We are going to live on faith."[5]

Aimee left Roberta with Minnie. The couple returned to Providence with two-year-old Rolf. They sold off their furniture and dishes and most of their clothing; Harold quit his job. Aimee and Harold had reached a compromise—they would live their life in pursuit of salvation, as she wished, but they would do it together as husband and wife, as he wished. There was no longer a need to argue, because the answer to their questions came through prayer, mostly through revelations as interpreted by Aimee. Everything, according to Aimee, was charged with a cosmic intention—where they would travel for her to preach, where they would stake their tent, how they would go about their day—it was all God's will, as translated to Aimee. They shed all vestiges of worldliness and bought a tent, which would serve as Aimee's church, leaving baby Rolf for weeks at a time with Harold's mother.

They pitched their canvas tent at a dozen outposts along the New England coast, but the crowds Aimee had hoped for did not materialize. Within a few months, Harold had to find work to pay for food and supplies, but their circumstances only made Aimee more motivated. When a storm in Providence blew down her church tent and tore it to shreds, she saw it as a sign that God was testing her just as he had her beloved biblical figures. She stitched the tent back together, gathered money from the collection plate, and continued to preach. During these early months on the road, Aimee was beginning to find her voice. She saw the way that people would come in when she stood outside and shouted her message that Christ was on his way to earth. She began to crave the magical silence when she connected to those gathered, calling out, "Oh Lord, send the power."[6]

The first people who came to see Aimee preach were drawn to the novelty of the "lady evangelist," mostly unheard-of at the time.

Aimee ignored the jeers and the insults as she traveled from one small New England town to another. Inevitably someone would stand and say a woman shouldn't preach. She would respond with biblical evidence to the contrary and move on.[7]

Inside her tent, she felt the power her words had over others. When she laid her hands on people, their bodies shook. She began to write down her sermons and musings, which she composed with stream-of-consciousness intensity, hammering them out quickly. She submitted them to Pentecostal magazines, which published a few of her articles. She began to receive fan letters and invitations to preach. Aimee was finally getting something she had always wanted: an audience. "How they came! Choking the aisles, laying silver and paper money upon the open pages," Aimee wrote.[8] Soon, she had raised enough money to travel to Florida—where her prophesies had told her she must go.

7

NEW ROAD REVIVAL

Jacksonville was shocking: hot and hedonistic. The dazzling reds, pinks, and oranges of the tropical flowers, the spikes of the palmettos, the ornate fountains spraying geysers of sparkling water into the crystal-blue sky in front of palatial new hotels—the extravagance of it all overwhelmed Aimee's senses. In the crowds, she saw sin everywhere. Sunburned men and women gathered around card tables on sidewalks; grifters and hustlers called out to passersby to place bets; city streets were roped off at night for dancing as cigarettes and alcohol were passed from hand to hand, lost souls being taken down, one after another.

In that last winter before the United States entered the Great War, Florida was a fecund and strange place. More than a million men had already perished on the fields in Somme, France, in one of the deadliest battles in human history, and in just a few months' time, President Woodrow Wilson would ask Congress to declare war on Germany. For those Aimee met in Florida—recent transplants and tourists—the time felt portentous, ripe for new ideas about heaven and hell. Aimee was one of many rising religious stars in Florida then, traveling along what had become a spiritual circuit.

Aleister Crowley, the infamous British occultist, was traveling the same swampy roads. "Having witnessed the bedevilment of New Orleans," Crowley wrote in the early months of 1917, "I was sent to Titusville, Florida, to complete my contemplation of the unspeakable degradation of humanity which is constantly being wrought by Christianity and commerce." Crowley lived with his cousin and his cousin's wife, born-again Christians whom he found superstitious and pathetic. "His wife," Crowley wrote of her, "hardly turned thirty, a wrinkled hag of sixty, with no idea of life beyond the gnawing fear for the hereafter and the horrible pleasures of venting her spite on her neighbors and thwarting and persecuting her children."[1]

Questions of the afterlife, of sin, of pleasure hung in the air in sharp contrast to the abundance of pleasures on offer. Still, it was fertile ground for those offering salvation. Also touring Florida around that time was arguably the most famous evangelist in the world: Billy Sunday. Sunday, who had been a professional baseball player, had established the twentieth-century role of American religious evangelical celebrity. Traveling across America in the early 1900s, Sunday drew immense crowds as he preached a fire and brimstone gospel. Athletic and handsome, he would race up and down the stage as he pantomimed beating the devil back to hell. Sunday was aware of Aimee even at that time, and while he was envious of her healing powers, he disapproved of her flowing robes and her tendency to "melodramatize her sex."[2]

The boat passage down the East Coast to Florida and the freight for their ragged tent had left Aimee and Harold broke. Traveling with three-year-old Rolf, they subsisted off canned corn, condensed milk, and crackers donated from congregations she'd visited in New York and New England. Their decisions about where to go and what to do were guided by Aimee's communications with God. At first, they traveled with other Pentecostals who had come south, hitching rides from town to town. They slept sometimes on the sand, sometimes in tents, sometimes in the homes of strangers. They did not know when their next meal would be or where they would sleep when night fell. Their only money came from her preaching—often offered in exchange for a blessing from the lady evangelist. This was hard living, and, as Aimee conceded, "I wasn't much of a businesswoman then."[3]

Aimee used her powers of persuasion with local authorities to erect her tent on the outskirts of the larger cities of Jacksonville and St. Augustine. She raised money to purchase lumber for building benches and an altar. She painted by hand a string of electric lights with bright colors and hung them outside the tent in the hope of attracting spectators.

One evening, as Aimee stood on the street, shouting invitations through a megaphone, her voice cracked. She'd been shouting for days, even months, on end, and for a moment the grind of the work caught up with her body. A young man who had been traveling with the group offered to help. He took the megaphone and shouted out to a pedestrian, "Say brother! Do you know you are on your way to perdition?"

The man walking past jumped, as if he'd been shot, then scurried away. Aimee snatched the megaphone back. "Why did you do that," she demanded. "Well, because he's on his way to hell, isn't he?" the young man responded. He, like so many evangelicals, believed the world was on the brink of doomsday. He saw conversion as possible only through the fear of damnation. "How do you know?" Aimee asked. "And even if he were, one can do more with the bait of love than with the club of bombastic preaching."[4] The distinction was important. Back in that little Canadian country church, when she'd first heard Robert preach, it was love that had overtaken Aimee—body, mind, and soul. As she continued to evolve her theology during this time, she increasingly emphasized this personal, loving relationship with God—not the judgmental and fearful trembling of a sinner but instead one of closeness, tenderness, and grace.

Farther south, she and Harold built an encampment in a clearing in the swamps twenty miles outside of Tampa. They spent their days making signs and handing out tracts in town. As night fell, the sound of frogs and locusts filled the air; stars studded the vast sky. Their advertising worked: cars loaded with people arrived from all directions around Tampa as word of mouth spread that something extraordinary was happening out in the woods, something worth seeing.

Their tent sat like a celestial orb, patched and illuminated against the dark of the tropical night. Aimee decorated the outside with flowers and palm fronds, giving it a fairy-tale quality. Inside, the air was tight and electric, sweaty and filled with a sense that something was going to happen, a nervous ecstasy rippling through the crowd. They all knew of the Great War across the Atlantic. They had heard of the famine and bloodshed and disease that were spreading across the world. So much change was happening so fast—cars were speeding down new highways, cities rising up overnight with gleaming metal buildings that reached for the sky, and individuals leaving behind generations of family to construct their own modern futures.

Outside Aimee's tent, a handmade sign read "Get Right with God." At the front, Aimee's arms rose up toward the sky as her words reached out into the air. The people in the audience were at a precipice, Aimee told them, a moment of divine importance, predicted by the Bible. Just like the Apostles two millennia before, they were at a turning point in history. If they opened their hearts and souls to Jesus, they would experience an incredible gift of transformation. The Bible had prophesied this time. The moment was now: *this is that*.

Aimee was spellbinding, hypnotic, powerful. People stood on tiptoe to watch her. She was like an ancient priestess, conjuring elemental and divine powers and funneling them down into the tent, to the heart-hungry multitude.

"My signs are written in the sun, moon, and in the stars. My signs are written on the stormy billows that break on the shores. My signs are written in the storm-clouds, in the tornadoes, the flood, the drought. My signs are written in the caterpillar and locust. My signs are written in my saints, gathered together in my name to wait for the Rapture," Aimee would shout out to the crowd, casting her vision as mystical, the times as urgent. "Behold the Pharisees and the hypocrites of the world cannot discern the signs of the times, but I am in the midst, saith the Lord."[5]

As people cried out in response to Aimee's prophetic words, anticipation of what was about to come next took hold. Women and men screamed and moaned, their hands outstretched like vines shooting into the air. Aimee prayed over men with crippled limbs and diseased children, she wrote. She observed real transformations that she recorded for posterity: "Two young men were healed, one of a broken arm, broken at three places and dislocated at the wrist: the other of a broken hand. Both removed the plaster and the splints before the audience, convincing everyone that they were made every whit whole. One sister was healed instantly of cancer."[6]

Divine healing had become a widespread popular movement across a variety of denominations by the late nineteenth century. Amid a confluence of forces, faith healing became an accepted part of life following a societal shift in ideas of pain, suffering, and invalidism. For centuries, the notion of suffering had been one of the highest forms of Christian piety. But innovations in medicine, surgery, and the treatment of pain began to chip away at this concept.[7] More and more, the ideal Christian was seen as a perfectible being—strong in spirit and body as they worked to spread the gospel. Divine healing was popular across economic and racial divides, and women were a significant force in the movement. Particularly when it came to the realm of "female conditions," divine healing offered opportunities and answers when the Western medical establishment was still in the dark ages.

In the face of Aimee's miraculous healings, the audience responded in kind—filled with the Holy Spirit as they would reach out to touch the spellbinding evangelist. The crowd fed some appetite inside her. All eyes were on her. Soon, according to Aimee's recollection, the gift of tongues would quickly fall on the audience. Harold, from the back of the room, would watch astonished as the collection plate filled.

Aimee used the money from the altar call to purchase a car in Tampa. On its side, she and Harold painted "Jesus Saves!" She called it her Gospel Car, and it became her traveling billboard. In St. Petersburg, Aimee watched as a line of automobiles gathered for a Mardi Gras parade. "Suddenly the Lord spoke to me," she recalled, "and said: 'Decorate your car and join the parade!'" She commanded Harold to drive them over and join. With the top folded down, Aimee played a tiny organ she had placed in the back seat. She shouted to the onlookers, "Oh get ready, get ready for Judgment Day." "After the first astonished stare," Aimee wrote, "the people began to laugh and clap their hands and cheer, and that night the tent was packed, and we had no more trouble getting crowds."[8] Aimee was building her repertoire, unencumbered by a sense of propriety.

Aimee spent the next few months traveling up and down Florida in her Gospel Car. In her writings, there's little mention of the baby or of her husband—her focus was on the work and the growth of her audience. Usually, Harold would do the manual labor of setting up the tents and organizing the printing of the tracts that Aimee wrote. He would fish for food and work odd jobs to pay for supplies. Aimee would stay at the camp with Rolf and type her sermons. The small details of their life on the road in her memoirs are given as evidence of destiny. The farmer who miraculously appeared to tow their car out of the river, the donated food and clothing that arrived just when they were penniless—for Aimee, all of this felt providential.

Doubt for Aimee was just another spiritual test. Sometimes at night, she wrote, the devil whispered to her that this was too hard, too much for her and her young family. Inside her mind, Satan tempted her with images of "others with comfortable homes and warm beds, and points in scorn to our hard canvas cots, with no home comforts, points to our smoky campfire, and says the price is great." But Aimee's belief kept such seduction at bay. "There is no desire in our hearts to go back, for we are happy with Jesus alone, and just one glimpse at the altar, filled with seekers after God, more than repays."[9]

As she and Harold crisscrossed Florida, the crowds grew bigger, and her voice grew louder. In the spring of 1917, Aimee felt called to head back north. They made their way up to Savannah, Georgia, with thinly sketched plans to return to the Northeast and their contacts in New York and Rhode Island.

Throughout her travels, Aimee continued to submit her sermons and essays to the evangelical publications that were flourishing at the time around the United States. The shift in the mid-nineteenth century from hand-operated to steam-powered printing presses led to a radical shift in the mass production of printed materials. The creation of a mass media opened up the public sphere—suddenly anyone could become famous. Popular preachers were some of the first to seize on the opportunity for national fame with this newly affordable medium. More than others, preachers had a constant stream of new material: their weekly sermons. Publishers were pleased with the steady stream of content, readers enjoyed the teachings and piety, and the ambitious evangelicals used the medium to propel themselves to newfound celebrity.[10]

Within this throng, Aimee offered something special—her tone was intimate and confiding, drawing in male and female readers alike. In her words, the divine voice sent a message quoting a passage from the Old Testament: "Write the vision and make it plain, that he may run who readeth it." Aimee initially resisted the call, feeling that there was already a proliferation of Pentecostal tracts. But the message from above was clear: "Nothing is impossible."[11]

So Aimee followed an instinct that would be important throughout her career: she worked to control the means of production to disseminate her message. Instead of submitting sermons to an evangelical publication, she created her own outlet. Aimee understood her role as a messenger for God. The voice in Providence had told her to go out and do the work of an evangelist, to spread the gospel as far and wide as possible. She was absolutely convinced that her voice was fundamental to the fate of humanity. With those stakes, she embraced every opportunity and technique to amplify her voice. She did so at this pivotal moment in the early twentieth century when America was just starting to have a sense of itself as a unified mass that could be spoken to through media.

She received step-by-step divine instructions for how to create a magazine. People were sent to her who could actualize her vision. In Savannah, she met a man who was so inspired by her preaching that he offered to print her pamphlet for the cost of paper. Aimee was convinced once again that it was destiny, that her fate was being guided. But for all the fatefulness, she was also making shrewd commercial moves, building her audience through every available form of communication.

The first edition of her magazine was a four-page, black-and-white, seven-by-ten-inch pamphlet. As they traveled around the South, Aimee sold those who came to see her a year's subscription for twenty-five cents. The magazine offered sermons delivered right to the reader's doorstep, filled with Bible passages and interpretations. Aimee composed the text in bursts of revelation, much of it in the passenger seat of her Gospel Car.

The cover of the first issue featured a drawing of Jesus, floating in the clouds, with text below his feet that read: "And at midnight a cry was made, BEHOLD, THE BRIDEGROOM COMETH! GO OUT YE TO MEET HIM! —MATTHEW 25:6."

The idea of Jesus as a beloved being, as the bridegroom, formed the foundation of Aimee's gospel. As born-again believers, her followers were like blushing newlyweds, waiting for their loved one to come. She named the magazine *The Bridal Call.* Aimee's words were a sort of heavenly come-hither, a promise of intimacy with the divine, a lifting up away from all the darkness that was gathering in the world. The title was taken from one of her favorite passages in the Song of Solomon. *The Bridal Call*'s tone was above all a seduction, an invitation into a new way of seeing and being and believing. Aimee was a skilled writer who employed sensorial description and romantic language. Her tone was often girlish and innocent. Her prose was amorous, adjective-laden, and woozily swooning. She balanced this with herself as a protagonist, rendered as a larger-than-life character, at once down-to-earth and transcendent. She emphasized her fallibility, always—she was prideful and prone to make foolish mistakes, but all of this made her more adorable and magnetic. Readers could relate to Aimee's faults and in doing so emulate Jesus's love for them: forgiving and unconditional.

"Can you not hear His voice sweet as the rushing of many waters calling you? He is saying, 'Rise up my love, my fair one, and come away.' Oh, precious voice! How our hearts are stirred at its bidding!" Aimee wrote, in what would become an established romantic refrain of her sermons. "Rise up from a life of flirting with the world, and dallying with the flesh, and come away to the chambers of the King; away to a life of wakefulness and watchfulness; a life of separation and love, unto the soon coming Bridegroom. O' dear ones, can you hear the Bridal Call? Then rise up and come away."[12]

American readers were confronting urbanization, the mechanization of their work, and the dissolution of traditional gender roles and societal norms; she gave them a nostalgic space for retreat. She gave them a god who was on their level—their own personal Jesus.

The first issue of *The Bridal Call* was published in June 1917. In her inaugural column, entitled "Signs of the Times," Aimee described the contemporary world as biblically prophesied. "What shall be the sign of thy coming, and the end of the world? In answer to this query the Lord tells us of many signs whereby we may recognize the season. Amongst others he tells us there will be Wars and rumors of wars; that nation shall rise up against nation, and kingdom against kingdom: we see this prophecy fulfilled in a startling literal manner."[13]

She continued to write about the worsening famines in Europe, the smallpox epidemic, and even of shipping challenges, as signs of an impending day of judgment. Evidence was everywhere that they were living in the last days of the Bible. But Aimee's genius was that even as she painted a picture of a darkening world, on the edge of ruination, she emphasized the bright joys of salvation instead of the fear. *The Bridal Call* was not a screed, filled with hellfire and damnation, but an invitation to a blossoming spiritual relationship with Jesus. She beckoned readers toward a realm of eternal love and forgiveness if they just stepped toward the light.

Aimee was acutely conscious of how she presented herself, and she fashioned her own image to embody her budding theology. She dressed often in white, with a lace-trimmed collar, like a bride. Her face had a captivating sweetness, with eyes large and bright. At twenty-seven, she was athletically built and appeared older than her years. She piled her auburn hair in a prim bun on top of her head. To many of the men who came to watch her preach, she appeared as an enchanting country girl. To many of the women, she embodied a sentimental apparition from their own wedding days.

When the evening service was finished, Harold would find a quiet place to park the car off the road. They would unpack and build a campfire. Once she put the baby down, Aimee would usually work on the newsletter, leaving Harold to cook and prepare for the next day's travels. The next meal was always a question; they lived day to day on donations of food and loose change. They spent months like this, driving the Gospel Car across rivers and fields, traveling up and down the Eastern Seaboard.

On Christmas Eve of 1917, they camped on the sand in Palm Beach. Harold built them shelter out of fallen palm fronds. They decorated a little palm tree and hung a few toys on the branches for Rolf to find in the morning. From there they headed toward Miami, where she decided to do something radical. She held two meetings—one for a white audience and one for a black audience.

At the turn of the twentieth century, as Florida became a sun-drenched fantasy for domestic tourists, strict racial segregation largely divided African American residents into separate communities. "To the first meeting thronged the rich and fashionable in their automobiles and fine clothing," Aimee wrote of the white Miami crowds. "A tent meeting was a novelty. They came to be amused," she said triumphantly, "but many remained to weep and pray." Still, it was her second meeting, for the "colored saints," that seemed to give her real pride. "Because of the strong racial feeling, the dear colored people did not feel free to attend the white meeting," Aimee wrote in Miami. "The Lord put such a love in my heart for the colored race that it was almost impossible for me to pass one of them on the street without such floods of love welling up in my heart that I had to step up to them and inquire: 'Have you ever heard of the latter rain outpouring of the Holy Spirit, the baptism of the Holy Ghost, and of the soon coming of Jesus?' I think they must have felt my love for them for they flocked about me whilst visiting and distributing tracts in their neighborhoods." Aimee wrote that her gospel was for people of every creed and color but added that her interest and ambition were on the level of the soul and salvation—not social change.

Aimee felt a sense of real accomplishment after delivering her sermons to the African American community in Miami, writing proudly of the two hundred converts who had received the baptism of the Spirit. She was then invited to Key West, where she again boasted about erecting her tent at the "colored camp," a settlement on the other side of town. Photos show Aimee watching as an African American preacher baptizes Rolf in a river. "So for the first time in the Island," Aimee concluded happily, "the white and colored attended the same place of worship and glorified the same Lord side by side. We arranged seats for the white people at the sides, reserving the center for the colored people, but so interested became the people in the meetings that reserve was a thing unknown."[14]

These occasions were significant for Aimee, and she wrote about the experiences in depth in her memoirs over the years. She reprinted the photos taken of her in the camps and often used them as evidence of what she called her "color blindness." But Key West also stands as a clear moment of myopia for her. Florida was a place of incredible danger and violence for the African Americans living there—in the years between 1889 and 1918, 178 African Americans were lynched in the state.[15] In Key West, white law enforcement officers had launched a brutal vendetta against the camps, killing people and driving them from their homes. When Aimee arrived to preach that winter, self-defense was probably top of mind for the African American residents living in Jim Crow Florida.[16] While she would write of these interactions for years to come—of her crossing of the "color line"—she does not mention the hard realities that were affecting the "colored saints" whom she ministered to and photographed. This kind of convenient obliviousness would become a pattern for Aimee as she navigated her own ambition in a society full of racism, sexism, and prejudice, all of which she largely ignored in her preaching, even as she propelled herself forward.

Around this time, as the crowds grew, and Aimee's fame spread, tensions between her and Harold reached a breaking point. Too often Harold found himself in the back of the tent, watching, with sometimes hundreds of people standing between him and his wife. One night, as he walked away, he heard someone ask, "Who is that man?" and the answer was, "Oh, he's just the preacher's husband."[17]

In Key West they stayed up late one night fighting. Harold said he'd had enough—he was tired of traveling, never knowing when their next meal would come, worrying for the baby's safety. The next morning, he left early to go fish for their food. When he came back, Aimee had taken the car and Rolf. Each would claim to have been abandoned. Heartbroken and angry, Harold made his way home to Rhode Island, where he tried to make a go of preaching alone—a few local newspaper advertisements tout Evangelist H. S. McPherson.[18]

Despite the separation, Aimee listened to the voice of Jesus and remained convinced that she was on the right path, and she reverted to her standard solution for any crisis: she wired her mother to come help. Minnie was back in New York with Roberta, who hadn't seen Aimee in almost two years. In a week, they were on a coastal steamer. They arrived in Key West, and Minnie immediately imposed her financial rigor on Aimee and set out to organize her burgeoning community of Pentecostal believers. From then on, all invitations for Aimee to speak were answered with a brief letter from Minnie requesting money: "Sister McPherson will be happy to accept if you can send a small check to cover her travelling expenses."[19]

Minnie and Aimee were together once again, along with both of Aimee's children. Roberta, eight years old, later recalled seeing her mother for the first time after the long absence:

> I gazed in breathless admiration at the copper-haired, white clad angel on the platform above me. Mother's arms were

> outstretched as she blessed her humble congregation, her face aglow with some mystical inner light, her voice vibrating, joyously alive. Sometimes it boomed like a mighty surf, and sometimes it fell to the hushed whisper of a butterfly's wingbeat, but always it pulled me toward her with the force of an invisible magnet . . . Could this glorious creature really be my own, my very own mother? Was it true that I was going to live with her forever? What happened from now on, I knew beyond a doubt that my life would never, ever, be ordinary again.[20]

Minnie and Aimee traveled throughout the South and East Coast that year with Aimee's young children in the back of the car. There were setbacks—poverty, lack of shelter, the Spanish flu, frequent hunger, and tropical storms. In July, Aimee attended a monthlong national camp meeting for Pentecostals in Philadelphia. The crowds reportedly totaled more than ten thousand, with people driving in from twenty-five states.[21] Aimee played an instrumental role in helping organize, and she preached and danced with the crowds. They left with invitations to Pentecostal churches across the nation. Aimee bought a new, more powerful car and painted it with her favorite slogans. On one side, in dripping white paint, it read WHERE WILL YOU SPEND ETERNITY? On the other, it read JESUS IS COMING SOON—GET READY. Then, in November 1918, after three years' living on the road, the voice in Aimee's head told her to drive west, to the promised land of Los Angeles.

8

CITY OF ANGELS

When Aimee drove into Los Angeles on December 21, 1918, she had only, as she would say time and again, "ten dollars and a tambourine." In the back seat of her Oldsmobile Touring Car were Roberta and Rolf, along with Mabel Bingham, an assistant. Minnie sat beside Aimee in the front. She served as the ballast to Aimee's spirit-filled wanderings, procuring money and supplies and mapping the road ahead. The women were some of the first to have driven across the country's new highways without a man, adding to Aimee's mythology as a swashbuckling evangelist adventurer.

The trip had taken nearly two months. Stopping every hundred miles or so, they had slept either in the homes of evangelical compatriots or camped by the side of the road. In the towns where they stayed, they encountered families depleted by the Spanish flu, which would kill more than five hundred thousand Americans over the next two years. "We were called into houses where poor people were lying so low their eyes seemed glassy and the rattle in their throats," Aimee wrote of the pandemic victims she encountered. But in the same breath, she praised the miracle of healings, for with her help,

"The Lord marvelously raised them up."[1] Aimee had contracted the virus in early October but quickly recovered; she took this as a sign that her body was blessed by a higher power. Before they'd left the East Coast, Roberta had been diagnosed with double pneumonia, and Aimee watched in distress as her daughter became increasingly ill, sometimes seeming just "an hour from death." Still haunted by Robert's sudden death eight years earlier, Aimee had stood over her daughter's feverish body and searched for a sign. She felt the voice of God telling her that the journey was destiny: she must go to Los Angeles.

Roberta recovered, and the children spent weeks on the road, waiting in the living rooms and kitchens of strangers as their mother stood over countless bedsides along the way, stroking bodies and summoning a higher power. As her ministry grew, Aimee was called upon to do more and more healings. She would work in one room of a home with the sick, while Minnie took down names and addresses of the patrons and signed them up for subscriptions to *The Bridal Call*. Mile by mile, they built a following through miracles and magazines.

Los Angeles at that time was not only one of the fastest-growing cities in the world but one of the fastest-growing cities in the history of the world. In the span of thirty years, it had gone from a dusty outpost inhabited by a few thousand ranchers and farmworkers into one of the wealthiest places on the planet. The last stop on the trail of westward expansion, Los Angeles sat between the desert and the ocean, a dry valley that settlers had just begun to shape into a fantasy of civilization and abundance. Unlike other American municipalities, Los Angeles, it seemed, had manifested itself through pure desire. It wasn't an outgrowth of an existing waterway or a railroad terminus but a wasteland that had been reimagined as a paradise. To borrow a perfect analogy from the historian Kevin Starr, Los Angeles was "the Great Gatsby of American cities."[2] It was a destination for those seeking second chances, opportunity, and reinvention—the perfect place for Aimee to build a following.

As Aimee turned her Oldsmobile toward downtown Los Angeles, she was passing over roadways only recently created by engineers and real estate speculators. Los Angeles was still being parceled up and sold to the rest of the nation as an oasis.

Aimee marveled at the oil wells and the palm trees, the groves of citrus as they made their way into the City of Angels. She would later write, "I had the feeling that here I would meet my destiny."[3]

As she crossed the hills into the San Fernando Valley, Aimee was reborn as a Californian—all previous heritage vanished. She would be remembered as an Angeleno, not a Canadian. She later penned a song to express her feelings about her adopted home:

California—
Where the golden sun is shining, shining all day long,
Where the song-birds fill the happy air with golden song,
That's California! My California!
Garden spot of God and Man,
Favorite Child of Uncle Sam,
That's my sunny, that's my honey,
That's my sunny California.[4]

In the back seat, Roberta cradled her doll, Dorothy. For girls and dolls alike, *Dorothy* was one of the most popular names in America in those years. The country had fallen in love with the heroine from the book *The Wonderful Wizard of Oz*. The story of the orphaned country girl who was transported, via cosmic forces of nature, to an enchanted urban metropolis where she fought entrenched evil struck a particular chord for the fifty million Americans who had moved in the past decades from rural life to the cities. Millions of those people were pouring into California, their lives shifting from the agrarian to the urban, and that meant a transformation of everyday life—the houses people lived in, the food they ate, the clothes they wore, the work they did, the crimes they feared.

L. Frank Baum, the author of *The Wonderful Wizard of Oz*, had himself decamped to Los Angeles shortly after writing the modern-day parable in 1900. Los Angeles felt like all that was enchanting about Oz, with its wide-open spaces, sunshine-soaked days, and balmy nights. Aimee's children's dream of what Los Angeles could be was sugarcoated and simple—they would have a yard, a rosebush, and a canary. After living on the road with their mother and grandmother, eating fish from a river, sleeping in the Gospel Car—what they dreamed of most of all was their own home. Aimee was buoyed by a sense of predestination, writing in her first memoir of the "guard of angels" who kept watch over them through the journey.

Aimee, exhausted but full of hope, sailed into town at an incredibly fortuitous and fecund moment. It was the beginning of a century of monumental growth—for both the city and Pentecostalism. The spiritual landscape of Los Angeles was ready-made for her.

The city was a breeding ground for radical ideas on how to connect to God and self. Much of this came from its image as a place that would give renewed life to the ill with its sparkling clean air and balmy ocean breezes. Rapid industrialization and crude coal-burning technologies had made many American cities filthy places, with streets covered in soot, lungs heavy with disease. Many Americans were obsessed with the healing power of clean, fresh air, and Los Angeles had it in seemingly endless supply. It was a modern civilization built on advertisements printed by real estate agents and sold to folks on the East Coast and in the Midwest. The pitch was a healthy utopia, "the smokeless city," a place where the sun shone all the time, and the desert warmth eased the spirit.

But the full blossoming of Los Angeles as a city wasn't possible until the water came to the desert. The vision of a modern Los Angeles was initially the stuff of smoke and mirrors—a real estate speculation advertised to the rest of America but without the infrastructure to yet make it real. That water is Hollywood history now, but in 1910, the city of three hundred thousand was straining at capacity. William Mulholland's aqueduct opened in 1913, five years before Aimee's arrival. The engineer stood beside the geyser of water, stolen from the farmers of far-off Owens Valley, and uttered words as if he were a prophet: "There it is, take it."

Mulholland's water ushered in a century of growth and transformation for Los Angeles. As Aimee drove toward the ocean, she crossed land that was only just then being sold by ranchers and farmers to developers to become Beverly Hills, Culver City, and Hollywood. The motion picture industry in particular made it a city that defined the way stories were told and gave shape to the hopes and dreams of people in every corner of the globe. Los Angeles became a mirage factory, a place that exported dreams, transforming the way that people in the coming century would dress, talk, argue, dream, and make love. Amid all this mythmaking, it also became a place that dramatically shifted ideas about how to believe in and worship God.

Dating back to the eighteenth century and the Spanish colonization of California, Los Angeles was predominately Catholic until the 1880s, when midwestern Protestants began to settle in the area. By the time Aimee arrived, Los Angeles was run by a WASP elite—more than 90 percent of elected officials declared themselves Protestant. Most were Episcopalians and Methodists. But from its earliest days, Los Angeles was a place where spiritual searchers flocked, and unusual beliefs blossomed. "It is a young city, crude, wildly ambitious, growing," wrote the critic Louis Adamic at the time, with scathing insight. "It has halitosis and osmidrosis; and to kill the stench it gargles religious soul-wash and rubs holy toilet-water and scented talc between its toes."[5]

As the birthplace of the Pentecostal movement, Los Angeles marked a spiritual homecoming for Aimee. Pentecostalism had expanded among working-class folks in Los Angeles who had uprooted themselves from their rural communities and families in their search for economic stability. Aimee gave herself just a day to recover from her epic cross-country trip before she embarked on her preaching career in her new city. She deposited her mother and children in the home of a family of subscribers to her magazine who had offered to take them all in. She headed to a Pentecostal mission downtown, where she found the pastor-in-residence floundering, sloppily dressed and preaching to a dozen half-awake congregants.

Ushered to the front of the room, Aimee buzzed with the energy from her tent revivals. She was costumed as a prim, virginal sort of nurse. "Call me Sister," she said. She swished her ankle-length navy cape and wore her hair in a bun piled high on her head, tendrils of hair curling around her face. Mixing intensity and yearning, Aimee's brand of worship was something the recently arrived folks of Los Angeles feasted upon as she spoke of her childhood on the farm, the taste of fresh cow's milk, and the wondrousness of being alive in this biblically chosen moment. Within a week, the auditorium was so full that people were being turned away. Soon, another Pentecostal group invited her to move her services to a hall that seated 3,500.

Azusa Street was just a few short blocks away, a narrow alley on the outskirts of the booming new downtown. As quickly as the African American preacher William J. Seymour had ignited a religious firestorm in the Azusa Street mission in 1906, he'd encountered challenges to his leadership. Much of that conflict centered around race. The early days of the revivals were remarkable for their free-spirited, unencumbered interracial worship. There had been a fleeting hope that the outpouring of Christian love would conquer racial divides. But Seymour's rising celebrity quickly created jealousy and greed from early white Pentecostal leaders, including those who had once served as his mentors.

In the fall of 1906, Charles Parham, the white pastor from Kansas who had helped fund Seymour's trip to Los Angeles, arrived in the city to share in the religious outpouring. Seymour welcomed Parham, his former teacher, even offering him space to preach. But the good feelings didn't last. Parham angrily denounced the racially mixed congregation in Seymour's Pacific Apostolic Faith Movement, declaring he was repulsed by white women commingling with Black men at the mission, and he expressed contempt for the "holy-rolling dancing-jumping, shaking, jabbering, chattering, wind-sucking and giving vent to meaningless sounds and noises," which he equated with animalistic baseness. "God is sick to his stomach," Parham said.

Seymour tried to resolve the situation, but ultimately asked Parham to leave.[6]

Following his departure, another white midwestern founding father of Pentecostalism, William Durham, presented himself in downtown LA, also looking to share in the glory and excitement that Seymour was generating. But Durham—who had ordained Aimee back in Chicago—also fell out with Seymour, this time over control and tenets of the faith, needling doctrinal questions about the exact sequence of the predicted end-times. These fractures and the entrenched white supremacy soon divided and dissipated the Pentecostal movement in Los Angeles and beyond. Seymour's interracial congregation shrank, his power waned, and in the ensuing decade, the fervor lessened. Seymour never had much interest in fundraising, and the mission fell on hard times. Seymour's vision of an interracial Pentecostal church was never realized. In 1914, at a meeting in Arkansas, three hundred delegates from Pentecostal missions around the United States organized themselves into Assemblies of God, intentionally separating themselves from the African American Church of God in Christ.[7]

In the dozen years since the Azusa Street revivals, Seymour had maintained his Apostolic mission there, despite an onslaught of challenges. Over time he had nurtured his core constituency of African American members. He had also written of his disappointment that white Pentecostals had emphasized sanctification through speaking in tongues above all else. For him, the real miracle of Azusa Street had been about the breaking down of the rigid social barriers of class, race, gender, and creed.

"The secret is," Seymour wrote of Pentecostalism, "one accord, one place, one heart, one soul, one mind, one prayer."[8] For him, the true church was one that reflected and encompassed the diversity of humanity.

With all the noise around glossolalia, and the healings, and the signs of the times, he felt that Christian love had been forgotten. Seymour's reputation was of gentleness and contemplation, but he felt a profound concern for the frightening increase in racial violence in those years. To create awareness, the NAACP published a study that year, looking back at the past thirty years of lynching in America, during which time 2,522 African Americans were killed. In 1918, there had been a string of high-profile violence, including the sadistic execution of Mary Turner, a pregnant Black woman in Georgia, and the torture and murder of Jim McIlherron in Tennessee. Seymour, who traveled nationally during this time, was keenly aware of this violence. In 1915, he had published his ninety-five-page *Doctrines and Discipline of the Azusa Street Apostolic Faith Mission*, in which he mourned the turn to racial division among the different Pentecostal branches. "Our colored brethren must love our white brethren and respect them in truth so that the word of God can have its free course, and our white brethren must love their colored brethren and respect them in the truth so that the Holy Spirit won't be greaved [*sic*]. I hope we won't have any more trouble and division of spirit."[9]

In a complex baton toss of history, records show that Seymour went to see Aimee preach when she first arrived in Los Angeles.[10] There's an account from a white congregant who knew Seymour from the Azusa days and was thrilled to see "Brother Seymour" at Aimee's revival. She noted only that he said he wasn't feeling well, and that his heart hurt. He would die a few years later from a heart attack—although his followers said it was truly of a broken heart over the loss of what could have been. There's no record of Aimee interacting with the man who was responsible for the faith that had transformed her life. She never wrote of Seymour, who in turn never wrote of Aimee, nor asked for recognition. Aimee had grabbed hold of the spirit of Azusa, supercharged it with her charisma and fundraising abilities, and repackaged it for a mostly mainstream white audience. The experience she offered connected quickly to her California congregants.

"Such weeping and singing and dancing!" Aimee wrote of these first days in Los Angeles. "The windows of Heaven were opened; sinners were saved, believers baptized with the Holy Ghost, ofttimes from twelve to twenty in a single meeting. The shouting and the heavenly singing of the people, with its attendant cloud of glory, so filled the tabernacle that at times the priests and the Lord's ministers could not minister."[11]

Loveless couples embraced and wept, their marriages and souls saved. Drunks, filled with the Holy Spirit, renounced their sins. Attendees lost control of their bodies and their voices as they fell to the floor, slain under the power. They saw souls descending into hell, shrieking and crying out to be rescued. They saw God as a farmer, harvesting grain and cutting down fruitless trees. And soon they were shouting her name, not Jesus's: "Sister Aimee! Sister Aimee!"

One Sunday night in January, a young woman leapt to her feet in the Pentecostal mission and yelled out, "The Lord shows me that I am to give a lot to Mrs. McPherson. I have four lots of land and do not need them all. I am not called to preach the Gospel, while she is, and by giving the land that the little ones may have a home and she may be free to come and go in the Lord's work, I will share in her reward."[12] Excitement rippled through the crowd. Men from the audience rose and said they would build the foundation of her home, do the construction, the lathing, craft her bed, her tables, her chairs by hand. Service for Aimee would be an honor, a spiritual act in itself.

By April, Aimee's followers had built her a bungalow on Orange Grove in Hollywood. The home gave the children the stability that they had been missing. Aimee's heart was not in child-rearing or homemaking, and she quickly hired a housekeeper who stayed with the children while she traveled the revival circuit, often with Minnie. "I was never away from my children more than ten or twelve weeks at a time, though my returning necessitated a trip of three thousand miles," Aimee later wrote. "As soon as I had loved and cuddled the kiddies and seen to their welfare on these hurried trips home, I would start back again for the next revival."[13]

She drove her Gospel Car up and down the California coast. She took overnight trains along the Eastern Seaboard and even quick puddle jumper flights to reach her destinations. She held multiday revivals in Tulsa, Chicago, Scranton, Baltimore, Washington, DC, Atlantic City, Montreal, St. Louis, Dallas, and dozens of small cities and towns. She preached wherever she was invited, whether it was in an opera house in Akron, Ohio, or in a revival meeting in Oakland, California. If there was an audience, Aimee went—during her first year in Los Angeles, she attended more than two dozen revivals outside of the city, many in the Midwest and on the East Coast.

Carey McWilliams, whose book *Southern California: An Island on the Land* is considered the definitive account of Los Angeles during this time, saw Aimee as an ingenious populist and saleswoman. Following many visits to watch her preach, he described Aimee as one of the first to name and create an identity around the "folks," the working-class midwesterners who came in droves to the city at this time. "She made migrants feel at home in Los Angeles, she gave them a chance to meet other people, and she exorcised the nameless fears which so many of them had acquired from the fire-and-brimstone theology of the Middle West."[14]

In February 1919, a wire service story on the "Feminine Evangelist" set the pattern for how the press treated Aimee early on and how she both played to and undercut their expectations. It made the exaggerated claim that Aimee was "the only woman evangelist in the United States." The writer asked her why a woman should be allowed to preach the gospel. Her response was a feat of logic that harkened back to her first argument with her mother over preaching. She conceded that women were responsible for humanity's fall from grace, which was the central reason that evangelical churches had given for denying women access to the pulpit. But then she went further, arguing that because of the mess women had made, they were responsible for cleaning it up. "Women brought sin into the world according to the Bible. It was Eve who fed Adam the forbidden fruit. So, it's up to the daughters of Eve to undo that evil and help remove the curse of wickedness from the world." Aimee's account of traveling the back roads of the nation was dramatized for readers in romantic language. "Although she had not a cent of money and no financial backer, she bundled herself and her children into the 'gospel car' and set out."[15] Blurry photos showed her standing in front of her car in a white dress, her head tilted demurely, her hands full of pamphlets.

Aimee's entrance into Los Angeles coincided with one of the great newspaper wars in the country, pitting the *Los Angeles Times* against the *Los Angeles Examiner*. In the years to come, she would both succeed and suffer from the rivalry: her endless appetite for spectacle made great copy for the hometown papers. The *Times* was owned by Harry Chandler. Republican, Protestant, shrewd, elitist, and exceedingly private, Chandler was instrumental in bringing the aviation and film industries to the city.[16] During his lifetime he helped to make Los Angeles a true metropolis, putting his political and social weight behind such projects as the Los Angeles Aqueduct, the Los Angeles Coliseum, the Hollywood Bowl, San Pedro Harbor, Caltech, and many others. At the height of his power, he was the largest private landowner in Southern California; he built an empire that would amount to half a billion dollars by the time he died. No one wielded more influence in the city than Chandler, and the paper was his mouthpiece.

But he wasn't without his challengers. William Randolph Hearst, the owner of the *Los Angeles Examiner*, was loud, outlandish. He loved to be the center of attention. Hearst—whose father had been a wealthy miner and US senator from California—had used his inheritance to transform journalism in San Francisco and New York with his taste for the sensational and populist. When he printed his first edition of the *Los Angeles Examiner* in December 1903, he held a parade in downtown Los Angeles, with a band, fireworks, and people chanting "Hearst for president!" In contrast to the Republican-leaning *Times*, with its dry, erudite prose, the Hearst papers were decidedly antiwar, pro-labor, and Democrat.

But the crowds that gathered around the country for Aimee soon attracted the attention not just of the *Times* and the *Examiner* but of the papers back east. Soon newspapers were comparing her to the most famous evangelist of the day, proclaiming her "the female Billy Sunday," which stuck and quickly made her a darling for feature writers on slow news days. Aimee had a natural ease when dealing with the press, an ability to connect through humor and self-deprecation. Even in her earliest newspaper photos, she is connecting with her public, gazing into the lens with a large smile and thrusting a Bible toward the heavens. She shed any rural hesitation and began to make urbane jokes and jabs with journalists. She acknowledged her childhood theatricality and wondered why as a woman she could perform on a stage but not in the pulpit. "Before I consecrated my life to this service of love for God and humanity, I was an elocutionist. No one questioned my right to amuse the church congregation with witticisms and comical recitations. That was 'speaking in church,' wasn't it?"[17] Still, stories about her usually ran in the women's pages, alongside articles about "frivolous blouses," "nagging men," or "beauty tips for schoolgirls."

Aimee loved the publicity, believing it helped her mission. She hammed it up for photographers, shaking her fist in the air with the Bible clutched against her chest. She disagreed with Billy Sunday's emphasis on sin and the fear of eternal damnation. It was the opposite of what she offered her followers: a loving invitation into an intimate relationship with Jesus. More than anything, she didn't want to be the female version of anybody. She was a star in her own right. Standing in the wings, her mother did everything required to help her shine.

The Personal Testimony of Aimee Semple McPherson, a small pamphlet, was published in 1916. Aimee's ability to hold people's attention with her own story made them feel close to her, her experience of Jesus universal and transcendent. Just beneath the surface of her observations was the sense that she was just like her dear readers. In 1919, she expanded upon that pamphlet with a 685-page book: *This Is That: Personal Experiences, Sermons and Writings of Aimee Semple McPherson, Evangelist*. "Cloth and gold bound," it sold for three dollars each—about eighty-five in today's dollars. It was a significant investment. Aimee was careful to give her version of the economics, telling her followers that her publications were sold at a loss, and that the price of subscribing to *The Bridal Call*—fifty cents a year—was far less than her actual printing and mailing costs.

As she developed her narrative style, Aimee stopped using "I" and switched to the first-person plural. "We are bewildered," she wrote of her experience of seeing large crowds gathering to see her. "What will we say? What will we do?"[18] At first, in those early days of national travel, the "we" mostly meant Aimee and her mother. Answering correspondence, collecting and counting money, arranging travel, and much more, Minnie was manager and administrator and assistant. Aimee presented her mother in these stories as an anchoring figure, someone who was beside her, behind her, bolstering her. But Minnie saw the two of them as equal partners in the work. She loved and believed in her daughter and saw the power that she had over people—Aimee was Minnie's tool to do God's work—just as she had promised and prophesied in the snow thirty years earlier.

9

FAITH HEALING

With the help of the press, Aimee soon had a national reputation as a miracle worker. "Blind Woman Has Sight Instantly Restored at Lyric Revival," read one headline from Baltimore. "Paralytic Woman Claims Limbs No Longer Useless," read another. "Lame Man Skips." "You can imagine the results," Aimee wrote of the increasingly hyperbolic coverage, celebrating her as a "Miracle Woman." "Hundreds of sufferers and cripples flocked from far and near and I, well, I was never so frightened in all my life. Taking one look at the throng of sick people, I ran downstairs, buried my face in a chair in the corner and began to weep."[1] She prayed, worried that she would not be able to help the growing crowds. But the voice of God reassured her that it wasn't her doing the work—it was Him. Over time, she and Minnie had honed a detailed system of operations as they traveled. As the revivals grew, Minnie's main job became organizing the pandemonium that surrounded her increasingly famous daughter.

In the spring of 1920, they traveled to Dayton, Ohio, where Minnie had booked a three-thousand-seat hall. The meeting was remarkable only in that Aimee took the time to write down an eight-thousand-word account of what took place there. A pastor in Dayton named A. B. Cox had written to Aimee that the city was in the throes of a multiyear revival. He wanted her to come for a few weeks. Aimee (or Minnie, more likely) wrote back a passionate form letter. "Write again if the Lord lays definitely upon your heart the matter of my coming there. We can only pray the Lord to guide us so that not a moment's unnecessary time be wasted, for surely today if ever the King's business requires haste."[2]

Aimee came to Ohio in early May. According to newspaper accounts, more than four thousand people, who had traveled from twenty states, crammed into Memorial Hall, a massive Beaux Arts auditorium with two-story pillars outside the entrance and a soaring arched ceiling. Aimee knew that many had come because they had heard about her ability to heal the sick and the lame.

The first morning of the services, a limousine lent by the local pastor took Aimee from her hotel to the hall. The route was thick with ambulances, trolleys, buses, cars, and hearses, all of which contained people in search of a miraculous transformation. From the car window, Aimee saw bodies splayed out on cots and stretchers being carried in. The mass of suffering overwhelmed her. "Oh God," she whispered, "is the whole world sick? Are they all coming to the Memorial Hall to Thee for healing?"

As the limousine inched toward the back entrance, followers pressed against the car. "Oh lady! Pray for me. Oh!" they shouted. "Lay your hands on this man and pray just for a moment." It was a chorus of anguish and misery, people desperate for miracles. "We have brought this child forty miles, surely you can let us in."

As she exited the car, police officers linked arms and formed a pathway for Aimee to walk through the crowd. She dashed toward the entrance, seeing people in a blur, but she noticed that the officers' faces were close to tears with pain as the anguished throng threw themselves against their backs, trying to get to her. The door slammed behind her, but she could still hear the moans.

Aimee made her way toward the stairwell. There, she looked down into the basement and saw a horde of people in wheelchairs and on gurneys. Amid the chaos, Minnie moved about with focus and authority, directing nineteen female ushers, all wearing crimson sashes across their chests. Just as she had during her days with the Salvation Army, Minnie brought a regimented order to God's work. The ushers gave each person a card to fill out, listing their name, church, and disease or ailment. Finally they were asked if they were willing to accept Jesus as their personal savior that day.

Once the cards were completed, the ushers gave each supplicant a number. Then, on a series of blackboards, they hashed out a seating chart and a run of show, slotting people into a numbered system to receive Aimee's divine healing.

Aimee greeted her mother, and the two made their way up the stairs. She passed by a security guard, who apologized for the lack of air, explaining that the windows had all been closed to keep out the crowds. "We had to lock them Sister," he told her. "People were passing the sick through the windows." The press of people, the lack of air, made it hard for Aimee to breathe, and she felt dazed, "as if in a dream." She glanced at her wristwatch—a pragmatic gift from her mother—and heard the pianist beginning to play the dulcet chords of the opening song.

This was Aimee's cue. She made her way out into the dazzle of lights of the hall. Standing on the stage, she looked down and saw the space reserved for the seven hundred people who had come to be healed. Beyond that were thousands, seated and standing, all with their heads bent in prayer. Aimee looked up to the high arch of the ceiling and blinked at the afternoon sunlight flooding in from windows. Immediately, she was filled with a supernatural charge as she felt the hum of the crowd fusing with something inside her. She felt caught in the nexus of human suffering and sublime redemption. Christ must be seeing the crowd just as she was—with compassion, pity, and forgiveness. She dropped to her knees and prayed, summoning that energy into her body. Flanking the stage, the choir stood and sang, their voices filling the hall: "What a friend we have in Jesus / All our griefs and sins to bear."

Pastors and audience members who had encountered Aimee in other cities stood up and shouted out their testimony of how Sister Aimee had healed them—tumors, cataracts, disease, all had miraculously vanished. The groundswell introduction felt spontaneous. That day, Aimee decided to skip a sermon and instead simply described back to the audience the electricity that buzzed all around them: God was in the room, right there with them, and His supernatural power was available to them if they could accept the healing balm of salvation.

"Christ is the great physician for body, soul and spirit," she shouted out. "It is He who forgiveth our iniquities, and heals all our diseases." People in the audience were weeping, their hands outstretched toward Aimee. She moved as if in a trance, as if she were a divining rod, summoning down celestial forces into the hall in Dayton. As the audience heaved and swelled, Aimee transitioned seamlessly to the altar call, when people were invited to the front to announce their devotion to Jesus. In her white dress, with a rose corsage and blue cape, she was their Heavenly Sister, walking them toward redemption. "The people are leaning forward in their seats," Aimee wrote. "Every face is turned expectantly toward the pulpit. Eagerly, they drink in the words we bring them from the sacred page." When it was time for the healing, two hundred people rushed the stage, and as they approached Aimee, she shouted, "Jesus is the same yesterday, today and forever! The things He loved to do when on this earth, He still loves to do today . . . Only one thing hindered the workings of His power, when He walked the shores of Galilee, that thing was unbelief."[3]

Aimee wrote that she sensed God all around her that day. "The atmosphere of that room was simply charged with divine power," she wrote. "You could feel the very presence of God the moment you entered the room."

"That's it, Brother! Don't wait a moment," she cried. "Come, Sister, come, Brother, that's right, don't be ashamed of the tears. Come as you are. Here bring your wounded heart. Here tell your anguish. Earth has no sorrow that Heaven can't not heal." She spoke to two audiences—to those in the room but also to the holy being all around them. "Here they come, Jesus—they are coming to you now," she narrated. "O, who could stay away from such a Savior as Thee! Who could resist such unfathomable love."[4]

As men and women lined up to receive her blessing, Aimee's staff discreetly enacted a set change. A cot and a table and a silver urn of anointing oil were placed onstage along with seven chairs for those who came to be healed. Clutching their paper numbers, the hopeful trembled with apprehension and wonder. The great stream of injured and unwell solidified into a thick line that wove around the great hall.

They came one by one. Blind, bodies bent, eyes filled with tears as they shuffled toward her. She held them individually, tenderly—by the hands, by the shoulders—sometimes rubbing oil along a crooked spine, caressing their ears, massaging hands and legs gnarled by paralysis. She was motherly and sweet with all of them. *The Dayton Journal* described the scene: "So many were appearing for aid that each necessarily received brief attention and only the machine-like and orderly manner in which group after group went forward enabled the evangelist to prescribe for the many she did before the services closed."[5]

Aimee's white dress dripped with perspiration and the grime from all the bodies that had touched her. She had her process of connecting to the divine: she envisioned the individual free of disease; she tried to take the power that she felt all around her and transfer it to the broken bodies before her. "In the name of Jesus," she shouted. "You shall walk. Rise, and you shall be healed." Aimee wasn't working alone. The "we" in her narrative had evolved; it was the one that did the work—Aimee and Jesus, within one body. "We kneel in prayer and lay our hands upon those weakened limbs. But we must not stay to watch! Pray on and on, for hundreds are yet feverishly watching the clock."[6]

Newspapers gave a rapt account of the service—a girl crippled from birth who could walk, a woman blind from cataracts who could see, a man with a degenerative disease who handed his crutches to his son and began to walk across the stage. Aimee made a list of the afflictions she tried to cure that day. The list conjures a postwar hellscape of suffering:

> Weakness, spinal trouble, neuritis, kidney trouble, deaf and dumb, hip diseases, varicose veins, disease of the throat, ulceration and paralysis after effects of the flu, meningitis, St. Vitus dance, crippled, loss of voice, cataract of eyes, palsy, afflictions of ear, diabetes, crossed eyes, curvature of the spine, paralysis, rheumatism, nervous diseases, locomotor-ataxia, loss of finger nails, hand and foot disease, broken hand, bronchitis, asthma, heart disease, tumor on arm, deafness, blindness, goiter, tuberculosis, growths on different parts of the body, valvular heart trouble, gall stones, epilepsy, dislocated hip, shell shock, stiff knee, chronic disease, dropsy, cancer and inflammation of the stomach, liver trouble, broken ankle, etc.

She worked past six o'clock, but the line never seemed to get shorter. Finally, Minnie tapped her on the shoulder, wiped the sweat from Aimee's face, and whispered, "You really must stop now, dear. The car is waiting to take you to your room." A new crowd was already gathered outside for the evening service, set to begin in an hour. Police officers and her small entourage helped Aimee move through the hordes, pushing her past those who yelled for her to make an exception, to let them be the last one healed.[7]

She rejoiced in the crowds. They were a confirmation of destiny. The multitudes were a miracle. It was the kind of success she had dreamed about since she abandoned her housewife life back in Providence. But after she left Dayton, she described the experience in *The Bridal Call* in terms that hinted at a subtle unease with what was increasingly expected of her. "If you were once caught in a crowd like this, if you then went to the doors and saw the crowd outside was still larger than the crowd inside, and they pressed you, wouldn't you just realize how Jesus had to get into a boat and push away from land, in order to preach to the people." In her writings she often described the outreached hands as grasping at her. The transformation that she saw on those stages powered her incredible ambition, her relentless, nonstop travel and preaching schedule. But the endlessness of the need, the vast horizon filled with those who wanted her to heal them, these ceaseless waves of demands from the public, also began to erode something inside her.

10

A LADY BUILDS A TEMPLE

Aimee dreamed of a California home for her preaching, a place where people would come to her rather than her having to perpetually travel and develop new audiences. The dream remained an abstraction until one day when Aimee was out driving with her mother. The two women passed a small lake in a neighborhood called Echo Park. The area was working-class, somewhat bohemian, largely avoided by the city's elite. A decade earlier, it been the preferred site for the newly emerging motion picture industry. Not far from the lake had been Keystone Studios, where Charlie Chaplin, Gloria Swanson, and Douglas Fairbanks had all passed through. But by 1920, the stars and the studios had moved west and north to Culver City and the San Fernando Valley.

When Aimee pulled up her car by the park, she was struck by the dappled light that fell on the water, which was thick with lilies. Willow trees blew in the breeze, and there was a shadowy hush. Although just two and a half miles from downtown and located near trolley lines, the area felt "strangely peaceful and quiet."[1] She thought of the sun-scorched sidewalks and the great crowds that she drew, and how they would be so comfortable as they waited for services in this bucolic, shaded neighborhood, an urban oasis. Aimee and Minnie located a lot for sale that overlooked the lake, and Aimee immediately pulled up the "For Sale" sign and began to sketch her vision on the back. It would be a semicircular structure in the shape of a megaphone—a church that would carry her voice.

By 1920, Aimee had become a national name on the revival circuit. She wrote that she sometimes puzzled over why the Holy Spirit hadn't chosen a more central or populous location for her to live—the Midwest or the Northeast—instead of California. But as always, Aimee knew that her actions were divinely ordained, and the divine voice told her to build a temple in the City of Angels.

Initially, she questioned the desire, wondering if it was her own ego that wanted a physical monument. "When this burden first came from heaven, I tried to shake it off, supposing that the idea might be of *self*. But the call persisted," she wrote. "Who ever heard of a woman without earthly backing or any organization behind her undertaking the raising of funds and the erection of such a building?"[2]

Aimee didn't write much about the worldly limits that society placed on her, but her doubts went beyond whether her heart was in the right place. Before the Civil War, a woman's assets belonged to her husband in most states. In the following decades, a series of state-based laws began to allow American women to hold property individually. By the time Aimee was a high school student, at the turn of the twentieth century, at least a third of the United States still did not have any specific provision that allowed a woman to hold assets individually. In 1920, as Aimee began to dream of buying land, courts were known to interpret the laws that did exist loosely, often to the disadvantage of women, and women were not able to access a line of credit from banks without a man as signatory.

On January 4, 1921, the *Los Angeles Times* ran a short piece about Aimee's intentions—"Pentecostal Faith-Healer Dedicates Lot for

Tabernacle." It described her holding a ceremony with "100 friends" who prayed and marched around the new lot on Lake Shore Avenue. "She says God has told her that there is a great future for Los Angeles and has shown this city as the center of a great radiating religious enterprise and so she selected it without any guarantees or known means in sight for the building."[3] Funds for the endeavor were limited, so initially Aimee proposed a 2,500-seat wood structure that would house a round-the-clock revival.

Aimee and Minnie worked out an unusual financial arrangement with their contractor; they would pay in installments as they raised the money from revivals. The construction company—Winter Construction—was making most of its money from building the new grand movie palaces around the city. As they were building Aimee's church, they were also erecting Grauman's Chinese Theatre in Hollywood a few miles away. But Aimee's project was considered an "important job" for the expanding firm. The general manager came to see one of Aimee's sermons as the company was at work. "We have our big auditoriums devoted to the drama, to song, to other purposes. Oh, but how few auditoriums are devoted to the Word of God," he wrote in a letter published in *The Bridal Call*.[4]

That January of 1921, Aimee had been invited to San Diego, 140 miles south of Los Angeles. Always thinking of how to increase her audience, Aimee saw it as a great opportunity to attract tourists who visited California during the winter. "How far-reaching would be the effects?" she wrote in *The Bridal Call*. "Like tying messages to homing pigeons and sending them abroad unto their different homes in every quarter of the globe."[5]

The legendary social critic and journalist Carey McWilliams had a bleaker estimation of why Aimee chose San Diego: it was full of sick, desperate people. "Chronic invalids have always been advised to go to California," he wrote in his 1934 essay "Don't Shoot Los Angeles." "And once there, they drift to San Diego. From San Diego there is no place else to go; you either jump into the Pacific or disappear into Mexico. Seventy per cent of the suicides of San Diego have been put down to 'despondency and depression over ill health.'"[6] In other words, a population interested in faith healing.

Minnie's choice for a venue was unorthodox: she booked Aimee in the Dreamland Arena, a state-of-the-art boxing ring that took up a city block, with stadium seats encircling the stage. Aimee wrote later that she was filled with doubt as she and Minnie arrived on a Wednesday night while a boxing match was being held. During the intermission, the master of ceremonies nervously asked Aimee to make her pitch to the gathered fans to come to her services the next morning. The arena was mayhem, full of men jostling and howling, accompanied by "hard-faced women" who smoked cigarettes, while "laughing intimately into the faces of their escorts." The whole place reeked of sin. "How can words be found to describe those hideous 'yowls' that rent the night," wrote Aimee, in her florid prose. "Men were fighting—fighting with bleeding nostrils—fighting till one went down and took the count, and was carried limply from the ring, uttering weird animal cries of pain and distress."

Aimee had prevailed in small-town chapels, in urban auditoriums with vaulted ceilings, in canvas tents, in cypress groves. But here in the boxing arena, she had come to the most profane of places—a devil's playground full of bloodlust and drinking—to preach her gospel. As her silky white slippers stepped onto the blood-spattered canvas, she crossed a new threshold toward larger opportunity: she wanted every soul she could get, no matter how soiled.

Aimee's instinct for audiences was canny. Dressed in her Sunday best, she asked them to bring "the worst sinner to be found in San Diego" to her services. Bawdy laughter reverberated through the crowd as they shouted back at her: "That's him over there, Sister!" "No! That's him over yonder!" They were elated that this preacher lady had come to them, had spoken to them where they were—not waiting for them to show up hungover and repentant on a Sunday morning. Her boldness, she wrote, led the people to begin to cheer for her. She was a good sport, insisting playfully that they all come the next day.

After the crowds left, Aimee turned to Minnie, their faces mirroring each other's, caught between joy and fear. "Well, thank God, that's over!" Aimee said. Late into the night, they worked with a small crew to transform the arena into a heavenly domain. With a set designer's flair, Aimee arranged to truck in boughs and branches. The flora was wrapped around the pillars and posts, to give the effect of "a cool forest, fragrant, restful and inviting." The bloodstains were scrubbed from the canvas, and flowers sprouted from vases at each corner of the ring—calla lilies, carnations, and orange blossoms. A grand piano was placed at its center. Aimee removed the advertisements for restaurants and jewelry stores that hung on the walls and replaced them with "a new one advertising Jesus."[7]

The next day, the bloodthirsty boxing fans brought their friends and families, and within a few hours the three-thousand-person arena was filled. Over the next three weeks, the crowds grew in what became known as Aimee's "Fight Against the Devil in San Diego." She and her mother had to move to a hotel after people found out where they were living and came banging on the doors of their host's home in the hope of getting an audience with the lady evangelist. Aimee wrote of the increasing intensity and hunger of the crowds—of her tripping on crutches and wheelchairs, of congregants grabbing at her dress, begging for a healing, of voices from every side asking her for something.

In Aimee's writings of San Diego, she described the crowds that came to see her in darker terms than on previous occasions. While the throngs had once been miraculous, bountiful, and joyous, they were now characterized as more insatiable and rapacious and deeply broken. "Mounting the platform, we look down upon those pale and emaciated faces," she wrote. "Some are almost skeletons upon beds, upon chairs, sick babies carried on pillows; the sufferer who has been unable to lie down for years and has to sit bolt upright on air cushions in her chair because of rheumatism; the blind, the halt; the lame, the children whose little bodies are devoured with the results of Tia Juana's sins; the sufferers from cancer, tumor and all manner of disease; the young woman whose limb is decayed and poisoned and must be amputated unless Jesus heals it; the human bodies in cages of steel and plaster . . ."

The revival at the boxing arena was a turning point for Aimee, a moment where she more consciously carved out a new space of religion for the masses as entertainment. But her popularity was giving her pause. Aimee sounded alone in her "we," the divide between her and the multitudes more concrete, the view from above more frightening. Still, she tamped down whatever anxiety and alienation she felt. For the most part, what comes through in her writing from that time is her resolution to bring the gospel to as many people as possible. "You must not break down or give way now!" she wrote, speaking to herself and her audience. "We are going to need every ounce of energy, faith, sympathy and endurance before this day is o'er."[8]

Just when the San Diego revival was ending, Aimee's advertising instincts led her to something even bigger. On a Friday afternoon at the end of January, Aimee told newspaper reporters to meet her at Aviation Field in San Diego. There she gave a short sermon and then fearlessly climbed into a plane and took off—this was at a time when commercial air travel was rare. From the air, she dropped fifteen thousand leaflets onto the city of San Diego, announcing that she would preach the following week at the largest urban park available in the area: Balboa Park, a 1,200-acre green space in the middle of the city.

The following week, the crowds at Balboa Park grew. Marines from nearby Camp Pendleton volunteered to help, and they worked alongside Minnie's female attendants as Aimee laid hands on as many as she could. She described the blur of bodies, goitered and tumored, the jumble of canes and wheelchairs and crutches as the hot sun sank slowly down the sky, the shadows stretching into evening, and she continued to work.

On the last day, the crowds pushed against the barriers that kept them from the stage. Aimee fainted from exhaustion and heat, her white dress soaked through with sweat and filth. As night fell, Minnie tenderly took her away from the crowds, wrapping her in dry clothing, as had become their custom.[9] Over those days the crowd had expanded to thirty thousand people—almost half the population of the entire city of San Diego at the time.

Aimee went back to Los Angeles with $5,000 in cash from collection plates—about $75,000 in today's money. She told her contractor to start building a real foundation for her temple—it would not just be a tabernacle with wooden stands. She appeared at a groundbreaking ceremony in a cloche hat, a stiff high-necked dress, and a coat, her smile gleaming as she jammed her shovel into the earth. Aimee's construction plan was to build the largest space she could afford—piece by piece.

The ever-growing multitudes were meaningful to Aimee. The large crowds that came to see her were seen as a sign of the miraculous. Size had not been a constant in American religion. Martin Luther had railed against the vast gilded structures built by the Roman Empire as symbols of corruption and excess. Early American Protestants in the eighteenth and nineteenth centuries were proud of their small churches and intimate, close-knit congregations as signs of purity and zeal. A confluence of historical factors shifted the modest notions of congregational size, including the transformation of the country from rural to urban. Between gleaming skyscrapers and densely packed tenements, urban tabernacles looked to serve the masses with larger churches that would provide space not only for worship but also for services such as education, commissaries, and other amenities.

Aimee took this idea of bigness and went further—her church would rival the ancient cathedrals in size and elegance. With this new, grander vision, fundraising became a focus. She sold signed photographs of herself, along with subscriptions to her magazine. She came up with the idea of creating "chair-holders," her clever twist on shareholders. She sold the concept to thousands; for twenty-five dollars, they would receive a number that corresponded to a seat inside the Temple they could call their own. Amid the stock market mania of the early 1920s, Aimee told them that they could own a piece of God's temple and the glory of the good that would be done there. Their investment would be amortized in heaven. "Do you know that some poor discouraged sinner may sit in your chair and be converted?"[10]

She proposed the most meaningful return on investment. Over the course of fourteen months—revival to revival, love offering to love offering, chair-holder to chair-holder—Aimee raised the funds she needed to erect her ambition.

As soon as she returned home from San Diego, she received paperwork from Harold: he had filed for divorce, claiming desertion and extreme cruelty. He wrote that she had repeatedly hit him, tore his hair and clothes, and threatened to kill him and herself. "Her mother also threatened to take my life," he wrote in careful cursive. "I never gave either of them any cause at all for their abuse of me."[11]

On the advice of her lawyer, Aimee countersued, accusing him of abandoning her. The proceedings seemed to have little effect on her emotional state—she did not speak of her divorce, even though as a Pentecostal woman this was highly unusual. But somehow Aimee's charisma and force seemed to put her beyond the expectations of the ordinary folks to whom she preached. She went on the road again and spent that spring and summer in Ohio, Mississippi, Arkansas, Texas, and Colorado. As she traveled, the building of her temple became Aimee's obsession. Her vision had expanded beyond just a wooden tabernacle; she wanted something that would become a monument, a building that would serve as a legacy. When she returned late at night to hotel rooms and guest apartments, she pored over the designs. It would be a 5,300-seat auditorium with marble and stained glass and a massive arched ceiling. She kept its megaphone shape and insisted that the acoustics be state-of-the-art.

Aimee, though, never touched the money. That job was Minnie's alone. She was the only one who was allowed—for years—to handle the collection plate offerings. Minnie often worked until three in the morning counting what they brought in, storing the cash in a safe at the Temple. Many speculated that she carried a gun. Minnie harnessed Aimee's charisma and helped her build her vision into a financially viable enterprise.

As Aimee's fame expanded, so did her message. While she emphasized the importance of the Holy Ghost baptism—that visceral experience of Jesus taking possession of one's body—her style was starting to change. By the mid-1920s, on the larger stages, she rarely spoke in tongues. She even pushed back against the more unruly aspects of the Pentecostal style of worship, criticizing the verbose behavior and "fleshly manifestations." There are accounts of her silencing rowdy worshippers who came onto her stage, for which Aimee was criticized as "quenching the Spirit."[12]

But the vast majority seemed to admire Aimee's sincerity and the well-run order with which she conducted her services. At the front of the room, Aimee herself was now the focus of the miraculous; there was less and less of spontaneous gifts breaking out in the crowd, as they once had in the hedonistic atmosphere of the field revivals. Traveling the country, she was invited to join a variety of different born-again religious denominations. These churches—Methodist, Assemblies of God, Baptists—wanted to tap into the evangelical fervor Aimee created.

All these denominations shared Aimee's belief that each person had a personal connection to Jesus and the sense of urgency that biblical times were being enacted. In Aimee's earliest travels through the South, with her tent and Gospel Car, she was "ordained" by several born-again denominations, including the Baptist Church and Assemblies of God. She took these designations happily, like someone collecting honorary degrees, but by the fall of 1921, she began to change her thinking. She started to draft plans to create her own denomination. It was less about conflict with any particulars of belief and more about centralizing control under her own organization.

Aimee shouted to the crowds that the time was urgent, the moment now, but she did not dwell on theological specifics. "My work is not denominational," she told the *San Francisco Examiner* in 1922. "I preach the old-fashioned religion, belief in God, and the Bible and I attack no one. The healing I try to keep subservient to the preaching, for I think spiritual help is the most important."[13]

From the beginning, Aimee made clear that her appeal was that of a direct relationship to the Holy Spirit, rather than dogmatic specifics. The doctrine Aimee preached was defined in many ways by what it was not. "It is so simple, so very simple. I believe in the Bible as the inspired word of God, believe every word of it, believe it from cover to cover! I believe in a personal God and a personal devil; I believe in the Fall of man and his Redemption through the blood of the Saviour; I believe in immortality, in a very real Heaven and a very real Hell. I believe that the gift of God is eternal life through Jesus Christ our Lord, that we are all sinners and may gain salvation only through Divine Grace, through the boundless merciful love of the Saviour who died for us."[14] She was the Goldilocks alternative—not too hot, not too cold. The just-right message on Jesus.

In September 1921, Aimee and her mother registered the Echo Park Evangelistic Association as "a religious and benevolent corporation," with Aimee and Minnie as equal and joint owners. A few months later, in January, she returned her Assemblies of God credentials, going so far as to mail them back to the headquarters in Springfield, Missouri. She was beginning to have a vision of what her own church could be and needed to shake off the claims of the others. That summer of 1922, she attended a ministerial conference at the Trinity Episcopal Church in Oakland. There she organized a group of one thousand fellow religious leaders to form the Foursquare Gospel Association. Her Foursquare Gospel was so named for the four cornerstone beliefs of her faith: personal salvation, Holy Ghost baptism, divine healing, and the belief that Jesus would return to earth soon. Those were the four corners of Pentecostalism, but even to a secular person it sounded positive—honest and patriotic.

On New Year's Day 1923, Aimee celebrated the opening of Angelus Temple—the largest church in America. The building was unlike anything else in the city of Los Angeles. The Temple had cost approximately $340,000, according to the records of Aimee's contractor—equivalent to more than $6 million today. Around town, it was known as "the Million Dollar Temple." A vast, Colosseum-like neoclassical structure, the Temple resembled both a place to worship an ancient Roman god and a theater in which to watch a grand European opera. It was a perfect assemblage of Aimee's sensibilities—dramatic and celestial. Visitors entered off the street through one of seventeen arched entryways. They passed through a hushed low-ceilinged foyer, with thick-pile red carpeting, and through a series of small doors into the vast, soaring domed auditorium, with stadium-style seating up to the rafters.

Looking up, visitors would gasp when they saw that the ceiling was painted blue like the heavens, dotted with puffy clouds, giving the sensation of an outdoor revival. A subtle sparkle danced in the walls from crushed seashells that Aimee had asked to be mixed into the cement. The dome spanned 107 feet across and 110 feet high. From the center of the dome hung a massive crystal chandelier, its hundreds of lights flickering like a celestial orb. At the front of the Temple, her congregants worshipped at a vast stage, hung with heavy velvet and brocade curtains. Behind the stage sat a giant Kimball pipe organ—installed at the exorbitant cost of $22,000 (nearly $400,000 in today's dollars)—whose deep, reverberating tones could be felt humming in the bodies of all who entered.

"When we planned the edifice that is now Angelus Temple," she later wrote, "we decided to break with the traditions of ancient church architecture, to banish mystic darkness, discomfort and dank corners, to make the Temple as bright, as modern, as cheerful, as homey as planning and skill could make it, and to emphasize in it not the torments of hell but the deep abiding joy of salvation, the glory that comes with complete surrender to the love of the Lord."[15]

She had manifested her dreams into a physical institution. She had built a megachurch, the first in what would become a long line of massive places of worship that would be erected over the course of the twentieth century—a remarkable achievement for a woman whose right to vote had been granted just two years earlier. Aimee had reconstituted the centuries-old tradition of large-scale tent revivals, once the stuff of rural country fields, into an urban physical monument. It was a savvy thing to do at that particular moment in history.

The monumental population shift over the past decades created the ideal conditions for the mass audiences that Aimee envisioned and desired. In 1850, there were only six cities in the United States with a population larger than one hundred thousand, but by the time Aimee built her temple, there were sixty-eight such cities, with half of the American population living in urban environments. Aimee shared the burgeoning American obsession with growth and quantification as signs of progress.[16]

From all over Los Angeles, thousands came for the first service. Aimee felt powerful yet isolated. In her writings from the time—her essays for *The Bridal Call* and her ongoing memoirs—she wrote of being very much alone in the crowd, but also connected to a divine power.

"A door in the front of the Temple is opened," she wrote. "Willing hands are there to assist the Evangelist onto the platform. Won't you come up with me, we ask several timidly. No. Sister, you must go alone, they answer. A final push and we are alone on that improvised platform looking down into that great sea of upturned faces."[17] Minnie is nowhere to be seen, and Aimee herself has become the main character, alone on the stage.

Aimee had been called delusional, crazy, a woman who did not know her place, but she had persevered. And here she was, just a decade after she first heard that voice in Providence. The opening of the Temple was one of the greatest events of her life, she wrote. It was "the day of days—the day we had all waited for with such earnestness of prayer and expectation—the greatest—the crowning day of fifteen years of ministry—the day when the seemingly impossible had become possible, the glorious dream a living fact and the wondrous vision a concrete reality."[18]

11

THE BEST SHOW IN TOWN

Angelus Temple buzzed with the thrills and demands of serving entertainment and spiritual solace to thousands of people a week. By the end of its first year, Aimee's church was employing more than a hundred people, and daily visitors numbered more than seven thousand. The temple was a veritable city unto itself: twenty-four departments made up the corporate body, ranging from administration and finance to the on-staff electricians to the vast musical theater production department. There were several breakout rooms for prayer, including the "120 Room," a place people could pray for the baptism of the Holy Spirit—and discreetly experience the gift of tongues. As the main theater became more mainstream, this room became a more private place for more demonstrative worship. Nearby, in the "Miracle Room," discarded canes, crutches, casts, and wheelchairs were displayed as evidence of divine healing.

On the first floor, phone operators at two phone lines took calls day and night from anyone in Southern California in need—supplying milk, blankets, and, of course, salvation. There was a publishing department that printed all of Aimee's literature. Along with the monthly *Bridal Call*, a weekly newsletter was added—the *Foursquare Crusader*, with reprints of Aimee's sermons, temple news, and various advertisements from neighborhood merchants. Aimee had three ministerial assistants and a board of seven elders, along with twenty-one deacons—fourteen of them women.

Everybody had a part to play. Her people, Aimee said, "must be kept as busy as I [am]. Then they w[ill] be as happy as I [am], happy with the business of achievement . . . And keeping them busy [is] a big job for me by itself."[1] Aimee saw her role as the conductor of a fabulous orchestra of energy and hope, a space where anyone and everyone could come and find a way to plug into the divine grid. "In God's great employment agency, we are each one called, each one given a work to do," read an early *Who's Who* pamphlet on the temple. "He never turns one away—there is always room for one more."[2]

In the brochure on the temple, Aimee wrote a swooning tribute to her mother's role in helping build it. "Men have criticized women and derided their ability yet when men purpose to erect a half million dollar building and organize a unit one-half the size of the Angelus Temple they are assisted by committee upon committee and hold consultation after consultation. The entire financing for the building of the Angelus Temple was executed by Mother, during which time she was also directing the international revival campaigns of her daughter . . . It is through her foresight and guiding hand that Angelus Temple has come to be the most competently organized church in the world today."[3] For a time, both women seemed to love this way of dividing their shared ambition, conquering the world together.

Aimee was a spectacle in a city that was becoming an industry of spectacle. Angelus Temple became known as a place for first-class entertainment for the masses. The temple had a fourteen-piece orchestra, a brass band, and a hundred-voice choir, two-thirds female, all dressed in white. The whole point was to dazzle and overwhelm.

According to Morrow Mayo, one of the city's most gimlet-eyed early chroniclers, the brass band was "bigger and louder than Sousa's," the organ was "worthy of any movie cathedral," and the choir "bigger and more beautiful than the Metropolitan chorus."[4]

Near the top of the giant domed ceiling, Aimee opened a small room that she called "the Watch Tower," where continuous prayer took place, in two-hour shifts, with male volunteers at night and female volunteers during the day. Minnie scheduled 320 slots a week, with a waiting list of volunteers, all of them eager to sit in the room and reach out to God. They were like ecstatic factory workers, an assembly line of good.

Aimee had originally intended to have the temple conduct services four days a week, but her followers demanded more. They camped on the sidewalks of the temple during the off days until she relented, reorganized, and opened the doors around the clock, seven days a week, with programming created for each day. The theater often held as many as 7,500 people at a time. Initially, the free Sunday school had 136 pupils; but within two months more than 1,200 children were registered. Following the morning service, children from the Sunday school would march through the streets outside the temple, banners in hand, shouting and singing, "We are McPherson's boys and girls."[5] Aimee would come to the balcony of her parsonage and stand and wave at them, a queen of her realm.

To those who came to worship at Angelus Temple, Aimee was the focal point. She sold herself as "the just right option"—more comfortable than the Holy Roller Bible thumpers who yelled about sin and hell, but also someone who embraced the pure fundamentals of Christian faith. She was "Everybody's Sister," and her audiences would sometimes recite a cheer before she came onstage.

With an "S"! With an "S"!
With a "Sis"!
With a "T"! With a "T"!
With a "TER"! Our SISTER![6]

Once Aimee built Angelus Temple in Los Angeles, she cut back on her national travel. She was asking local audiences to come to the temple every week, and in doing so she lost some of the allure of being a fleeting attraction. When she'd been traveling on the revival circuit, she had more than sixty sermons that she'd written that she could perform for her ever-changing audience. But anchored in Los Angeles, she felt the pressure of producing new material.

She needed to create a steady stream of content—sermons, programs, classes, workshops—that would bring in new people and keep them coming back for more. Her innovation was the illustrated sermon—part spectacle, part feel-good homily—delivered every Sunday night. Mimicking the state-of-the-art technology and techniques of Hollywood, she delivered a gospel that felt relevant and immediate to her audience.

Aimee hired a stage manager, Thomas Eade, who had trained in vaudeville, to design her elaborate skits. They rented costumes and scenery from nearby Hollywood studios. Aimee drew on popular culture and everyday life and wove current ideas and debate into sermons. She depicted life in Los Angeles as biblically prophesied and infused with meaning. Her critics called her the P. T. Barnum of Christianity. She used live camels, tigers, lambs, palm trees—whatever it took to bring the ancient world to life on her stage. Aimee's sermons were soon considered the best show in town.[7]

"Many objected—even some members of the Angelus Temple felt a little uneasy—to the novelty of the illustrated sermons every Sunday evening, sermons in which the lesson of the text is driven home through the eye as well as the ear," she told *Sunset* magazine. "What matters the trail, so long as the goal is reached? If we can hold the wavering attention and reach the heart of just one sinner through the costumes, the scenery and the properties of the illustrated sermon, the gain is worth all the efforts."[8]

One of Aimee's early illustrated sermons was so revolutionary it made local headlines and cemented Angelus Temple as a place where the spectacular happened. Aimee drew on the most mundane of incidents to create the sermon: she had received a speeding ticket. She and Roberta were driving to Venice Beach, a place Aimee liked to go to clear her mind and come up with ideas. That day, Aimee was preoccupied, trying to come up with new material for sermons. "Keep an eye out for motorcycle cops. I can think best when I'm driving fast," she told fourteen-year-old Roberta. Soon they heard the wail of the siren. Aimee pulled to the side of the road, and the policeman walked over and said, "You're arrested for speeding."

"I've got it! I've got it!" Aimee responded.

"You certainly have, Sister. Here's your ticket."

"No, I mean I've got my sermon inspiration," she said. "Come to the Angelus Temple, and you'll hear the best sermon of your life."

The following night, the temple was packed for the Sunday evening service, often geared to a wider and worldlier crowd. People took their seats, and there were murmurs of confusion as they saw an actual motorcycle parked on the stage next to the pulpit. Aimee entered, wearing a policeman's cap and jacket and a navy skirt. She asked her audience to raise their hands if any of them had ever gotten a speeding ticket, and laughter filled the auditorium. It wasn't the worst sin to confess. "Then you know exactly how I feel. I was worrying about what I'd preach the other day, and before I knew it, I was speeding . . . and I got arrested for speeding." The audience gasped. "That's how I got the idea for this sermon. It's going to be one of the best the Lord ever gave me. Because I believe He had me arrested for a purpose."

Aimee wheeled the motorcycle across the stage. "If Christ were alive today, I think he'd preach modern parables about oil wells and airplanes . . . the things that you and I understand. Things like being arrested for speeding." She reached out to her motorcycle and hit the siren, and shouts of excitement and laughter filled the temple.

"See what I mean? Everyone understands what that sound means. It means Stop! It means Danger Ahead! Stop rushing down the highway to death and destruction. The broad highways of sin are crowded with men and women rushing along at breakneck speed . . . Many times, God tries to stop us, to force us to pull over to the side of the road and think about what we are doing."

As she said these words, she walked back over to the motorcycle and sat astride it. Photographers in the audience from the local papers—whom Aimee had invited—clicked their shutters rapidly. She moved back and forth across the stage, calling out to the audience, asking questions, getting shouts and hallelujahs as she preached about the fast pace of modern times and the destiny that brought them there for that evening's sermon.

"God sent you here for a reason. I, too, am one of God's patrolmen! Every preacher is! So . . ." She hit the siren again. "I'm here tonight to say to you, 'Halt!' In the name of the Lord! Stop your rush into the life of selfishness and sin . . ." The crowd was electrified. Applause and cheers rang out, her message driving people to hilarity and ecstasy. "This may be your last chance!"

She then moved on to the altar call: "I want you to step out in the aisle nearest you. Then I want you to march right down the aisle to the altar, kneel right here and say yes, 'Yes, Lord! I need your help to live the good life!' Come on everybody . . . Don't one single person sit down. Don't you dare! This may be your last warning."[9] Hundreds of people poured into the aisles, weeping and shouting, the crowd heaving toward the pulpit as others fell to their knees and prayed. Gone was any sense of church as small or rigid—Aimee ushered in a century of worship as spectacle.

A dozen Foursquare churches had opened in California by the end of 1923, and each week more than a thousand volunteers conducted prayer meetings at the county jail, at hospitals, and at prominent businesses, such as the Ford Motor Company.

The collection plate callout at Angelus Temple became a thing of operational mastery. "If you can't afford to support God's work just let the collection plate go by," Aimee would say. "If a nickel is all you can afford to give, then give it and the Lord will bless you. But don't put in a nickel if you can afford a dime and don't put in a dime if you can afford a quarter."[10] The average Sunday morning collection ran around $1,890, which worked out to about three cents a person, with the silver platters full of small coins and an occasional expensive diamond ring. The weekly numbers equated to more than $85,000 in today's dollars. By the end of 1925, estimates put the annual collection at $1 million ($18 million in today's money), and the value of Aimee and her mother's property holdings were estimated at more than $1.5 million ($27 million today).

As the demands of the Temple expanded, and the money poured in, Aimee acted more and more like a Hollywood star and director rolled into one. Much of her time was spent writing and producing and enacting her sermons. Aimee lived next door to the Temple, in the attached 2,750-square-foot parsonage. There, Aimee, Minnie, and Roberta lived in three small bedrooms upstairs. While the home was simple, there were luxuries hidden inside. Aimee's bathroom in particular was like a portal to another world—floor-to-ceiling handmade black tiles were bordered by intricate gold embossed clouds, waves, and luminescent ceramic fishes. It felt like a spa, fit for an ancient queen. But downstairs, the home was communal, open at all hours to temple staff and visitors, who came and went without knocking. Rolf, an adolescent, had been sent off to live with a congregant on a farm in the Central Valley. Aimee never wrote about sending her son away—Rolf, Harold's son, merited little mention in his mother's early writings, compared to his older sister. Later the church explained that Rolf was sent away to protect him from his mother's growing fame. For her children, Aimee was a remote, theatrical, and somewhat authoritarian presence. She loved the occasional sentimentality and emotion of motherhood but eschewed most of the day-to-day grind of parenting. When her children were babies, she wrote of her fears that she had endangered them by choosing to live life on the road. But later, she wrote little about what it was like to work and raise her children.

Roberta, a young teenager, sought out moments when she could be alone with her mother. Often this was when her mother prepared for a sermon. They would lock themselves in Aimee's bedroom as she dressed in her silky gowns and put on makeup. She would spritz on her perfume, Quelque Fleurs, an expensive Parisian scent, and arrange her hair. Watching Aimee watch herself in the mirror would be one of Roberta's most cherished memories.

12

RADIOLAND

Inside a dark room in Oakland, Aimee faced a large microphone. A photographer stood by to take pictures, and a crowd of spectators had squeezed in to watch her: the first woman to preach over the "wireless telephone," according to the announcer who introduced her. It was April 1922, and Aimee had been invited to give a guest sermon at the Bay Area's popular new Rock Ridge radio station. Aimee was struck by the potential of the technology, how a single radio broadcast could reach significantly more souls than even a weeklong revival meeting. In the broadcasting room, as a crowd of technicians fiddled with the dials around her, Aimee was on edge. Could she be as effective in this tiny room with no audience to engage, no audience responding to her words?

But as she had so many thousands of times, Aimee shifted her being out of the room and directed her focus toward the heavens, like an antenna. "After putting them all out except the operator, I felt more at ease," she wrote. "That is, as much at ease as it is possible for one to feel facing that great horn and having only its dark, mysterious-looking depths for a visible audience . . . In a moment I found myself talking into that great receiver—talking somehow as I had seldom talked before. The room with its electrical apparatus was forgotten . . . and I prayed and preached and prayed again and did most everything but take up the collection."[1]

Always attuned to new technology, Aimee believed it was her duty to find the loudest amplifier to preach her message. Radio had a magic she instantly recognized: it compressed space and closed the gap between the presenter and the audience.

Long before the advent of television, films, or the Internet, radio made the remote immediate and the powerful intimate. With the flick of the dial, Aimee saw how she could be in people's living rooms and kitchens, her voice in the ears of her listeners as she described how Scripture outlined a plan for modern existence and how the news of the day fulfilled biblical prophecy. For a woman who had succeeded by making herself so accessible, the radio was the perfect amplification tool. It allowed Aimee to connect directly on a new scale: her message could reach the masses in an instant.

After Oakland, she began making appearances on the *Los Angeles Times* radio station and on stations in other cities she visited. Over the next year Aimee began asking around about how she could start her own radio station and inquiring about the costs. Minnie did the calculations on equipment, airtime, and programming, and they came up with a budget. Then they began to fundraise. Aimee used the language of magic to make her sales pitch, telling her followers that "these are the days of invention! The days when the impossible has become possible! Days more favorable than any that have ever been known for the preaching of the blessed Gospel of our Lord and Savior, Jesus Christ! Now, the crowning blessing, the most golden opportunity, the most miraculous conveyance for the Message has come—The Radio!"

The campaign also dabbled in fear. Aimee sent out circulars that warned that "the world" had already used motion pictures to depict distinctly earthly pursuits—greed, adultery, sexuality, and vice. For Aimee and her fundamentalist followers, "the worldly" were people who lived without a connection to the Holy Spirit. Certainly, the libertine demi-monde of early Hollywood fell into this category. "Shall we let them have the Radio too? Or shall we say: 'No, this is Father's Air and Earth, and we will send the Message upon its breezes to spread the Gospel in this wholesale and miraculous manner.'"

After over a year of fundraising, Aimee launched KFSG (Kall Four Square Gospel), a $25,000 state-of-the-art radio station, on February 6, 1924. Twin steel towers with five-hundred-watt antennas bridged the 250-foot temple dome. The visual effect of these massive towers over her megachurch was striking, a futuristic vision of worship.

Aimee was the first woman to hold a radio license in the United States, and KFSG one of the country's first radio stations for a religious organization. It was the third licensed station in Los Angeles. Wanting the radio station to be of the highest quality, Aimee and Minnie hired a radio operator—a job that was equal parts engineer and programmer. She wanted someone with a reputation who could make KFSG dominate the California airwaves. She found her ideal candidate in Kenneth Ormiston, a suave twenty-eight-year-old she hired away from the *Los Angeles Times* radio station—which he had helped launch.

Her first broadcast was from the luxe Los Angeles Biltmore hotel during the Los Angeles Radio Exposition. "The time drew near," Aimee wrote of the occasion. "A button was pressed, a little green light flashed, and all was readiness. Then the evangelist, heart throbbing with the import of the moment, sent out these words—the first ever spoken into a microphone at KFSG: 'For God so loved the world, that he gave his only begotten Son, that whoever believeth in him should not perish but have everlasting life.'"[2]

Aimee used the launch as a networking opportunity. She invited a parade of city power brokers onto her show. Harry Chandler praised the evangelist's "God given powers." The president of the Chamber of Commerce and her friend the Superior Court judge Carlos Hardy spoke as well. (Soon Hardy would be given his own half hour time slot, when he would pontificate on the law and God and religion as a "crime eradicator.")

"Draw up your fireside chair, adjust your earphones and tune in, for the great Angelus Temple Revival is now on the air!" read the announcement in *The Bridal Call.* Indeed, for the thousands of congregants gathered in the Temple and around their home radios, Aimee's disembodied voice was spellbinding. By one o'clock in the morning, an elderly man had arrived at the parsonage and asked to see Aimee so he could tell her that he had heard her on the radio and that the glory of God had fallen upon him. He had found salvation in her voice. Others followed. The response was far-ranging, immediate, and visceral. The church received telegrams and letters from listeners as far away as Mexico, Canada, Alaska, Panama, Hawaii, and the South Sea Islands, who said they could hear the evangelist as clearly as if they were inside the Temple.

People who had never seen her preach started to write to her, to visit the Temple. They would approach her, saying, "Sister McPherson, I am a radio convert. I heard the story of Jesus Christ and His love coming over the air. I listened in and have now through those messages accepted Jesus Christ as my personal Saviour."[3] These stories multiplied and created a sense within the Temple that their testimony was doing work beyond their walls, that their faith had put them on the technological forefront, at the cusp of a radically new and massive salvation campaign.

Aimee's vision of Christian media as a replacement for small-town Christian community was prescient, as was her programming. In addition to her Sunday morning sermons and baptismal services, she included Sunday school lessons, speeches on the state of Los Angeles by civic officials, lectures from Boy Scout leaders, and in-studio performances from a multiracial mix of musicians performing spiritual ballads, such as frequent guests the Negro Swanee Jubilee Singers, or a sacred opera performed on the massive organ inside Angelus Temple. Listeners could enjoy *Children's Hour*, Minnie's Sunday school program. Minnie became known simply as "Ma Kennedy" on the program and around the Temple. Perhaps most radically, Aimee was one of the first to convey faith healing—perhaps the most physical form of worship—through the radio. She asked listeners to kneel in their living rooms and touch the hard metal of their radio sets, using her voice and this new technology to create a sacred space for individuals as far as her words could carry across the airwaves. Aimee used the medium of transmitting sound to establish a new realm of spirituality. "As I lay my hands on this radio tonight, Lord Jesus, heal the sick," she intoned nightly, her words hushed and reverential. "Bridge the gap between and lay your nail-pierced hand on the sick in Radioland."[4]

More than any other preacher, Aimee emulated the commercial radio world. On the dial, Aimee's sermons would coexist alongside studio serials such as *The Green Hornet* and *Superman*. In response, Aimee tried to take on these secular offerings with her own sacred versions of popular entertainment. The Temple even began producing its own versions of radio plays such as *The Red Comet* and *The Adventures of Jim Trask—Lone Evangelist*.

As the importance of the radio station within the organization expanded, Kenneth Ormiston became one of the most central members of Aimee's staff. He was the first person she saw every morning, when she delivered her *Sunshine Hour* radio sermon. She seemed to value his judgment more than others'. Minnie watched as her daughter regularly stopped into Ormiston's office at the end of the day after finishing her services. She was troubled when she heard Aimee ask Ormiston for notes on the Temple productions of her illustrated sermons. Minnie could not understand why her daughter would be asking this secular and flirtatious man for an opinion on God's work.

In the Temple, where jubilant cries of "*Hallelujah!*" volleyed back and forth between the congregants endlessly, Ormiston was a bit of an outcast. A tall, bald man with large, piercing eyes and cupid lips, he dressed like a dandy. He wasn't a member of the temple, or any church. He enjoyed working at KFSG but had no interest in the ideas that he helped broadcast across the West Coast. Reserved and urbane compared to the giddy go-getters who made up most of the administration, he isolated himself in his tower and spent most of his day inside the office, tinkering with his radio technology. Ormiston obsessed over sound and engineering, writing an occasional column on radio for the *Los Angeles Times*, and, briefly, published a small-circulation technical magazine called *Radio Doings*.

Despite large ears and a significant limp from a childhood bout with tuberculosis, Ormiston enjoyed a reputation as a ladies' man. He had high cheekbones and an intense, unencumbered gaze. He was married to an Australian ice cream heiress, but rumors were that he got around. He saw the potential for Aimee and her ambition to use the radio to reach a massive audience, but he didn't speak in the reverential tones that her followers used with "Sister." He spoke as a peer, calling her "Mrs. McPherson" with a hint of flirtation. It was their "low-voiced remarks,"[5] during choir practice, that began to make people in the temple uncomfortable. More and more, Sister was a being that was beyond human, a figure of reverence and worship who possessed supernatural powers. At Angelus Temple, Sister was a saint, and her followers wanted her to stay that way.

13

POWER AND PUSHBACK

Over the airwaves, on the streets, and in Angelus Temple, Aimee became a powerful voice in a city where, in the early 1920s, power was very much contested. Establishment preachers, city hall operatives, and gangsters were united in their irritation with the lady evangelist who kept shouting about corruption and vice on her radio station. Myriad forces were eager to exploit any vulnerabilities of the increasingly famous Aimee.

All the elements that made Los Angeles glamorous and wild and full of opportunity in the 1920s also made it a frightening city. "A bright and guilty place," observed Orson Welles in *The Lady from Shanghai*. These are the same years when Raymond Chandler, an alcoholic bookkeeper, also came to the city and worked his way up in the brand-new office towers of downtown, until he became a vice president of the Dabney Oil Syndicate. Chandler, who would later become one of America's most beloved chroniclers of California noir, saw Los Angeles as a mysterious and derelict place. "Outside the bright gardens had a haunted look," he wrote, "as though wild eyes were watching me from behind the bushes, as though the sunshine itself had a mysterious something in the light."

How dangerous was Los Angeles? The Los Angeles attorney Bernard Potter famously said the city was "the dumping ground for the riff-raff of the world, racketeers of every type, bootleggers, bookmakers, black market operators, thugs, murderers, petty thieves, procurers, rapists, fairies, perverts, reds, confidence men, real estate sharks, political carpetbaggers and opportunists. Ask for any violator of any law and we can promptly fill the order."[1] By the end of the 1920s, the official murder rate had tripled over the decade, according to the LAPD.[2]

Los Angeles in the 1920s specialized in the so-called sporting life: drugs, prostitution, and gambling were readily available to all. Los Angeles had been toying with prohibition since the turn of the century, and by the time it took effect the *Los Angeles Times* claimed that the city was only 30 percent "wet," even though arrests for intoxication were more than twice those of San Francisco, which was supposedly 80 percent wet. By the time Aimee had built Angelus Temple, the underbelly of the city had been cemented into its noir form. With Hollywood scandals such as the rape and murder trial of Fatty Arbuckle and the murder of the prominent director William Desmond Taylor, the city was finding what would become its repeated refrain: the broken dream.

Unlike the flashy organized crime syndicates that existed in Chicago or New York, Los Angeles gangsters kept a low profile in the early 1920s. Chief among the powerful syndicate bosses was Charlie Crawford, described by his mistress as a "big bluff handsome man."[3] Crawford avoided publicity. While Capone and Siegel were making themselves into nationally recognizable figures in the newspapers back east, Crawford did the opposite. He toned down his style of dress when he arrived in LA from Seattle, getting rid of his pinkie ring, and kept his name out of the press. In the late teens and early twenties, Crawford controlled Los Angeles City Hall—literally. He had shrewdly hired a handsome, socially gifted young lawyer named, ironically, Kent Parrot to serve as the fixer of all his public interests. Parrot handled the statecraft while Crawford ran the underworld.

The East Coast–born Parrot was a former USC football star, big bodied and magnetic. He passed the bar in 1910 in Los Angeles, and his first wife became a screenwriter. By 1915, he was being written up in the *Los Angeles Times* social pages by the columnist Alma Whitaker. He represented a hodgepodge of business interests in Los Angeles. Throughout the decade, his name appeared in the papers as he "mastered the art of the unorthodox floating coalition," wrote the historian Jules Tygiel, "merging liberals with conservatives, church leaders with underworld figures, union officials with open-shop zealots, and prohibitionists with liquor interests."[4] He was considered unique in that he could deliver the Pentecostals, the rumrunners, the bourgeois Babbits, and the African American vote.

Parrot groomed a local politician named George Cryer and through much effort had Cryer voted in as mayor, despite strong opposition from the *Los Angeles Times* and a consortium of well-to-do businessmen. But Cryer had Parrot, and that along with a thin résumé and some man-of-the-people marketing made him a powerful man in Los Angeles. Newspapers referred to the "Parrot-Cryer" administration daily without any need for a backstory—everyone in the city understood that Mayor Cryer had Parrot behind him. As Parrot ran the political machine, Harry Chandler and other elite businessmen saw him and everything he embodied as the enemy. "Los Angeles does not need a boss," the *Times* wrote in a 1925 editorial, opposing Cryer's reelection. Still, he won. This meant that Harry Chandler had to look for other ways to exert his influence outside of the mayor's office. He poured his money into supporting members of the LA County Board of Supervisors—a competing seat of power that governed the larger Southland metropolis and included the San Fernando Valley. The clash between these two municipal entities would come to define politics in the city of Los Angeles for the coming century.

Behind the scenes, though, Charlie Crawford ran the show. He held a regular meeting with Parrot in an apartment at the Biltmore hotel. Crawford lived with his family in Beverly Hills and set up an opulent brothel in Hancock Park with his mistress, Beverly Davis. The

Evening Herald wrote, "He knew everybody. Judges, lawyers, bankers, beautiful women, theatrical magnates, chauffeurs, politicians, and bootblacks were familiar acquaintances and friends. He was genial, happy and at home wherever he found himself."[5]

Los Angeles City Hall and its shady police force connected all these strivers. The law in Los Angeles in the 1920s openly engaged in a symbiotic relationship with the underworld. Before the rest of the country passed the Eighteenth Amendment, most of the cities in LA County had already outlawed alcohol, thanks to the national temperance movement. At the same time, California was the largest alcohol producer in the nation. Los Angeles was slick with speakeasies and distilleries. Rumrunners and gangsters worked the beaches nightly, from Redondo to Malibu, importing liquor on boats, often with bribed LAPD officers standing guard.

Through her congregants—largely working-class—Aimee said she knew more about the underworld activities in Los Angeles than most anyone.

> Ladies with their soft hands and sparkling diamonds, gentlemen with their formal garb and business airs, may raise their brows questioningly when one speaks of "the under-world," but it is no myth to one who has kneeled beside penitents at the altar and heard the sobbed-out stories of crushed hearts and broken lives which have been ground down by the ruthless wheels of this giant evil force. Being a woman evangelist, I have held in my arms scores of trembling little forms and listened to stories which it is doubtful a masculine evangelist would ever hear. To me this kingdom which exists just beneath the thinly veneered surface is a grim reality. It is a definite foe with a definite leadership, a real force with which to reckon.[6]

It wasn't just gangsters who didn't like the lady evangelist nosing into the drinking and gambling and sexual habits of Los Angeles. Aimee had also aroused the ire of the wealthy elite, men such as the oil tycoon Edward Doheny, who hoped to make LA an erudite city on the hill—not a place for fringe religious figures. This informal oligarchy controlled the water and land rights in the city, as well as the press. They sent their children to private schools—the Harvard School for boys and the Marlborough School for girls. They were members of a host of social clubs that emulated eastern establishment tastes but shimmered with new money from oil and film. The California Club, the Jonathan Club, the Sunset Club, the Midwick Country Club, the Flintridge Riding Club—these all become sites to parade the birth of the new West Coast gentry. They had an image they wanted to project of Los Angeles back to the East Coast—white, educated, cultured.

Aimee worked to integrate herself more into these rarefied corridors of power. She was ordained as an honorary chief by the Fire Department. In July 1924, Aimee welcomed a special guest to the temple stage, LA's district attorney, Asa Keyes, who spoke to a packed audience on "The Part of the Church in Law Enforcement." She was showing herself as a kingmaker. She developed a close friendship with the local judge Hardy, whom she invited to all her events.

But in 1925, Aimee pushed further into the political realm, sending shock waves around the city. She waged a campaign to ban evolution from being taught in California public schools. That July, the nation had been riveted by a Tennessee case that prosecuted a high school science teacher, John Scopes, for teaching evolution in a state-funded public school. The trial was a staged spectacle, with the three-time presidential candidate William Jennings Bryan arguing for the prosecution, and Clarence Darrow, a prominent attorney and member of the American Civil Liberties Union, arguing for the defense. Soon known as the Scopes Monkey Trial, it pitted those who accepted Darwin's idea of evolution against fundamentalist Christians who believed in biblical inerrancy. The trial and the coverage divided the nation in two, with half of the country seeing the other half as either godless heathens or illogical blind believers.

The latter was not the vision Los Angeles's elite had for their new city. They were building stately, important museums such as the Huntington and institutions like Caltech, which would attract world-famous scientists, including Albert Einstein. In the face of that, Aimee telegraphed Bryan her support and invited him to share her pulpit. The city fathers feared her ecstatic revivalism would turn their mecca into a joke, their residents into bumpkins.

But perhaps Aimee's fiercest critics were those closest to her cause, the establishment preachers: men of faith who jealously dubbed her a "lady charlatan" and accused her of stealing their congregants with her sensational revivalism and her promises of healing through the power of faith. There was one man who built his reputation, in part, on hating Aimee. Like Aimee, "Fighting Bob" Shuler had traveled throughout the South as an evangelist before moving to Los Angeles in 1920. He ran the large Trinity Methodist Church, starting in 1920, with a congregation that soon grew to over five thousand. Shuler was a fundamentalist conservative bullhorn. He used pugilistic language, focusing his invective on political corruption, Hollywood, theological liberalism, the ordination of women, Jews, Catholics, and jazz. In his magazine he defended the Ku Klux Klan, writing that they were necessary to protect the nation, as "they have found the Jew gradually taking over the nation financially and the Roman Catholic Church as surely taking over the nation politically. So they are here."[7]

But it was his virulent hostility toward Aimee that became his signature. In 1924, after what he called an extensive investigation into her, he published the first edition of *McPhersonism*, a book that proved, he said, that she was "neither honest nor genuine." Accusing her of using her "hypnotic powers" as she played "on every chord of emotionalism that there is left in human nature," Shuler depicted Aimee as a wicked con artist who was duping the masses with her witchy feminine tricks. He alleged that she kept electric gadgets in her baptismal tank that would give a jolt to make converts shout, and that she had a "padded room" for "fanatics" who would be released into the audience during her sermons. He even accused her of paying people to say they'd been healed by her.[8]

With his rival—albeit smaller—radio station, he mocked Aimee and her ministry's focus on women, and her inclusion—albeit limited—of minorities in the congregation. Shuler was disgusted by

Aimee's softer, more emotional and inclusive approach to faith. To Shuler, Aimee's romantic language between herself and Jesus was self-important and silly. He snidely remarked, "She does not wear white for nothing. She wears white so that she will have on the wedding garments when the Lord returns for His bride."[9] But he couldn't stop the people from flooding her temple each week, draining his audience—and thus his coffers.

While others would seek to enrich themselves in this murky new economy through real estate, oil, or entertainment, Aimee's ladder to success was built on people's desire to connect to one another and to the divine and to transform themselves in the process. Aimee called out and connected to the souls of the regular folk, the working class, the poor, the everyman. She was spellbinding as she spoke to her "heart-hungry" multitude, the impoverished newcomers from the Midwest and soldiers who were returning from the Great War, who had come to find their fortune out west, only to see a corrupt elite taking more than their fair share.

Aimee was relentless in her quest to expand her reach, to get her version of the gospel out to as many people as possible. She and Minnie decided to build their own in-house education system—it would be the best way to assemble a legion of Foursquare missionaries who would open more churches and spread the gospel. The L.I.F.E. Bible College started teaching classes in 1923 and was formally incorporated in California in 1924. The finishing of the new campus in January 1926 marked a high for Aimee. By the time the five-story structure next door to Angelus Temple opened, it had enrolled over a thousand students, with dozens of staff and teachers.[10] Aimee wanted to educate the next generation of evangelical missionaries who would spread her message around the globe—many were women like her.

As her congregation and fame grew, Aimee wielded incredible influence in a city that often operated as if it were still an outpost of the Wild West. The Nineteenth Amendment was ratified in the summer of 1920, ensuring women in every state the right to vote. Ahead of that, California had granted women the right to vote in 1911, and in 1918, four women were elected to the California State Assembly. The conversation about women's rights, birth control, and the place of women in society was happening in homes and churches across the state, and around the country, as Aimee rose to power.

Aimee navigated her own course through these cultural flash-points. As a religious fundamentalist, Aimee officially held a conservative view of a woman's role in society. She avoided discussion of suffrage and birth control. But belief in herself was Aimee's central worldview, and she privately supported suffrage efforts. Although there is no record of her support for the suffrage movement in the Foursquare archive, her daughter, Roberta, has said that Aimee privately funded the effort.

Despite the progressive moment, to be a woman in Los Angeles in the early 1920s was to choose between two identities: sister and sinner. Many women left the punitive existence of domestic servitude and escaped to the booming city by the sea. They chopped off their hair and smoked and danced and even, it seems, had a fair amount of premarital sex. The world of vice was alive and well, and as a young woman in Los Angeles, one could easily find oneself ensnared by the temptations of libidinous sex, opium, heroin, and crime. On the flip side, there was a bumper crop of "career girls," women who were pushing the workplace boundaries. For Aimee, all of these were potential converts.

But as Aimee's profile in the city grew, what went on with her life when she wasn't preaching became a subject of great public curiosity. Her sex life and chastity came under question more frequently. There, "Mother Kennedy" gave her excellent cover, acting as a perpetual Victorian-era chaperone. Aimee later wrote that she was aware of the suspicion of her as a single, divorced woman, and she always made sure that a female temple member slept in the room across from her. Her power was becoming something those around her looked to protect.

Alma Whitaker was a British-born housewife whose husband

became ill when she was twenty-nine years old. She managed to talk her way into a junior reporting job with the *Los Angeles Times* sports editor, Harry Carr, in 1910. Within a few years, Whitaker had worked her way up to having her own reported column, brassy and popular with working-class white female readers in Los Angeles. Her editors regarded her as a "spit fire." Whitaker lived with her family on a hilltop in Echo Park, with a clear view of Angelus Temple. When the paper decided to profile Aimee, Whitaker was the perfect reporter to take on the omnipresent evangelist who was the talk of the city.

Whitaker spent days trying to arrange an interview with Aimee through the church press agent. She was repeatedly rebuffed. So she decided to do what any good journalist does: she just showed up. She knew Aimee held visiting hours in the evening at the parsonage, and Whitaker joined the line of people waiting to speak with her. Based on Aimee's reputation, Whitaker had expected a carnival barker, maybe a vaudeville star, or a Barnum-like hustler dressed as a virtuous schoolmarm—someone who had duped the city's feebleminded. If nothing else, she wanted to see evidence of the strange cult of personality that surrounded this woman. But Whitaker was quickly struck by Aimee's genuine sweetness and the intensity of her work. The evangelist sat at a desk, with her long, thick hair piled in what had become an old-fashioned bun. Dressed in white, she resembled an angelic Red Cross nurse, Whitaker wrote in a column in 1924 titled "Reveals Intimate Charm of Angelus Temple Head."[11] They spoke at length, forming a connection that would last for years.

Whitaker tried to draw Aimee into the cultural crosshairs, asking the evangelist if she thought that bobbed hair was wicked; Aimee replied that it wasn't, she just found the new boyish fad of women's hair "undignified and unsuitable." When Whitaker asked her if she'd been a flapper in her girlhood, Aimee demurred, saying she had been an honors student but then admitted she had loved to dance. "I think she seemed a bit wistful in naughty memories," Whitaker wrote in her column, taken in by Aimee's warmth and relatability. Aimee grew nostalgic about her childhood as she spoke, telling the reporter that she'd never really grown up. "The longer I talked to her the more I realized how engagingly young and childlike she really is," wrote Whitaker.

Whitaker, through reporting and close observation, quickly grasped that Minnie served as many things for Aimee—business partner, personal assistant, nanny, chief operating officer, mom-ager—and was crucial to her daughter's success. The reporter seemed to have astutely observed the dynamic between Aimee and her mother, writing that the fact that Minnie ran the show with a heavy hand had allowed Aimee's vulnerability—remarkable for such a powerful person—to have been preserved. Minnie's role as enforcer, she wrote, explains "why Aimee Semple McPherson can keep her sweet smile, why she is free to lead, free to preach, free to heal, to console, to inspire, to enthuse." She also compared the way that Minnie controlled her daughter's career to the era's most famous stage mother: Charlotte Pickford.

Whitaker wrote that Aimee and her mother lived frugally, sharing the small apartment in the parsonage, which had been built in 1925 on the ever-growing temple complex. Aimee told her that all the money that poured into the temple's collection plates was used to support its work and expansion. Even the press agent she employed at fifty dollars a week was a necessary expense, for she was helping Aimee spread the gospel. When Whitaker began to ask questions about her divorce from Harold, Aimee refused to say anything, besides mumbling that Harold worked in "automobiles."

The evangelist told her she slept from 2:00 a.m. to 7:00 a.m. When the reporter left at 11:00 p.m., there was still a line of people to see Aimee. "She just seems to love everyone," Whitaker wrote. The journalist concluded that there was something exceptional and authentic about Aimee but also something deeply restless. "She looked very tired, rather wistful."

14

BURN OUT

On October 9, 1925, Aimee celebrated her thirty-fifth birthday. Angelus Temple treated it as a major holiday, with thousands flocking to that evening's service, where Aimee had promised to preach a new sermon, entitled "The Story of My Life." It was a story she had told since her earliest days of preaching, using her experiences as testimony to the work of the divine. That night, traffic stretched for miles, all the way to downtown, with every car headed toward the temple. The streetcars were packed with followers headed for the celebration. Many members had brought large bouquets of flowers to give to Aimee, so that the inside of the temple resembled a lush country garden. The atmosphere was adoring, as described dramatically in that month's *Bridal Call*.

> Music, the scent of flowers, a restless rustling of papers and wraps as the great congregation waited patiently, then—
>
> Ah, there she is!
>
> Oh! Look! Isn't that too sweet for anything!
>
> Why it's a milk pail she's carrying.

Aimee appeared onstage in a large sunbonnet and a coquettish calico dress with big sleeves. She carried a milk pail as she walked in, escorted by a dozen little boys and girls, who bore a long chain of flowers and greenery alongside her. Part nature goddess and part country maid, Aimee sang along with the audience for the opening hymn. When the final notes died out, each member of the temple band approached Aimee and gave a verbal tribute to her, describing her magnificence and their gratitude. Flowers were dropped from the upper tiered balcony like a heavenly shower, and soon Aimee's hands were so full of bouquets that she heaped them in piles at her feet. She launched into the story of her life, which for the thousands listening in the room—and the tens of thousands listening on the radio—was as well-known as any story from Scripture. Still, they were moved by Aimee's emotional retelling, which was "punctuated by tears, smiles, and downright hearty laughter." At the end of the evening, Aimee cut slices of a four-hundred-pound birthday cake and passed them out to her audience members.[1]

But as 1925 came to a close, there was trouble in Aimee's world. Her friendship with her engineer, Kenneth Ormiston, had become an object of gossip in the temple and around the city. During services, as the choir sang, Aimee would whisper remarks to Ormiston on the in-house intercom from the dais to the control room. She thought no one else could hear. But the acoustics of the Temple, which Aimee had obsessed over, ensured that her commentary to Ormiston could be heard by the people sitting in the balcony next to the radio room. According to a later newspaper interview with Minnie, an older lady, who always sat at the front row of the balcony, was scandalized to hear Sister Aimee and this man chitchatting and cooing to each other during the service. Word of these conversations reached Minnie, who was the only one with the authority to speak to Aimee about her behavior. Minnie reminded her daughter that Ormiston was a married man and that, as an evangelist—especially a famous female one—Aimee needed to be unassailable.

But the talk did little good. One day, when Minnie was looking for

Aimee, she went upstairs to Ormiston's office, and, through a small square of glass in the door, she saw the two of them sitting close together. When Aimee spotted her mother, she slumped into the chair and made "a petulant face as a child being caught in a naughty trick." Afterward, Minnie told her daughter, "Whenever I want to find you, I always know where to look."[2]

While the five-story structure meant to house the Bible College was being built next door to the parsonage in 1925, Aimee had started spending the night at the fashionable four-hundred-room Ambassador Hotel a few miles away. A small distance seemed to be opening between Aimee and her work. According to Minnie, she disappeared often after the Friday sermon, seeking privacy at the Ambassador and returning just before the Sunday morning sermon. By the end of the year, Aimee had become fidgety and distracted during choir practice, and temple members noticed her hands sometimes jerking erratically during meetings. She began to lose weight, her figure leaner, frailer.

Minnie was especially worried about the changes, having witnessed the aftermath of her daughter's mental and physical collapse years before in Providence. Aimee had begun to complain to her mother that she was tired. Her schedule was a nonstop round of preaching, writing, broadcasting, and meetings with the rapidly growing temple staff. At the end of 1925, Rudolf Dunbar, the choir chaplain at Angelus Temple and a wealthy insurance executive, publicly voiced concern about Aimee's edgy moods. He offered to pay a well-known Chicago evangelist, Paul Rader, to come to the Temple and preach for a few months so Aimee could take a vacation. She resisted, but after several weeks she agreed. Minnie was miffed that she wasn't invited. Aimee instead said she was taking Roberta, whom she planned to deposit in Ireland with Robert's parents while she went on to England, France, and the Holy Land.

As Aimee's travel plans were cementing, Ormiston quit his job, with no explanation. Minnie was relieved to be rid of him. Aimee set out on her Holy Land tour on January 11, an expensive gift paid for in part through a collection taken from her congregation. Her time in Los Angeles and her increasing success changed the way she presented herself to the world. Throughout her years of traveling in her Gospel Car, pitching her tent in far-flung fields, she had worn floor-length white dresses—a costume of simplicity and accessibility, unadorned by anything except her feverish love of God. But these days she rarely wore this uniform outside the Temple, opting instead for tailored coats and long, dark dresses. Aimee's adherents mostly enjoyed her transformation. Her reserved dignity and the growing crowds were signs of divine blessings on her and those who sought her light.

Newspapers more and more wrote of her beauty, taking time to describe her bedazzling eyes and her captivating smile. She had once been called out as "motherly" or as a "matron," but reporters newly noted how comely she was, how there was an element of seduction to her shows. On her trip to Europe, she began to wear lush, finely crafted, modern silk suits and even a few pieces of jewelry. As a fundamentalist, she'd renounced "worldliness" and "sophistication" as emblems of an elitism that would destroy Christianity. The press in Europe began to take note of her outfits, her "coiffeur that might have been done in Bond Street, pale yellow silk jumper, black silk gown, short skirts, and flesh-colored stockings." In Paris, she bought shoes and lingerie as reporters took note of her visit to some of the city's most "exclusive" shops.

The London papers hailed her as "the greatest woman preacher in the world," with one claiming that she had "shocked the orthodox" with the sophisticated "short skirts" that she wore to give a dramatic and emotional sermon on the resurrection.[3]

The European papers celebrated this exciting and strange American import—a sexy lady preacher—but Minnie was increasingly afraid of a scandal. Aimee's secretary, Emma Schaeffer, took her aside and said that she had heard that an unnamed local gossip magazine was planning on running a story alleging that Aimee was having an affair with Ormiston and that they were traveling together in Europe. Such a story could destroy everything they had worked for. In a panic, Minnie called Thomas Cook and Son, a global travel and tourism agency, and asked that they provide a security escort to accompany

Aimee, starting immediately. The idea was to have an official sort of chaperone. She also telegrammed Aimee, who was in France en route to Palestine. Aimee wrote back to her mother in a telegram dated February 25, 1926, from Nice.

> CABLE JUST RECEIVED SHOCKED AT INFERENCE WHAT NEXT KNOW NOTHING OF ET [*sic*] WAS EN ROUTE FOR ROME NAPLES PALESTINE BUT UNDER CIRCUMSTANCES COMBINED WITH LONLINES RETURNINE [*sic*] FOR ROBERTA TONIGHT VIA PARIS . . .[4]

Aimee returned to London, and on Easter Sunday was invited to an evangelical revival. She was said to be the first woman to hold services at the Royal Albert Hall, preaching to a crowd of ten thousand. She collected Roberta from her grandparents. No story appeared. But Minnie couldn't track down Ormiston.

Minnie thought she had things under control, until Ruth Ormiston, Kenneth's wife, showed up at the Temple and demanded an audience. She told Minnie that Kenneth had vanished weeks earlier, and she believed he was with Aimee. She had already filed a missing-persons report with the Los Angeles police, telling them that he was with "a certain prominent woman." The police concluded it was a domestic matter and were not pursuing the case. But now, Ruth said, she would name Aimee in the divorce filings she planned to submit. Minnie begged her to wait and let the Temple try to find the radio operator for her.

Time passed—less than a fortnight—and then one night "the radio boy," a young man trained by Ormiston, came running to Minnie to tell her that the former radio operator had sent a message from the state of Washington, a blasé statement saying only that "the program was coming in fine."[5] Minnie sent word demanding that he return and make an appearance around the temple, do a radio show or two for broadcast, so that people could see he wasn't with Aimee and the gossip would end. She sent Ormiston money, and he returned to Los Angeles in February for a brief spell. Meanwhile, the press coverage of Aimee's tour in Palestine was well orchestrated—the captivating prophetess walking amid the biblical landscape, an icon in her spiritual home.

Aimee returned from her nearly three-month travels on April 24, 1926. When she arrived at the train station, a crowd of twelve thousand awaited her. Judge Hardy gave a speech on the train platform welcoming her, and Boyle Workman, president of the city council, was there to shake her hand. Minnie beamed, and Roberta smiled prettily next to her mother, holding a bouquet of flowers. Newspapers ran photos on the front page of her smiling, writing that believers thought her a "direct manifestation of divinity," and even skeptics admitted that she was "remarkable."

Aimee told those gathered that she had been heartened by postwar Europe. "The people are seeking the good old-fashioned religion of our forefathers," she told the crowd. Reporters asked if Aimee, a proponent of Prohibition, had seen much public drunkenness, and she responded that she had not, but it was up to America to be a model of sobriety for the world. Aimee headed back to the parsonage and within a few hours was standing at the pulpit, speaking to a full house about her observations in the Holy Land. The following Sunday, over the course of three services, more than fifteen thousand people came to hear her stories.

Immediately after her return, Aimee inserted herself brazenly into local politics, rallying her followers in the temple and on the airwaves to vote against an upcoming ballot measure that would allow dancing on Sundays in the newly incorporated neighborhood of Venice Beach. Aimee raged against the measure, declaring that she'd rather see her daughter dead than in a dance hall. The measure passed, and on Sunday, May 16, dancing resumed in Venice. Two days later, Aimee decided to go to Venice Beach for a swim. On the hot sand, she wrote of light and darkness, sketching the rays of a sun in the margins of her notebook. Then she walked into the ocean and her life changed forever.

PART II

SCANDAL

I believe there is such faith in Angelus Temple and loyalty to its pastor that if an angel from heaven were to come down and say, "Sister is not the child of God," they would not believe it.

—Aimee Semple McPherson[1]

15

ABDUCTION

The water had been glorious for Aimee, fresh and enlivening. She walked in from her swim, the surf swirling around her knees as she held her hand up to her eyes and scanned the shoreline for her secretary, Emma, and their umbrella. As she searched, two figures appeared in her periphery—a heavyset woman with a thick face of makeup and a man, clean-shaven and brown-haired.[1]

"Mrs. McPherson?" they called out to her as she stood in the foaming shallow waters.

Aimee's reverie was pierced, her name calling her back to life and her duties.

"Yes?"

"Oh, Mrs. McPherson," the woman cried, her voice supplicating. "My baby is dying. I would be ever so happy if you would just come over and pray for my baby."

Aimee said she would—she always did say yes—but first she needed to grab a towel and her things from the hotel, which sat about fifty feet up on the sand. She wore only her bright green swimsuit. She couldn't walk around in that, she explained politely. But the couple insisted, acting emotional and panicked as they urged her to come at once. For modesty's sake, the woman cast her large, heavy black coat over Aimee's shoulders. Without a chance to tell Emma where she was going, Aimee was herded off to the small boardwalk that ran parallel to Lick Pier. Aimee was used to being treated like an emergency service, even on her days off—whisked away to a hospital bedside, or an accident, to conduct healings.

As they walked, Aimee asked the couple how they had known to find her at the beach, and they said they'd just been to Angelus Temple, seeking her healing powers after a terminal prognosis for their child. Aimee's mother had told the couple where Aimee was and that she was sure that her daughter would tend to the sick baby. That sounded, Aimee said, like her mother—offering her daughter up for service on her afternoon off.

As they neared the curb, the woman ran ahead and climbed into the back seat of a waiting car, pulling what looked like a pile of blankets into her lap. That must be the baby, thought Aimee. A third man sat at the wheel, the car motor running.

Aimee leaned in to see the baby, setting her foot on the running board. Wham! She felt a strike on the back of her head as hands grabbed her face and held a wet sponge against her mouth. She struggled to breathe, but instead her lungs filled with some noxious chemical, a cloyingly sweet smell. Lights out.

She awakened to find herself in a decaying little room, vomiting on a mattress in an iron bed. She took note of her surroundings: a small window and a kerosene lamp. She heard the click-clack sound of a typewriter, and low voices somewhere in the next room. She heard mention of Calexico, the California border town. Then she collapsed again into unconsciousness.

Time passed; she didn't know how long. When she next awoke, she found a woman in the room, whom she would learn was called Mexicali Rose. Rose was hefty, large breasted, a woman with a professional demeanor and a dark bob. When she saw that her prisoner was awake, she called out to the next room: "Steve!"

A man entered: skinny and fedoraed, Steve told Aimee she was their prisoner, and he called the shots. He said they had kidnapped her because she'd been causing so much trouble with her crusading and evangelizing. She'd disrupted business as usual in the California underworld, he told her. He implied she'd made life hard for their "white trafficking" ring.

"You've taken enough of our girls, and turnabout is fair play," he told Aimee. She understood then that—of course—the kidnapping was revenge for her good works. But that wasn't all—he then told her that he'd asked her mother for half a million dollars in ransom money. She told them they were foolish, wept that she did not have that much money. But Steve laughed cruelly and said he knew she and the temple were filthy rich. He'd heard about that collection plate, always full of cash. He slammed the door. She remained in the squalid room for days.

She was treated badly. Her abductors threatened to sell her to a "Mexican chief" called Felipe. One day Steve burned her wrist with his cigar. He tried to force her to reveal details of the temple's finances. But Aimee refused, and he gave up. He brought in a great, hulking man. This, Steve said, was Felipe. Aimee thought it was a bluff—hadn't they said Felipe was in Mexico City?

She begged them to take her home or telephone her mother. But the men laughed at her. Aimee paced the floor like a tiger. She was distraught, her fear and suspense not about her fate but about what would happen to her mother and children—and Angelus Temple.

Over and over, her captors threatened to sell her to Felipe, sending her to Mexico. "We're going to get that damned temple!" they cackled. They cut off a thick swath of her hair and threatened to take a finger next. She was bound with ropes and burned. For days on end, she was tied to the bed in her nightgown, sick and drugged. Mexicali Rose watched her sternly from the corner.

One night, Aimee was drugged again and forced to lie on the floorboards of a car. They drove for hours—she wasn't sure how long. She awoke to find herself in a small shack with a wooden floor. They were in the middle of the desert. It was very hot.[2]

Weeks passed; Aimee was desperate. One afternoon, Rose left the shack for supplies. Aimee pounced at the opportunity for escape. She saw a jagged can of discarded maple syrup and used the serrated edge of the lid to saw off the ropes that bound her. She crawled out the window of the cabin and raced across the burning sands of the desert, through the scorching day. The sun set, and on she went, into the cold, thick darkness of the night. She stumbled for twenty-two miles at least, a hike that lasted at least thirteen hours. She was exhausted but she was afraid to sleep, fearing the poisonous creatures in the sand. At last, she saw small buildings on the horizon. She came to a road. She saw a glow in the sky. Delirious, Aimee thought perhaps it was heaven in the distance.[3]

16

RESURRECTION

On June 20, 1926, thirty-three days after Aimee vanished into the ocean, her mother held a memorial service at the temple she had built. Minnie mourned her daughter's death wearing Aimee's own signature blue cape, a voluminous mantle that symbolized the transfer of power. Roberta stood by her grandmother's side, smiling bravely for the crowd. On the flower-strewn stage of Angelus Temple, Aimee's chair sat empty as twenty thousand people filled the pews and spilled out into the hallways and the lobby and onto the streets. Minnie's words crackled over the loudspeakers on the sidewalks and across the radio waves. She told the emotional crowd that a miracle had taken place: God had so loved Aimee that he raptured her body to heaven, whisking her away like an angel. Minnie used an old Salvation Army expression to describe what had happened: Aimee was "gone to Glory."[1] Minnie said it was up to them to continue Sister's work. "Carry on and re-dedicate your lives to a religious principle which still lives," she told the crowd.[2]

When the collection trays were passed around, the congregation dug deep. Aimee had changed their lives and given them faith. For many, she'd opened a portal, connecting them directly to Jesus, a gateway between their soul and a divine presence. For some, she had healed them of sickness and injury. According to newspaper accounts, those in attendance reached into their pockets and purses, calculated their gifts against their bank accounts, and even their future earnings, and gave. Some gave cash; others signed over deeds, loans, and mortgages. The love offerings that day amounted to more than $36,000—at least thirty times more than an average Sunday service at the temple and more than half a million dollars today.

"She is with Jesus now," Minnie said, over and over. She wanted to convey, she later said, a sense of spiritual uplift. But when the crowds left, Minnie did not feel joy. She went to her office inside the temple, but she could not shake a strange sentiment—a "premonition of evil."[3]

Less than two days after the memorial service, at one o'clock in the morning on Wednesday, the 23rd of June, a woman in all white emerged from the darkness of the desert.

She stumbled into the edge of a small town, just south of the Arizona-Mexico border, six hundred miles away from Los Angeles, where Minnie slept, fitfully. Inside his casita, the former Agua Prieta mayor and local bar owner Ramon Gonzalez was enjoying a bedtime cigarette. Above the sounds of his radio, he heard a voice cry, "Hel-loooo! Hello!"

Looking out his upstairs window, Gonzalez saw the woman. She was agitated and shouted to him in a rush of English, which he did not understand. She did not ask for water or food or a police officer—just a phone. She begged him to make a call to the authorities in Los Angeles. "Los Angeles" and "phone"—those were the words he grasped. He quickly dressed and went downstairs, where he found the woman lying by the garden gate, her delicate cotton dress pooled out around her in the dusty sand of his yard. She was unconscious, "cold and her body very loose." Ramon and his wife, Theresa, spent the next hour trying to revive the woman, wrapping her in blankets, rubbing her arms with alcohol, and moving her onto their porch.

The two border towns—Agua Prieta, Mexico, and Douglas, Arizona—were mirror images of each other. Prohibition had meant brisk business for Agua Prieta's bars, and the Mexican town had seen its share of American women stumbling through its dirt streets, doped up or dead drunk. Gonzalez, though, felt immediately that this lady was different. Her great pile of auburn hair was pinned neatly in a silk net.

When she finally came to, she began again with her torrent of words, gesticulating to him. All Ramon could glean was that she was from Los Angeles, and she had no husband. She drank "very little" water during this time, mostly focused on the need to make a phone call. Gonzalez left his wife with the woman and ran down the street. He found the current mayor, and together the men set out to look for a translator.

It was now past two o'clock in the morning. They asked an American who worked as a bartender at the Gem Saloon to help them, but he was too busy at work. Finally, an American taxi driver was found who could drive the woman across the border to Douglas.

The cab pulled up to the Douglas police station, where the watchman was just finishing his night shift. He peered in and saw a lady wilted in the back seat. The cab driver reported that she had just escaped kidnappers and fled across the desert. The officer directed them toward the Calumet and Arizona Hospital down the street, where he and another police officer hoisted the woman between them and helped carry her into the emergency room. There, the woman lifted her head and breathlessly proclaimed: "I am Aimee Semple McPherson."[4]

To the doctor, nurses, and police who gathered around her, Aimee recounted her bizarre and frightening story of being kidnapped from the crowded beach in Venice over a month earlier. She said she had been abducted, to be sold as a slave in Mexico.

She gave a harrowing account of events that sounded straight out of the black-and-white Hollywood movies she had disavowed for years. She described how she had reappeared six hundred miles away from Venice, escaping through the window of the shack she'd been held in and trekking through a desert whose daytime temperature hovered above a hundred degrees. In the coming days and months—and for the remaining years of her life—she would tell the exact same miraculous and terrifying story.

Aimee begged the people standing around her to call Los Angeles immediately. They didn't seem to realize the gravity of the situation, she said. The threat wasn't over—she'd overheard her captors outline plans to kidnap other famous people, celebrities just like her. They had named Mary Pickford. Aimee was also afraid that her teenage daughter, Roberta, might be in danger.

By six o'clock in the morning, an Arizona police officer managed to reach Captain Herman Cline of the Los Angeles Police Department. A brick of a man, Cline had joined the force in 1909, when Los Angeles had still been an outlaw town of dirt roads and adobes. He had worked his way up to homicide over the past fifteen years, and that February, he'd been appointed chief of detectives. Cline had seen it all, and his demeanor was unflappable. He had worked the McPherson case since the day she vanished on May 18. Even as rumors had swirled that Aimee had survived the ocean currents, or had been sighted in California, or even kidnapped, Cline had dismissed them as Hollywood gossip. He was sure she'd drowned. He was confident up until the voice on the phone that June morning said the missing evangelist had reappeared out of the Mexican desert. He was stunned.

Cline jumped in his car and drove to Angelus Temple. There, in the dawn light, he broke the news to Minnie that after more than a month gone, her daughter was alive. He told her Aimee said she had been kidnapped but had emerged unscathed from the desert just hours earlier. He watched carefully as a look of shock came over Minnie's face, her small eyes narrowing. After a month of wild tales, crazy letters, false alarms, and bunk news stories, Minnie's response was skepticism.

"I can hardly believe that," she said. "If they kidnaped her and held her for ransom, why did they not come forward when we offered

$25,000 reward for her return? It doesn't seem possible they could snatch her up unseen. She never listened to strangers, much less carry out their wishes." Minnie was tough, Cline observed, even at this miraculous moment. "How she was enticed into the hands of abductors is something she alone can explain to my satisfaction," Minnie said, sternly. It had been only a matter of days since Minnie had announced to thousands that her daughter was in heaven, only days since she'd raised enormous sums of money to honor her legacy. She couldn't quite seem to accept Aimee's resurrection.

The telephone lines between Angelus Temple and the Calumet Hospital were connected at 7:30 a.m. Inside the parsonage, Cline stood in the corner of the parlor room, with its heavy brocade curtains and ornate wooden Mission-style doors, and eavesdropped on the call. In a hushed voice, Minnie asked questions and then listened to verify that the woman on the other end was her daughter. Family history and the name of a long-dead pet pigeon were asked for and provided. When Minnie hung up the phone, her disbelief had melted away. She began to weep. "Praise God, It's Aimee!" she called out to those standing in the room. Quickly, word spread beyond the temple: Sister was alive! Outside, Cline heard reporters pushing against the door and shrieks of "Hallelujah!" from the sidewalk.

By mid-morning, four thousand people clogged the streets around Angelus Temple. Minnie went outside, her stance notably softened, more cheerful than she'd been with the detective. "When Sister gets back," she told the journalists, "we're going to have every one of you boys out to the house for a big dinner, and don't you forget it!"[5] Soon the crowd had fashioned a spontaneous anthem, which they sang on repeat all morning:

Coming back, back, back,
Coming back, back, back,
Our sister in the lord is coming back.
There is shouting all around,
For our sister has been found
There is nothing now of joy or peace we lack.[6]

Minnie delivered the news to Aimee's children. (Rolf had returned to be with the family after his mother's disappearance.) Their grandmother told them both to pack their bags and ordered tickets for the midnight train to Arizona. Upon hearing that Aimee was alive, Emma Schaeffer, Aimee's secretary who had been with her on the beach in May, sank into a chair in a corner of the downstairs room, her face ashen. She did not speak.

In Arizona, Aimee hung up the phone. The nurses helped her undress and meticulously documented her condition. They found her body surprisingly unmarked by the long trek through the desert or by the brutalities she had described. She showed them a small fresh scar on her hand, which she said came from being tortured with a lit cigar. On her wrists were thin red welt marks from the ropes that had bound her. Otherwise, her skin was smooth and pale, with no burns from the blistering desert sun. Her lips were not chapped, her body almost completely unblemished. Her heart rate and blood pressure were normal. An inventory of her other ailments by the nurses produced a short list: two small blisters on her toes and two or three cactus thorns in her ankles.

As Aimee sat propped up in her hospital bed, eating a poached egg, oatmeal, and an orange, the press war of the decade commenced. The editor of the *Douglas Daily Dispatch* arrived at the hospital and verified officially that it was indeed the lady evangelist—he had seen her preach in Denver a few years before. Over the wire service, he filed the biggest scoop of his career: Aimee Semple McPherson had returned to life.

When the bulletin that Aimee had reappeared hit the wire service, reporters at the *Los Angeles Times* and the *Los Angeles Examiner* reacted to the news as a major historical event. The papers of Harry Chandler and William Randolph Hearst treated the story as bloodsport. Editors bellowed commands that they needed to publish the first photographs of Aimee. The *Times'* plane took off from an airstrip in Los Angeles, while the *Examiner*'s took off from San Diego. When the *Times'* aircraft stopped in Tucson for gas and oil, its crew watched as the *Examiner*'s plane passed them overhead. The planes landed in

Douglas within an hour of each other, and the pilots raced to grab the rolls of film from their photo correspondents on the ground. But as they prepared to take off, the *Examiner* crew found they didn't have enough fuel to make it back to Los Angeles. The *Times* called it "one of the most remarkable battles in journalism history" as they breathlessly described their achievement in publishing photographs of Aimee before anybody else.[7] Not to be bested, the *Examiner* trumpeted its own triumph—the nonstop flight from Los Angeles to Douglas had been achieved in record time.[8]

Aimee's disappearance had made national news, but her resurrection made global headlines. In less than twenty-four hours, a swarm of reporters descended on Douglas, a town of dirt roads and a single traffic light. In the coming days, the press hordes would spend an estimated five thousand dollars calling their editors in newsrooms around the country, issuing updates, large and small, about the miraculous resurrection of the lady evangelist. Western Union set up eight extra telegraph operators to work around the clock as reporters churned out ninety-five thousand words with the Douglas dateline.[9]

After she finished breakfast, Aimee asked the nurse for a curling iron. Soon reporters and cameramen started to pour into the hospital. "Let the reporters in!" Aimee exclaimed to her nurse, who begged her high-strung patient to rest. "I just can't refuse to tell them my story. They will tell it to hundreds of thousands," Aimee responded.[10] The first photos of Aimee that morning show her smiling wanly, in a cotton nightgown with lace around the shoulders. She is wearing no jewelry, except a thin watch around her wrist—the gift from her mother. Her thick hair falls in gentle waves around her face, the morning light washing over her. There is something so intimate in these photos—the way Aimee gazes into the camera, relaxed and open. As the reporters gathered around her bed, Aimee said she would gladly tell her story. All she asked was that she not be interrupted.

The story was cinematic and riveting. The events she described were biblical, with their dichotomy between the insidious underworld and saintly Aimee, fleeing abduction. Her journey was an epic that began when she was snatched from the freedom of the ocean waves, climaxed with her torture in Calexico, and ended with her escape into the desert thanks to her quick wits. She described herself as targeted for her virtue and her beliefs. She had been punished for fighting evil in the City of Angels, but she had emerged resolute. The account was as allegorical as one of her Sunday sermons; it had an arc and structure, with characters straight out of a Hollywood movie. Her tale told, Aimee leaned back and smiled for photographs in the hospital.

But as quickly as the printers were typesetting the giant font of the special evening editions relating Aimee's saga, so came the scrutiny. When the press back in Los Angeles asked him for comment, the city's district attorney, Asa Keyes, wondered aloud to reporters, "How was a woman like Mrs. McPherson, known almost all over the civilized world, kidnapped in broad daylight from a crowded beach?" Keyes mused, "Why was a $25,000 reward offered for her safe return withdrawn, then re-offered and withdrawn again on June 12?" And his final question, tinged with skepticism toward the large amounts of cash flowing to the collection plate during Aimee's absence: Would Minnie return all that funeral money that she had collected?

Keyes—rhymes with "tries"—was forty-seven years old, an ambitious and gifted prosecutor. He was stocky, with broad shoulders, a thick neck, a large forehead with a receding hairline, and a bullfrog-like countenance. In the bombastic world of Los Angeles law enforcement, the district attorney was self-contained and subtle. Born in South Los Angeles near the harbor, he graduated from the University of Southern of California law school—where the city's elite sent their sons. He had immediately gone to work at the DA's office. When he took over as the head prosecutor in 1923, Keyes quickly remade the department as his own. He asked eighty-seven employees to resign, and then rehired twenty-seven of the men he trusted the most—giving the impression that he would clean up the corruption of the old guard. He held himself up as a no-nonsense prosecutor. But by the summer of Aimee's disappearance, the years on the job were starting to wear on him.

At first, Keyes seemed drawn to all the attention surrounding

Aimee's claims—likely seeing it as an opportunity to enhance his own public profile. He told reporters that his office would go over Aimee's story word for word. "The circumstances of the case in the opinion of the district attorney's office call for an investigation both to do justice to Mrs. McPherson and to the public and I intend to see it made,"[11] Keyes said on the day of her reappearance. He announced he would send one of his sharpest young prosecutors to Douglas, posthaste: Joseph W. Ryan.

Ryan was a striver, twenty-six years old, with pale skin and a square head of black hair that culminated in a slick widow's peak. Born in Brooklyn, Ryan moved to Los Angeles, and was admitted to the California bar in 1923—the same year that Aimee opened Angelus Temple. Like Aimee—and so many who had come to California to make their fortunes—he was determined to make his dreams reality. Having ascended quickly in the city prosecutor's office, Ryan had even greater political ambitions, with hopes of running for governor. Also, Ryan was married to Captain Cline's daughter.

On the afternoon of June 23, hours after Aimee had shown up in the hospital, Cline decided that—given how high-profile this case was—he would go to Douglas to interview Aimee himself. And so, father- and son-in-law, Cline and Ryan, met at the grand downtown Central Station to take the overnight train for Arizona. A special press car was arranged, which held fourteen reporters and photographers. The energy was kinetic—this train was headed toward the biggest story of the decade, and every passenger on board knew it. Minnie and her grandchildren were set up in the stateroom car. Just before Ryan climbed aboard, he was delivered an unusual handwritten message from Keyes, his boss: make no statement to the press.

17

DESERT SEARCH

On the morning of June 23, the Cochise County sheriff, J. F. McDonald, was at his office in Tombstone when he received a call from an officer in Douglas, saying that a woman had walked out of the desert and ended up in his territory with a story of being kidnapped for "white slavery." McDonald was a longtime sheriff in Tombstone, a place made famous by the Earp brothers' gun battle at the O.K. Corral. He was a gentle-faced cowboy who often made local headlines for his arrests of platinum thieves, robbers, and killers. He had seen all types of violence and deprivation and, yes, even a few kidnappings.

In a confidential memo he wrote to Asa Keyes five days later, McDonald gave a meticulous report of his investigation. When he first received the call about Aimee, he drove the forty-nine miles to Douglas and pushed past the crowds outside the hospital trying to glimpse the famous woman. His report was terse: "Mrs. McPherson was being cared for at the Arizona and Calumet Hospital, seemed entirely rational and without the signs of fatigue or sunburn to be expected in such cases. The place was surrounded by a curious crowd.

Mrs. McPherson was receiving callers, and it was impossible to get a complete and definite statement on account of the interruptions."

Sheriff McDonald was immediately struck that a highly articulate woman, who liked to talk so much, couldn't seem to give him much detail on her kidnappers. He listed her description of each of them:

"Number one, woman named Rose, age 40 to 43 years, weight 185 pounds, large arms, black bobbed hair, eyes dark brown, even teeth, deep voice, businesslike."

"Number two, man named Steve, broad shoulders, weight 200 pounds, height six feet, ruddy complexion, dark clothes."

"Number three, man, name unknown, flat-chested, dark complexion, bushy eyebrows, upper gold tooth, grey clothing."

He continued: "I thought possibly that as Mrs. McPherson is a public speaker and must have a considerable knowledge of English that she would be very apt to remember their manners of speech and detect any slang expressions or grammatical errors committed by her abductors. She could give me no information along this line."

The growing crowd of spectators and journalists made McDonald concerned about a mob overrunning the hospital, so he took the only evidence on hand—the clothes Aimee wore during her desert escape—and deposited them in a vault at the First National Bank of Douglas. The clothes consisted of a gray housedress of cheap material, a white princess slip, a simple white muslin undergarment, a pair of black slippers with rubber heels, a corset, a pair of stockings, and a hair net. From the bank, he drove ten miles across the border and out into the desert, heading toward the mountain that the Mexicans called Cerro Gallardo. There, he met up with the Agua Prieta chief of police, Sylvano Villa, and a team of police officers from Douglas. Rapidly, the search party grew to more than a dozen men—ranchers, cowboys, and desert trackers, both Mexican and American, who had lived on this land for decades and had deep knowledge of every rock formation and gully for miles.

Some of these men had been working since dawn, and as the sun rose in the sky, the doubts about Aimee's story spread through the search party. She had told investigators that she had walked for about thirteen hours without crossing a road. This, they knew, was nearly impossible. They did find "good impressions of a woman's footprints" about four miles from Agua Prieta, but the tracks seemed to appear out of nowhere, as if the person had been dropped by car. The tracks went in a circle, before heading directly toward Agua Prieta. Sheriff McDonald examined the tracks and found them to be like those made by the slippers Aimee had been wearing. When he had inventoried her slippers, he noticed that they, like the rest of the clothing, appeared to be relatively unused—except for a few light grass stains. The slippers were black kid, and on the bottoms the soles read, "New Era." McDonald described miles of red dirt and sand, rough and rocky terrain, which should have worn down and scuffed the soles—and a total absence of grass.

In his memo he mentioned a prolific scrub called catclaw. McDonald couldn't understand how Aimee's clothing and slippers were unmarred by the thorny yellow shrub, whose burrs covered him and his officers within minutes of walking into the desert. "Furthermore," he wrote, perplexed by the layers of clothing that Aimee had worn, "I cannot understand why she did not discard the corsets. The heat would have made their presence known to her and however excited she may have been it would seem she would have thought of taking them off and throwing them away."

For him, the real flaw in Aimee's story, though, was that when she had arrived in Agua Prieta, she had not done the one thing that every single person in his experience who emerged from a long trek in the desert does: beg for water. "I have helped revive people who have been exhausted on the desert and have been near the point of exhaustion myself. One symptom is always present—INSANE CRAVING FOR WATER."[1]

Over the next few days, the search party looked for the shack where Aimee had said she had been held captive, but they found nothing. "The Mexican officers in the locality know every foot of the ground and no shack could remain unknown to them for more than a few hours," wrote McDonald—certainly not one large enough to have a bathroom and a wooden floor. The sheriff's conclusion was concise: "I have no desire to cast any reflections on anyone, but my conclusions are that Mrs. McPherson's story is not borne out by the facts."

The next day, as McDonald was still scouring the desert, the overnight train from Los Angeles pulled into the Douglas station. Residents had gathered to watch the spectacle of Aimee's family arriving. Minnie stepped down from the platform and immediately made a fiery statement to the crowd and the reporters who followed behind her. "I am positive that she was abducted by interested persons in Los Angeles and that the ransom plot was only a subterfuge to screen a more subtle motive," she declared.

She described how before Aimee's disappearance, a Los Angeles minister had said he would "put the skids under Angelus Temple." The press filled in the blanks—everyone knew she meant Aimee's antagonist the Pasadena preacher "Fighting Bob" Shuler. Minnie implied that perhaps the gangsters and Aimee's rival pastors had teamed up in an unholy union to take Aimee down—or out.

Leaving reporters with that cliffhanger of innuendo, Minnie and the children were shepherded into a car that awaited them. Joseph Ryan and Herman Cline followed, with reporters and photographers close behind. Douglas had decided to treat the return of Aimee as a holiday. Shops were closed, and people lined the street as if awaiting a parade.[2]

When the cars reached the Calumet Hospital, a tall shingled-roof building that looked more like a cowboy saloon than like a medical facility, Minnie rushed ahead of the children, pushing past the jostle of reporters. She found Aimee lying in bed in a pale pink nightgown, her hair curled, as photographers took her picture. Minnie shoved them away, taking her daughter into her arms. "Mother! Mother darling!" Aimee cried. The two women clutched each other as law enforcement steered the journalists out of the small room. In the doorway, Aimee's children stood back, solemnly watching the reunion. The detective and the prosecutor listened as Aimee and Minnie whispered intently.

(Aimee, when asked, would later say that her mother was concerned whether she'd been sexually assaulted.) Once their exchange was over, Aimee motioned for the children to come and for the reporters to rejoin her family as flashbulbs snapped and she detailed her abduction.

The nurse attending her observed that the audience seemed to soothe the Aimee. "While she was talking and had people around her," the nurse later testified, "she seemed to be all right and self-contained. As soon as she relaxed or had no one around her she seemed to be in a nervous condition. She had twitching of the muscles."[3]

When Ryan, the assistant district attorney, first heard that Aimee had escaped kidnappers, he had accepted the fact at face value, like his father-in-law. But here amid the crowds, the whole thing felt wrong—Aimee's strange ebullience, the melodramatic story, the reporters buzzing around her, the theater of it all. The first tangible clue he had beyond just his instincts, though, came when he examined the clothing that McDonald had placed in the bank vault. In the pocket of the dress Aimee had worn in the desert, Ryan found an exquisite and expensive-looking silk hair net. How did she get her hands on this, he wondered? She said all her clothes had been given to her by her kidnappers—why would she have this fancy thing? His suspicion deepened when he rejoined Aimee and her family, and he saw that she was wearing a delicate leather wristwatch around her wrist. How had she been kidnapped swimming on a beach wearing such a hair net? And a watch?

As Ryan looked on, Aimee invited reporters outside to photograph her and her family. On the lawn, Roberta and Rolf were stone-faced as they flanked their mother, who sat in a chair, and their grandmother, who beamed for the cameras. The children's attitude troubled Ryan too—they didn't seem as excited as he expected they would be, having had their mother returned from death. Roberta "appeared bored and slightly embarrassed by the whole performance," he wrote later to Keyes.[4] Aimee was in her element—motioning for Ryan and Cline to join in the photos. When she stood up from her chair, she fainted—caught from hitting the ground by a policeman standing nearby. The flashbulbs exploded as Aimee lay draped dramatically in the officer's arms.

Cline did not share his son-in-law's growing suspicion. He told reporters he was "firmly convinced" that her story was true: "There is absolutely nothing that makes me disbelieve Mrs. McPherson's version of her abduction from that California beach."[5] Leaving the hospital, Ryan and Cline met with the Douglas police officer in charge, A. B. Murchison. Instead of tracking down suspects, Ryan scrawled questions he had for the evangelist: Why weren't her shoes scuffed or worn? Why were there grass stains on the insteps of the shoes? Why wasn't she dehydrated or even sunburned? Why weren't there sweat stains on her dress? But for the moment, Ryan kept his questions to himself.

That afternoon, Ryan and Cline took Aimee out to the desert, to see if she could help in the search for the site of her captivity. They met up with Sheriff McDonald, Officer Murchison, and the rest of the search party. Aimee led them to where the footprints had been found earlier that morning—the ones that had seemed to go in a circle before heading toward Agua Prieta. "She pointed out during this trip," Ryan later testified, "the places up to the place where the footsteps turned around. Beyond that, no point was familiar to her."[6]

She recognized the gully she'd crossed right before she came into Agua Prieta, but otherwise, she was lost. "It all looks alike to me," she said. The group turned back to Douglas, leaving behind a growing ragtag group of "shack hunters," a dozen or more men, excited for the sport of helping the famous lady evangelist and perhaps even solving the mystery.

Later that day, Minnie checked her daughter out of the hospital and into a large private suite at the nearby Gadsden Hotel. She told the front desk to keep the reporters away from Aimee. In her own interviews, Minnie struck an anxious and disheartened tone. She told one reporter, "I can't help but feel our years of hard work will be hurt as a result of what has happened. We were always so careful and conservative. It is so unfortunate it had to be Sister. If I had been at the beach, this would never have happened!"[7] Minnie felt her life's work slipping away from her. For a decade she'd carefully managed her daughter, her talents, her career, and suddenly it was all being exploded by sensationalism.

By nightfall, Aimee's story was on the front pages of newspapers around the world. WOMAN EVANGELIST ESCAPES ABDUCTORS, announced *The New York Times*. AIMEE TORTURED FOR HUGE RANSOM, cried the *Los Angeles Examiner*. EVANGELIST RELATES STORY OF TORTURE BY KIDNAPPERS; ANXIOUS TO GET HOME, read the *Los Angeles Times*. ALIVE AGAIN, punned *The Sydney Morning Herald*.

Aimee spent the following day wandering through the desert with an entourage of press and law enforcement trailing behind her. She again wore a white cotton dress, the wind whipping the fabric around her legs as she walked gamely through the scrub brush. She emphasized how comfortable she was, smiling for photographs and explaining how she didn't really need any water, how she was at heart a strapping Canadian farm girl who was unfazed by the brutal climate. She didn't even sweat, she said. A reporter, however, slyly noted that Aimee snuck back to her car after an hour and drank from a thermos of iced water with her mother.

18

SKEPTICISM

That Friday night, Aimee and her growing entourage—made up of her family, law enforcement officers, and a swarm of reporters—left Douglas for Los Angeles on the Golden State Limited. A boisterous six-hundred-person crowd at the train station sent her off, shouting her name, with local dignitaries handing her large bouquets. Aimee's miraculous appearance forty-eight hours before had been the biggest thing ever to happen to the border town—postcard and souvenir sales commemorating the occasion would continue for decades. All along the train route through the Southwest, eager onlookers gathered into the night to catch a glimpse of history in the making with the return of the lady evangelist from the dead. Newspapers described the crowds, with people in wheelchairs and on crutches, waiting in the stations and in the train yards in the hope of encountering the miraculous. A small boy who was seen bathing in a station faucet was interviewed by a reporter, whom he told, "I am getting ready for Sister McPherson. She will be along soon and I don't want her to see my dirty feet!"[1] For those who loved her, her presence was sacred.

But at one o'clock in the morning the train stopped in Tucson.

A man named B. P. Greenwood boarded and approached Captain Cline. He told the detective that he had seen Aimee days before her return, walking about freely on the sun-soaked streets of Tucson. Cline brought him into Aimee's train car, and there, in front of the assembled reporters, Greenwood announced with certainty that he had seen the evangelist earlier in the week. He was a well-respected building inspector, known locally for his meticulousness and honesty, so the captain listened to him carefully. "If it was not Mrs. McPherson," he said to Cline, "it was her twin sister."

Aimee was aghast. She appealed to Greenwood, pacing the aisles, clasping and unclasping her hands, asking him rapid-fire questions, saying anything she could think of to prove to him it wasn't her that he'd seen. For Aimee, it felt vital that above all, she was believed. "You must realize that I am fighting for my life," she pleaded.[2] With finality, Greenwood said he knew it was the evangelist because of the thickness of her ankles, at which point Aimee became less interested in establishing that she wasn't in Tucson and more interested in establishing that she didn't have thick ankles. Reporters witnessed the exchange and reported it in full for the next day's papers. Before the train left the station, Cline and Joseph Ryan questioned Greenwood and took down a statement. For the next hour, as the train rolled down the tracks, Aimee continued to protest the insult to her figure. "That is preposterous!" she said. "My ankles are not thick!" The reporters secretly disagreed, gleefully describing the evangelist in their stories on the confrontation as "having barrel legs."

At a stop in Colton, California, Aimee read aloud a telegram, purporting to announce the discovery of her kidnapping shack (which ended up being false). "Praise the Lord!" she cried. "Oh, dear friends it was bad enough to go through the ordeal but to have your word doubted is worse." Then she asked those gathered at the depot to raise their hands if they believed her. "There couldn't be any thinking person," she said, "who would think for a minute that these stories doubting the report of my kidnapping are true."

As the train drew closer to Los Angeles, Aimee seemed to realize that she needed to take firmer control over her own story. Special radio broadcasting platforms were set up for the evangelist to speak to the crowds at each stop—and to radio audiences—from her now flower-bedecked railroad car. "Praise the Lord," she said. "The day of resurrection has come." In the desert town of San Bernardino, she emphasized that she was a modern celebrity, recognizable to all. "I think I am the best-known person in the world. I say this not boastfully, but wherever I go, people always know me. I want to thank everyone who has been faithful to me." Rolling toward their last stop, Ryan observed Aimee dabbing dark makeup underneath her eyes, making herself look more exhausted. She was ready, he thought cynically, for the audience that awaited her.[3]

On Saturday afternoon, June 26, Aimee's train pulled into Central Station in downtown Los Angeles. At least 50,000 people filled the streets surrounding the building, with some press estimates as high as 150,000. The stationmaster would say that the crowds dwarfed any of those that had gathered for either President Wilson or President Taft. Squadrons from the fire department came out in their uniforms, along with LAPD officers and temple cowboys on horseback, all of them forming a corridor to protect Aimee. City officials stood on the platform to greet her.

Aimee stepped out of the rear train car, with her family and law enforcement following tightly behind her. She beamed from the guardrail as people screamed her name. An airplane flew low over the station and dropped flowers, as if from heaven itself. Cries of "Hallelujah!" echoed through the crowd. Aimee was carried from the train on a wicker chair, bedecked in red roses. The brass band played "Wonderful Savior." Aimee, wrote one journalist, was "like a god in a pagan procession."

The crowd's adulation registered as pure love, she would later write—a return on her own years of service. As loving hands lifted her up and showered her with flowers, she felt waves of gratitude. "The idea of my church officers carrying me over the heads of the crowd and lifting me into the car—me, who had carried *them* around, figuratively speaking, for so long!"[4]

Aimee's car ride to the temple, with the streets lined with jubilant crowds tossing flowers and paper, became a parade. When they reached Echo Park, she disappeared inside the parsonage for less than an hour before returning to the small balcony of her home. Framed by French doors and a scalloped awning, she blew kisses, laughed, and waved, all the while cradling a bouquet of flowers.

"Oh, I love you so much!" she said, swooning. "I am so glad to be back! My voice is still a little weak and I need rest and food, but I can't resist your appeal." She swayed, and two policemen moved to support her.

"How many believe my story?" she asked the crowd. "In all this surmise about me, there has never been one logical motive advanced to explain any voluntary disappearance on my part." She then asked the assembled a question that would become a mantra: "How many have been faithful and believed through all this?" A crowd of hands shot up. "Praise the Lord! God bless you!" she cried.

"There is absolutely nothing which I wanted that my followers would not gladly give me. I am queen in my own kingdom, and I am not boasting when I say so. I can ask anything and get it."[5]

Aimee went back inside the parsonage, but not for long. Minutes later, she strode down the aisle of the Temple, red roses in hand. The congregants, who had filled the pews just minutes earlier, screamed her name, sang, stomped their feet, and shouted, "Amen!" She asked everyone to turn to their neighbor and give a cry of "Happy day!" The Temple filled up with giddy proclamations, over and over, increasingly louder and more ecstatic. "Happy day! Happy day! Happy day! Happy day!"

After an opening prayer, Aimee told of her kidnapping once again. In the few days since her reappearance, the story had been tightened and burnished. Her followers roared with laughter as she described a Douglas policeman checking her breath to see if she was drunk and snickered when she mocked the Tucson building inspector who questioned her identity and called her ankles thick. As she closed her service, she asked again for all who believed her to raise their hands. Everyone did.

As the sun set on a very long day, Aimee slipped out of the

Temple, alone. She wore a large hat and a heavy overcoat. She looked exhausted. She got into a car with Ryan and Cline and drove to the beach. A cold fog hung in the air as she stood on the sidewalk with the two men and reenacted her kidnapping. Ryan was struck by how perfectly her story matched up to the one she'd given two days earlier in the hospital room in Douglas. Almost word for word, every detail stayed the same—the sticky waffle, the room key, the orange juice, the phone call, the green swimsuit, the hot sun, the draft of the sermon, the message sent to the Temple. Still, something about her story felt cartoonish to Ryan, especially when she described being taken by the kidnappers.

Aimee led them to 22 Navy Street, a spot surrounded by cottages and buildings. This wasn't the spot she had described to Ryan and Cline back in Douglas. There, she'd told them that the kidnappers' car had been right next to Lick Pier in a secluded no-parking zone—she'd been so specific about the location. As the three of them stood at the curbside, a woman cried out, "There's Aimee!" People began to gather around and watch. Ryan and Cline shared the same thought: How could this woman who lived in the public eye get kidnapped on a busy street by the beach? Everywhere she went, people recognized her. There should have been eyewitnesses. What kind of kidnappers would do something so bold? And get away with it?

The investigators bid Aimee good night and then covertly drove to the home of Asa Keyes, avoiding the press that had camped outside his office downtown. There, they raised their observations and concerns with the prosecutor. Meanwhile, Aimee drove back to Echo Park, where she preached again to a packed audience. The evening edition of the *Los Angeles Examiner* contained a barb pointed at Cline and Ryan. Aimee's friend and frequent radio contributor Judge Carlos Hardy was quoted announcing a reward for the kidnappers, saying, "The public wants the truth, and I think they will get it now. If left to the law-enforcement agents alone, I am afraid the truth might not come out."[6]

The next morning, a Sunday, Aimee was scheduled to preach. In anticipation of record crowds, a sidewalk speaker system was set up so that the thousands who could not fit inside the Temple would hear her. The streets around the building were blocked off from traffic. Radio sets across the western United States were tuned to KFSG, as hundreds of thousands waited expectantly in their living rooms. But Aimee failed to show. Minnie took the stage and described the debilitated state of her daughter. "Sister has lost fifteen pounds," she told the congregation. "She is still weak from her terrible experience. Her hair hadn't been washed since she left us on May 18; it was just like brush. She is dark under the eyes, and we may have to get some things from the drug store to make Sister look like herself."

The audience laughed in appreciation of Aimee's lack of pretense. They related to her; she was just like them—a fundamentalist Christian who only wore makeup in the direst of circumstances. Minnie also took the opportunity to discuss the memorial service she had held the previous week. Newspaper articles were pointedly asking about what had happened to the more than $36,000 given as a tribute to Aimee. Minnie said she had nothing to hide: "Bravely we did it, but with heavy hearts, and now it is as if she had risen from the dead."[7] The crowd cheered. Minnie added that, of course, if there were some who were not happy to have Sister returned home safely, they were free to get their money back.

When at last Aimee entered the Temple for the afternoon service, the congregation stood and applauded, giving her an ovation that just kept going and going. Aimee walked slowly down the central aisle, flanked by her son and daughter, supporting her on either side. She wore her trademark long white dress with her fluttering shiny blue cape. Carrying a bouquet of lilies of the valley, she gazed out at the crowd—seemingly at once shell-shocked and joyous.

Once onstage, Aimee quickly brought her enraptured audience into the action, describing the events as if they had all experienced them together. She—they! we!—were part of a crime of biblical proportions. She compared herself to Daniel, the Old Testament hero who had been torn apart and persecuted by unbelievers. This abduction, Aimee told them, was a modern-day epic—a war of the devil himself against them. They needed to understand that the questions about her kidnapping were not natural skepticism but persecutory, acts of hatred against not just her but also them. Why? Because their power was too much for the sin-riddled city of Los Angeles. It was Light against Darkness. She spoke of Satan and Job and Jesus and the snake in the Garden of Eden, intermingling Bible stories the audience knew well with the latest headlined specifics of her abduction, blurring past and present, personal and biblical. She laid out how her righteousness—their righteousness!—had made them targets of Satan. "I have tried to win people out of the white slave traffic, and thus have incurred the enmity of the evil powers that be."[8]

"The evil powers that be." This was a dramatic shift in tone from the woman who had once cautioned fellow evangelists not to use hellfire and brimstone when preaching alongside her. This was a different picture of the world and of herself than Aimee had ever presented. She had built her gospel on gentle language, offering an intimate, tender, sentimental relationship with the divine. The woman who had designed a house of worship that was specifically free of hellish imagery, the woman who had sketched angels by hand and whimsically asked that seashells be crushed into the paint to make the sky-blue ceiling sparkle, had pivoted. Now the world she painted for her followers was forbidding.

Aimee took her seat on a wicker throne, surrounded by a jungle of roses and lilies. A clutch of temple workers stood around her, serving her glasses of orange juice. She was dramatic about how thirsty she was now, even days after her return—a different approach from her argument to law enforcement that she really didn't need water. She was noticeably thinner and, some thought, transformed; she looked ten years younger. She told the congregation she was feeling better and had slept well. She made a point of admitting that she had gone against fundamentalist principles and applied a bit of makeup for the service, "So I might look my old self again for you."[9] Her tone with the crowd was cooing, confiding, and intimate.

Over the next hour, Aimee described her kidnapping once again, this time in vaudevillian tones, leaping from her seat and reenacting her careening through the desert, her narrow escape from captivity.

She circled back to how her heroic and righteous stand in favor of Prohibition and against vice had made her a target. Even her position against "coldness in churches" and "modernism" meant that the devil had her in his sights, turning all the other churches against her.

"For three years there has been a great revival," she declared, referring to the inauguration of the Temple. "Thousands have found their way to Jesus. You have seen big, strong men stumbling down the aisles. The Devil had lost his grip just standing there, pulling his mustache (if he has one!)."

Laughing, she intoned the devil's voice: "'What am I going to do to stop this revival . . . If I can get hold of Sister McPherson, if I could just get her away, the thing would crumble! . . . There she is. I have her alone for once. Her secretary has gone to telephone and she is alone on the beach!'"[10]

She cried out that the forces of evil hovered all around, pushing back, furious at the strength of their goodness. But like Christ, who lived in all their hearts, she and they would persevere. Nothing could stop them. A chorus of performers came onto the stage, their pounding footsteps reverberating through the audience. They performed a skit, the Temple versus the devil, and sang a version of a Salvation Army classic, "The Gospel Chariot":

We'll roll the old chariot along,
We'll roll the old chariot along,
We'll roll the old chariot along,
And we won't stop long behind.

If the devil's in the road, we will roll it over him,
If the devil's in the road, we will roll it over him,
If the devil's in the road, we will roll it over him,
And we won't stop long behind.

If the sinner's in the road, we will stop and pick him up,
If the sinner's in the road, we will stop and pick him up,

If the sinner's in the road, we will stop and pick him up,
And we won't stop long behind.

Aimee ran back and forth on the dais, pantomiming this cosmic battle. Her story was forbidding and frightening: she was the victim of a vast conspiracy—a martyr of prophetic proportions. In the coming days, she would compare herself to numerous biblical figures—Daniel, Saint Stephen, Shadrach, Meshach, Abednego, Peter.

But there was one person whose story intersected with hers, over and over: Jesus. Despite all her Christ-like qualities, Aimee remained fixated on the disbelievers, shouting how absurd it was to disbelieve her. Aimee then collapsed on the podium and had to be carried away. Her audience was riveted.

19

THE PUBLIC MIND

Every day, it seemed, photos of Aimee, Minnie, and police investigators appeared on the front pages of newspapers around the country, like a serial drama. Their faces soon became as recognizable as those of Hollywood stars, the intricacies of Aimee's kidnapping as well-known as the plot of the latest silent film. For daily news readers, the coverage was reminiscent of the rape and manslaughter trial of the Hollywood comedian Fatty Arbuckle five years earlier. That case had created a profitable template for publishers in selling celebrity Hollywood's true crime. (Seven years later, when the aviator Charles Lindbergh's infant son was brutally kidnapped and murdered, this sort of yellow journalism reached its horrific noir climax.) But that summer Aimee's kidnapping created an unprecedented level of fervor—especially given the questions it created around both female virtue and religious authenticity. Many remarked that the second coming of Jesus could not have been more astonishing.

While Aimee's story was a gold mine for the papers, it was a threat to others. Her seedy account of what had happened on the beach in

May presented an undesirable vision of Los Angeles—portraying it as a place where a young, attractive, and famous female who had crusaded against vice and corruption could be kidnapped in broad daylight, held captive, and tortured for weeks, and threatened to be sold into sexual slavery in Mexico. This was not the version of Los Angeles that its leaders were selling to the world. Downtown, in the corridors of power that yearned to be seen as "the Wall Street of the west," resentment grew with each new salacious headline.

In the summer of 1926, just as Aimee's story of resurrection spread around the globe, the most powerful men in Los Angeles were bidding to make their city the site of the 1932 Olympic Games. It was an unlikely and audacious campaign. The youthful metropolis had no real infrastructure to host the competition. To travel to California from Europe—home to most of the athletes who would be competing—would entail nauseating weeks' sailing across the Atlantic and then a rough weeklong train ride across the United States. Most people viewed Los Angeles as a provincial western backwater and for a reason—as a modern city it had been in existence only for less than thirty years, and it was far from other outposts of urban civilization.

The Olympic effort was led by the local real estate tycoon Billy Garland and included members of the Chamber of Commerce, Mayor George Cryer, and his shadowy backer, Kent Parrot, along with a host of other railroad barons, bankers, and real estate developers. Together these power brokers worked to project Los Angeles as a sun-soaked second chance for America's growing middle class. Garland had spent years negotiating with the European Olympic committee, trying to arrange for Los Angeles to become a host city.

"We're selling the sunshine," said Harry Chandler, who, along with building his media empire, had quietly aggregated one of the largest real estate holdings in California. These men were united in their desire for Los Angeles to be the western capital of North America. To sell Los Angeles as an equal to Stockholm or Berlin, these captains of industry were investing heavily and working quickly to build a real urban downtown, a grid of paved roads, streetcars, dazzling high-rises, and functional utilities. But even as the core blocks of downtown Los Angeles evolved into this envisioned metropolis, the hundreds of square miles that made up the rest of the city still had dirt roads, large swaths of orange groves, and farmland for as far as the eye could see.

Worried that Aimee's story threatened their bid, the members of the Chamber of Commerce pushed Asa Keyes to investigate Aimee's claims and reach a conclusion swiftly, getting her strange story off the front pages. Even though the newspaper barons profited off the daily sales, they wanted the crime solved and for Los Angeles to maintain its western Garden of Eden exterior. The reputation of the city was at stake.

For others, it was Christian faith itself on the line. Mainline Protestant ministers publicly weighed in on the kidnapping episode. These churches had long viewed Aimee with suspicion. The faith healing, the speaking in tongues, the fundamentalism, the sheer spectacle of her services, her fame, the love offerings, her gender—it was all unseemly to them. And this story of white slavery and her miraculous resurrection: she was turning Christianity and Los Angeles into a vaudevillian circus, one of her illustrated sermons come to life. The Church Federation of Los Angeles, a nondenominational coalition of local Protestant ministers, released a skeptical statement, demanding an investigation:

> . . . Whereas it is apparent to all that either a crime of the most terrible nature has been perpetrated against Mrs. Aimee Semple McPherson, or else a fraud and hoax that is a shame to Christianity have been attempted . . . Now, therefore, be it resolved . . . that we solemnly affirm that the district attorney, the sheriff, the police department, and the grand juries empaneled in Los Angeles County should make an honest, sincere and thoroughly adequate investigation of this whole matter . . . [1]

In the face of doubt, Aimee had one person she knew she could rely on: her mother. Minnie pushed back against her daughter's skeptics in the press. She was emphatic that she believed her daughter's story, and, more than that, she believed that the Temple was the center of Jesus's work on earth. "These ministers issuing this statement didn't build Angelus Temple, and it will take care of itself!" Minnie announced a five-thousand-dollar reward for the arrest and conviction of the kidnappers. Temple staff were offered five hundred dollars if they could find the shack in Arizona where Aimee was held, even though she admitted that she had given up all hope of ever finding it, explaining that the kidnappers had likely destroyed it. The *Los Angeles Examiner* and the *Los Angeles Times* also offered rewards for any evidence of the kidnapping.

Still, to quell growing public outcry, Aimee answered written questions submitted to her by the *Times*. Saying its editors wanted to address the persistent rumors, the *Times* asked the evangelist about why she had given different locations for where she'd been tossed in the car in Venice, about why she hadn't needed water coming out of the desert, how she had had the strength to escape the kidnapper's cabin, and how her clothes had remained unmarred. Aimee was detailed in her answers, giving extra color and context to her story. But then the *Times* asked her how she was in such great shape when she emerged from the desert: "Mrs. McPherson, you have said you were ill, in a state of nervous and physical collapse to a degree that kept you in bed . . . Making all possible allowance for the exaltation due to the opportunity to escape, your doubters say that one in such a condition of illness could not have traveled a mile in the sun without total collapse."

Rather than respond with more facts, Aimee performed a delicate flourish in logic, writing by way of explanation that she was both like the readers in so many ways and yet also superpowered. "You get in the same position and pray to the same God and have the same courage that I have, and you would do likewise," Aimee said. "My life and work are built along lines never duplicated by either man or woman. Many have said that a woman could not have built Angelus Temple and do these other seemingly impossible things—but I did. Before judging that I would have collapsed, look at the things which I have accomplished and at the courage back of it."[2]

For all his doubts and his public-facing bluster, District Attorney Keyes didn't want to go after the evangelist. Unbeknownst to many Angelenos, he had launched an investigation into the Los Angeles County Board of Supervisors that spring, looking into allegations that the entire board had conspired to embezzle government funds to build a private resort for themselves. This board was backed by Chandler and a handful of other business oligarchs who controlled the city's wealth at that time. Power in Los Angeles was—and is—more dispersed than in most East Coast cities, and the County Board of Supervisors often represented an opposing force to the mayor's office and the city council. Keyes was aligned with Mayor Cryer, and he had been told that the supervisors case would be the case that defined him—and potentially rewarded him with new political opportunities. Investigating the squawky lady evangelist and her absurd tale, however, would be a time-wasting distraction with little reward. If only she would just stop talking.

A week after Aimee returned to Los Angeles, Sylvano Villa, the chief of police in Mexico, released his report to the authorities in Los Angeles. The mayor of Agua Prieta, Presidente Ernesto Boubion, also issued a statement to the newspapers of the official findings of their hunt for the shack. It was damning. It read: "Mrs. McPherson was told by me . . . that the story of her wanderings as related by her to the American press and authorities could not be true."

He meticulously, step by step, explained what his investigators had found:

> Chief Villa and his men read the tale in the dust in the early hours before anyone else had passed over the road. Only one automobile had passed over the road. These tracks led to a wash slightly less than three miles east of Agua Prieta. Here the dusty road again told the whole story. The machine turned around and stopped. Footprints of a woman led from the

> automobile to the garita, a rurale shelter near the side of the road. The tracks were followed around the garita and then into the shelter. The footprints showed that a woman had walked about 300 yards from the automobile to the shelter, then the tracks returned to the automobile . . . Some distance from the slaughterhouse where Mrs. McPherson was first seen, the automobile again stopped and the woman's tracks again begin. For 175 yards they were followed by my men to about the spot where Mrs. McPherson says she stopped and called for aid. Then the tracks leave the slaughterhouse and head toward Agua Prieta, where they were lost.
>
> The tracks and footprints found by my men in the dust of the road were followed not only by Mexican officials, but the sheriff's office and they were the only tracks on the road where Mrs. McPherson says she was. I therefore believe that they were her tracks . . . If she did make them, then she could not have been wandering around all over the desert here but would have been the passenger in an automobile which drove her across the border and from which she got out and walked back from a point near the slaughterhouse, after having left the machine once before some few miles beyond.[3]

The report created enormous pressure on Keyes. Law enforcement officers in Mexico had declared that Aimee had made up the entire story—there was no shack, no kidnappers, no twenty-two-mile trek across the desert. Aimee had gotten out of a car outside Agua Prieta, walked around in circles, and then arrived under Ramon Gonzalez's window. Despite this damning version of events, Aimee's supporters were vocal that a terrible crime had been committed against one of the city's most famous women and the kidnappers needed to be hunted down and prosecuted, quickly.

On Tuesday, July 6, Keyes went to the grand jury and formally requested a hearing to investigate Aimee's alleged kidnapping. After listening to witness testimony, it would be up to the members of the grand jury to decide if and whom to prosecute. The *Los Angeles Evening Post-Record* reported that the sensational story was "being brought before the jury upon the theory that Mrs. McPherson's story is true in its entirety. However every angle of the case, including the beliefs of her critics, is to be investigated and heard."[4]

The grand jury for Los Angeles County served as an accusatory body rather than a trial jury. It generally comprised around two dozen citizens, and they were impaneled for a yearlong term. During that time, they spent their days and weeks downtown at the newly built, imposing, granite-clad Hall of Justice, hearing evidence brought by the district attorney and his prosecutors to determine who should be charged and whether there should be a trial. They met in private on the sixth floor, where they heard evidence, asked questions, and then voted on whether to indict. Already that year, the men and women on the grand jury had heard evidence on murders, robberies, and corruption. But Aimee's case was something completely different.

What Keyes was asking of this group that July was somewhat unusual—a preliminary investigation into a crime with no known perpetrators. It was an oddly freewheeling approach, where they would hear from every witness associated with Aimee's disappearance and reappearance. It seemed Keyes wanted the jurors to decide if Aimee's story—and by extension Aimee herself—was a hoax.

20

GRAND JURY

As process servers banged on the parsonage door with subpoenas for Aimee and Minnie, the papers blasted more bad news on July 6. Another witness had come forward, this one saying he'd seen Aimee traveling freely on June 18 in Mexico, days before her desert reappearance. C. A. Pape, the president and general manager of the Overland Motor Company, said that he was absolutely sure that he had observed the evangelist emerging from a club and walking toward a blue sedan with California license plates. He said he immediately recognized her "piercing eyes" and the "reddish sheen" of her hair. He was traveling with a friend, a doctor, and both men signed affidavits, saying that when the woman had realized Pape was looking at her, she'd ducked quickly and crouched behind the blue car. Presented with a photo array, Pape also identified one of her companions as H. D. Hallenbeck, a longtime handyman for Angelus Temple. Other witnesses told the newspapers that Hallenbeck had purchased a Panama hat in Tucson around the same time.[1]

Aimee may have proclaimed over the airwaves and in her sermons that she was helpless and victimized, but privately, she and Minnie were assembling a powerful team of lawyers to defend them. They gathered for a strategy session the day she received the subpoena. The team was initially headed by Arthur Veitch, a pugnacious defense lawyer. A group of Aimee's wealthy followers hired an additional attorney, Roland Rich Woolley, a focused and elegant Mormon, who shared Minnie's desire for Aimee to hunker down, give no comment, and end the investigation. The litigator Leonard Hamner, a former deputy district attorney, served as associate counsel. W. I. Gilbert, a trial lawyer who had represented Rudolph Valentino, among others, would later join the group. Also in attendance at the strategy session was Carlos Hardy, the Superior Court judge who was a close ally of the temple and had his own show on KFSG. In recent years, he had become a close friend and informal advisor, helping Minnie in business matters and advising Aimee on navigating Los Angeles's amorphous power circles.

The team of advisors was divided. Some of her lawyers thought there was no use in trying to keep Aimee from the stand—she was not an easy client to control. Minnie was vehement that she and Aimee should ignore the subpoenas, even at the risk of contempt charges. Aimee's story should stand for itself, Minnie thought. Her daughter had said everything she remembered and should leave the rest to law enforcement. The risk of her perjuring herself was too great. But Aimee was adamant that she would testify.

She had read the questioning news stories, she'd heard her rival Bob Shuler mock her story, and she was livid. More than anything, she needed to prove that she was telling the truth. Silence and retreat were not the way Aimee lived her life. She couldn't bear to be disconnected from the public—to let others tell her story. Over and over, in the days leading up to the grand jury hearing, she protested her innocence on her radio broadcast. "My story is true!" she said as she began to taunt Keyes and the police for being incompetent—or worse. Where were Mexicali Rose, Felipe, and Steve? she asked over the airwaves. Why had the authorities failed to find them?

* * *

On the morning of July 8, a squad of sheriff's deputies, requested by Aimee, arrived at Angelus Temple to accompany her downtown. The motorcade left just after 9:30 a.m. and headed toward the Hall of Justice. One of the tallest buildings in Los Angeles County, it housed the sheriff's department, the district attorney's office, the jail, the coroner's office, and all the city's criminal courtrooms. Sirens blared as Aimee's car pulled up in front of the building. On the sidewalks, her followers lined the streets and proclaimed their support as she made her entrance into the marble lobby.

She wore her signature uniform—a pure white nurse's dress with a wide collar and a long blue cape. Photographs of her outside the courtroom showed a woman whose features were sharper and hair more expertly coiffed than before. As she looked into the lenses of the cameras aimed at her that day, her eyes seemed more knowing, her expression franker and more self-possessed. She was no longer just a subject for the cameras—she was working them.

She was flanked by seven young women from the temple, dressed identically to Aimee, with their hair piled on their heads. They refused to give their names to reporters, their anonymity a key to the spectacle. It was intentionally confusing: Which one was Aimee? Who could really recognize famous Aimee? They formed a spear shape and marched up the steps, blue capes billowing behind them, holding their Bibles tightly to their chests. Trailing the women were Aimee's lawyers: somber-looking men in dark three-piece suits and slicked-back hair. Members of the church, the Foursquare Crusaders, also all in white, lined the hallways, holding up their Bibles and singing. It was a show of faith, force, and allegiance. Aimee grasped each of the temple women and kissed them one at a time. Inside the courtroom, Keyes awaited her. Aimee paused before walking into the chamber, turned back to the crowd, and cited Isaiah: "I am like a lamb led to the slaughter."[2]

At the front of the room sat Judge Arthur Keetch, the presiding judge over all the city's criminal courts and the director of the grand jury. The Liverpool-born jurist had escaped poverty in 1907, coming to America when he was twenty and putting himself through law school. He had served as Los Angeles's deputy district attorney from 1910 to 1918, just as the city was taking shape. That hot July morning, he was fifty-nine years old and exuded an old-world judicial dignity.

Aimee removed her cape and stepped up to the elevated witness chair. The grand jury foreman, William H. Carter, administered the oath to tell the whole truth, nothing but the truth. He then began to ask Aimee to take an oath of secrecy, often pro forma for grand jury witnesses. But Aimee stopped him. She refused to promise to keep silent about what might happen in the room.

"On what ground?" Keyes asked.

"On advice of counsel," she said, and then proceeded to explain that she would need to communicate her story and her experiences to her congregation. She could never keep silent with them; it was part of her sacred duty to describe the world she lived in to her followers. But it was more than professional obligation: Aimee knew her power lay in control over the story. She needed to be the narrator to her followers, as well as the public and the media.

"All right," Keyes capitulated. "I won't hold you to that." For someone who wanted the clamor of this investigation to stop, Keyes allowing Aimee to shape and interpret the story stereophonically from her platform and on the radio every night seems a decision that was at best shortsighted. His agreement to do away with secrecy and allow information to flow freely from the private grand jury room out into the world would transform the course of the hearing—and both of their lives.[3]

Keyes asked her to recount the sequence of events that had begun on that May afternoon on Venice Beach. Aimee was in full command, elegant, passionate, and yet sweetly innocent, as she began to narrate the kidnapping. Sitting in a semicircle around her, members of the grand jury took notes as Aimee described the night of May 18, her first in captivity, when she awakened in a stupor after being pulled into the running car at Venice Beach. Blinking awake that first night, she had no idea where she was, according to testimony documents.

> My face was red and sore for quite a while after they pressed that sponge with something on it against it. The room I awoke in was not large and had blue-striped wallpaper. I was and had been quite nauseous. I believe it was night. They told me I was being held for ransom. It was warmer there than Los Angeles. I heard the word Mexicali, but that's all. The first house was two-stories. I kept myself together at the first house, but then I was told that my mother had collapsed and perhaps had a stroke, and I was pretty much hysterical by the time I got to the second house.

That building, she said, was dark and run-down and filled with canned food. She would have no difficulty recognizing any of the people who held her, she assured Keyes. Her kidnappers included a "dark man" with a gold tooth and Rose, who was "rather professional in her manner," perhaps a nurse. "I tried everything I could think of to convince them to let me go. I tried to talk to her as a woman, and then I told Rose I would make it worth her while. I tried to convert them, too."[4]

After a short lunch break, Aimee returned to the stand. During the intermission, Keyes's office had assembled a large bulletin board with a map depicting the desert outside of Agua Prieta. Aimee was asked to pinpoint her twenty-two-mile journey through the desert. But within minutes of her getting into her escape story, Keyes began interjecting, questioning Aimee as if she were the defendant instead of a victim.

Keyes laid out a line of inquiry that indicated the prosecution's theory: Angelus Temple was in financial difficulty, and the kidnapping was a harebrained scheme to raise money. He read press stories that said Aimee would soon go on a global speaking tour. He stared at Aimee and then turned to the jurors. "One of the reasons that you might have for pulling a stunt like this is for the purpose of getting worldwide advertising or publicity for the sake of helping you in your work!" he bellowed. He began to ask her a series of rapid questions, zeroing in on the holes in her story:

"Did you have your wrist watch on after you left Angelus Temple to go swimming?" he asked her.

"I don't remember," Aimee said. "If I wore a watch that day, which I do not remember, I would most certainly leave it in my pocketbook . . . I believe I got it when I returned home. I think it was on the dresser."

"You don't believe then that you had it while you were in Douglas?" Keyes asked.

"I don't believe I did. I am not positive, but I don't think so."

"The reason I am inquiring about that is this," Keyes said. "If my memory serves me right, I saw a photograph of you taken in the hospital while you were in Douglas and on your wrist apparently was that wrist watch."

"Then Mother must have brought it, if she did," Aimee responded. "I didn't have any watch myself when I was found. Mother must have brought my watch."[5]

Each was performing for a different audience. For Keyes, he needed to show the grand jury and the press that Aimee wasn't bamboozling him, that he was aware that her story didn't hold up. He was the tough-minded, skeptical prosecutor, who would establish the truth no matter the evangelist's sway over the populace. City leaders could be confident he was asking the hard questions. At the same time, Aimee was demonstrating her innocence, animating the events with drama and emotion so that the public might imagine themselves in her shoes. When Keyes asked her about Kenneth Ormiston, Aimee conceded that his wife had been a jealous woman but insisted the rumors about them had no substance. When Keyes asked her if she had wired Ormiston $1,500 in May, just before her disappearance, she laughed it off.

"To begin with, I could not possibly get hold of money like that. I received for spending money twenty-five dollars a week."

"You don't handle the finances?" Keyes asked, surprised. Aimee was known around the city as a savvy businesswoman.

"I don't handle the finances, no. If I want any money, they give it to me like a child," Aimee said flatly. He proceeded to question her—about what she wore to sleep at night, about the number of bank accounts held by the Temple, about the number of corsets she owned, about the amount of the offerings she was given on the revival circuit. Aimee was clear and steady in her responses, even though the subtext of the questioning was invasive. Her account of her kidnapping did not have much evidence, but the implication by the prosecutor was that she was too much—too female, too rich, too sexual—to be an innocent victim. Always aware of her audience, Aimee looked to redirect. As the day drew to a close, she asked Keyes if she could say a few words to the jurors.

"I realize that this story may sound strange to many of you, may be difficult for some of you to believe. It is difficult for me, sometimes, to believe. Sometimes it seems it must have been a dream." She gathered herself and then continued. "I want to say that if character counts a little, that I want you to look back: my mother gave me to God before I was born; my earliest training had been in a Bible and religious work; I lined up the chairs and preached to them as early as five years of age . . ." Aimee continued on, using the trusted bedrock narrative of her life events as an allegory of her authenticity. As she detailed her life and then the kidnapping, she stood up, assuming a preacher's position. "I don't need to ask that you will give your most earnest consideration," she said, locking eyes with the jurors, "and that you will pray about it on your knees, because it concerns the church and concerns Christ, and the eyes of the world are on a religious leader and upon this case . . ."[6]

Finally, Keyes had had enough of the posturing and asked her to sit. But Aimee had made her point, both to the jurors and to readers of the next day's newspapers. She needed folks to understand that she'd been a victim of an evil and organized crime that had arisen because of her power—their power—to follow a righteous path.

The foreman, William H. Carter, exited the courtroom and told reporters that the group of jurors had found the evangelist a very pleasing witness, quickly dispelling any notion of secrecy in the proceedings. If Aimee wasn't going to take an oath of silence, it seemed no one else would either.

By the time Keyes dismissed Aimee, after five o'clock, the crowd outside the courtroom had dwindled to a few hundred. She appeared exhausted, posing for photographers briefly, telling them to "hurry as I have thirty people to baptize at the Temple tonight." Then she was swept away by her brigade of caped sisters into an awaiting car.

ABOVE LEFT: Aimee Elizabeth Kennedy, born October 9, 1890, near Ingersoll, Canada. By the time she was a teenager, she was a budding thespian.

ABOVE RIGHT: Aimee and Robert James Semple on their wedding day at her home on August 12, 1908.

Called by a higher power to leave her life as a housewife behind, Aimee used her "Gospel Car" as a billboard for Jesus. 1918.

In 1917, Aimee's daughter, Roberta, was baptized by a local preacher in a river. Aimee made a point of breaking with social convention by preaching to African American revivalists as she traveled the rural South.

Aimee drove her Gospel Car throughout the United States, often enduring hunger and a lack of all creature comforts as she preached the gospel. Here she is crossing St. Mary's River, between Georgia and Florida, with her Gospel Car in 1916.

Aimee and Harold McPherson in 1917, with the typewriter she used to write the first issue of her monthly magazine, *The Bridal Call.*

Aimee at a revival in Philadelphia in 1918 accompanied by her mother, her children, and her husband Harold McPherson. While she and Harold briefly preached together, Aimee quickly became the main attraction. They separated later that year.

Aimee at a tent revival meeting in 1919 in Los Angeles. As her fame grew, she ministered to tens of thousands, many of whom came to experience her divine healing services.

RIGHT: Aimee with her mother, Minnie, and her children, Rolf and Roberta, in California in 1919. In their first years in Los Angeles, Aimee and Minnie worked together constantly, building a national audience, a roster of real estate assets, and Angelus Temple.

BELOW: Aimee opened her Angelus Temple on New Year's Day, 1923. Arguably the nation's first megachurch, Angelus Temple seated almost six thousand people, with a vast staff that ran twenty-four departments and organized multiple services a day.

BOTTOM: Inside Angelus Temple.

Aimee used all the talent that Hollywood had to offer to help her bring her sermons to life at Angelus Temple, featuring elaborate sets, dancers, musicians, and wild animals. Her services were considered the best show in town. 1931. (Herald Examiner Collection, Los Angeles Public Library.)

A 1925 publicity photo for one of Aimee's most legendary sermons, "Arrested for Speeding," shows her posing on a motorcyle.

Aimee in January 1926, looking out the window of her newly built Bible College. Exhausted by her workload and the burden of her rising fame, Aimee left that month to take a vacation throughout Europe and Palestine, dogged by rumors that she was having an affair with her radio operator.

As news spread of her disappearance into the ocean on May 18, 1926, Aimee's followers gathered on the beach in Venice to pray for the evangelist's return. Here they watch as the surf is dragged for her body. (Herald Examiner Collection, Los Angeles Public Library.)

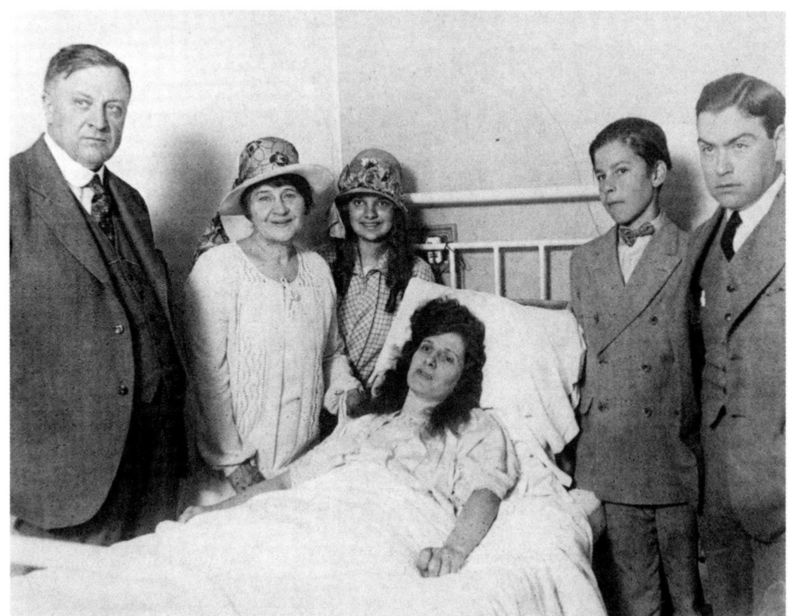

Taken at the Douglas hospital in Arizona, this photograph shows Aimee flanked by the LAPD's Captain Cline, her mother, her daughter, her son, and the assistant district attorney, Joseph Ryan. June 1926. (Bettmann Collection, Getty Images)

Aimee in the desert near Agua Prieta, Mexico. In the days following her reappearance, she worked with authorities to locate the shack she claimed to have escaped. It was never found.

After her miraculous escape from her kidnappers, Aimee returned to Los Angeles on June 26, 1926. The crowds that gathered for her dwarfed those that had come for presidents and monarchs, and as she stood on the train platform, people shouted, "Praise the Lord!"

When Aimee arrived back in Los Angeles after her disappearance, she was met by tens of thousands of admirers. She was hoisted in the air on a throne and carried through the throngs, as an airplane dropped flowers from above. (Los Angeles Times Photographic Archive, UCLA Library Special Collections)

A page of the sermon titled "Light and Darkness" that Aimee wrote on the beach on May 18, 1926, the day she disappeared. (Los Angeles Times Photographic Archive, UCLA Library Special Collections)

Aimee in court in 1926.

On the first day of testimony for the grand jury trial about her disappearance, Aimee entered the Hall of Justice with her lawyer, Arthur Veitch, and a brigade of women from her church who all dressed identically. July 8, 1926. (Los Angeles Times Photographic Archive, UCLA Library Special Collections)

Minnie Kennedy (left) and Aimee sit in a Los Angeles courtroom during the inquiry into Aimee's disappearance and alleged kidnapping in 1926. (Los Angeles Times Photographic Archive, UCLA Library Special Collections)

Los Angeles District Attorney Asa Keyes led the inquiry into the disappearance of Aimee Semple McPherson in 1926. (Los Angeles Times Photographic Archive, UCLA Library Special Collections)

Aimee and the radio engineer for Angelus Temple, Kenneth G. Ormiston. (Herald Examiner Collection, Los Angeles Public Library)

Los Angeles law enforcement officers examining the clothing Aimee was wearing when she reappeared out of the desert of Mexico in 1926. (Herald Examiner Collection, Los Angeles Public Library)

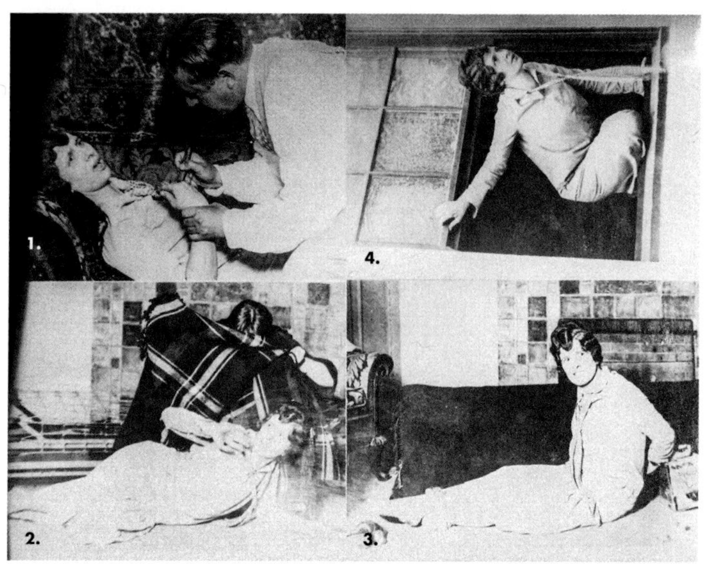

Aimee demonstrates how (1) her fingers were burned by a cigar wielded by one of her abductors, (2) the kidnappers swathed her in blankets, (3) she was then tied up, and (4) she managed to escape before struggling across the desert to safety. 1926. (Bettmann Collection, Getty Images)

RIGHT: In her "confession," Lorraine Wiseman-Sielaff (left) asserted that Aimee paid her expenses and promised her more money to produce a fake "Miss X" of Carmel. Lorraine said Aimee coached her to dress like the evangelist and do her hair the same way. 1926. (Herald Examiner Collection, Los Angeles Public Library)

ABOVE: A trunk found in Ormiston's New York hotel room was sent back to Los Angeles, where detectives sifted through a trove of women's clothes from LA stores—all in Aimee's size. 1926. (Bettmann Collection, Getty Images)

In the years following the inquiries into her kidnapping, Aimee cut an increasingly glamorous figure. She allegedly had plastic surgery and worked with a screenwriter to turn the events of her life into a film. 1938.

Built on the far outskirts of Los Angeles, the lavish home that became known as "Aimee's Castle" was her escape in the boom years just before the Great Depression.

Aimee and the baritone David L. Hutton share their breakfast with reporters the morning after their surprise elopement on September 14, 1931. He was her third husband. (Herald Examiner Collection, Los Angeles Public Library)

A line for Aimee's soup kitchen on Temple Street, 1932. The Foursquare Church estimates that it fed and clothed more than 1.5 million Angelenos during the Depression.

RIGHT: Aimee kneeling onstage praying for her followers during a revival in Boston in 1931.

BELOW: A huge revival event for Aimee in Minneapolis in 1933. Even as her third husband, David Hutton, filed for divorce in July, it was a time of enormous public work for the evangelist—she preached in forty-six cities in twenty-one states to more than five hundred thousand people in the second half of that year.

Aimee sits next to her business manager and eventual guardian, Giles Knight. Aimee was embroiled in a dramatic lawsuit brought by a former pastor, Rheba Crawford. December 12, 1936. (Bettmann Collection, Getty Images)

In the years following her kidnapping episode, Aimee dealt with dozens of lawsuits and increasingly dire financial difficulties. 1937.

Aimee standing on the dome of Angelus Temple with Giles Knight on New Year's Eve, 1938, burning the outstanding debt notices that they had finally paid off after years of financial turmoil.

Aimee and Roberta during a dramatic and ugly 1937 lawsuit in which Roberta sued her mother's attorney for slander. Aimee took the stand and testified against Roberta, thus severing ties with her daughter, whom she had hoped would take over her church.

Aimee and her son, Rolf, in a formal photograph. After her death, Rolf presided over the Foursquare Church for forty-four years. (Security Pacific National Bank Collection, Los Angeles Public Library)

21

SINISTER PLOTS

The grand jury proceedings into the kidnapping took place over the next two weeks, with three more sessions following Aimee's testimony. Asa Keyes, working with Joseph Ryan, devoted the majority of time to hearing from witnesses who called into question Aimee's version of events. They included a woman who said she saw Aimee speaking flirtatiously with a man in an extended conversation on Venice Beach the afternoon she went missing; a police officer from Culver City and his wife, who said they saw the evangelist driving out of Venice in the front seat of a blue sedan on that afternoon; a parking attendant from a Salinas garage, four hours north of Los Angeles, who saw her get into a blue car with a limping man a day after she was thought drowned.

Among the most dramatic was C. A. Pape, the Tucson automobile man. He declared confidently to the jurors that he had spotted the evangelist outside a Mexican roadhouse days before her reappearance in Agua Prieta. He and his doctor friend both testified to the sighting, describing, as he had in his affidavit, how the woman had tried to hide when she saw them looking at her. The jurors wanted to be sure, and a call was placed to the Temple, asking Aimee to come to the court. She was ushered inside the jury room for less than five minutes. Keyes asked Pape if he was certain that the woman he had seen was Aimee. "There is absolutely no doubt in my mind," Pape replied, staring at Aimee. "That is positively the woman who I saw in front of the Club International in Aqua Prieta."[1]

Rumors of incriminating evidence mounted in the newspapers—allegations of telegrams from Ormiston in code, his wife's threats of a divorce filing, accounts of Ormiston and Aimee cooing to each other inside the Temple. This sordid affair wasn't the only rumor. Equally explosive were stories of bad blood between Aimee and Minnie, of a power struggle over the increasingly valuable Angelus Temple. A witness told the grand jurors that while she had been a student at the Bible College, she'd seen Minnie slap Aimee in the church offices during a heated quarrel.[2]

To change public opinion and bolster her story, Aimee hired private detectives to conduct her own investigation. Aimee later wrote in a *Bridal Call* article that even that July she knew there was a vast conspiracy against her. She said that she'd been advised that the grand jury proceeding was a ruse to get her to testify under oath and inadvertently commit perjury. She knew that her testimony wasn't enough—she needed to provide evidence that would corroborate her story. With her lawyers and detectives, Aimee's team cast a wide net and soon focused on Russell A. McKinley.

When Aimee disappeared on May 18, the Temple had been inundated with phone calls, telegrams, and letters alleging every manner of sightings and theories and claims about Aimee's whereabouts. Minnie dismissed them all as bunk. But at the end of May, the LAPD chief of detectives, Herman Cline, came to the Temple with a strange story. He said that a blind lawyer named R. A. McKinley claimed that two men had just visited him at his office in Long Beach. They had picked him, they explained, because he was known to represent bootleggers and criminals. And most importantly: he couldn't see.

The men told him they were holding Aimee hostage and asked McKinley to serve as their go-between with the Temple. They had asked for "test questions" from Minnie to prove that they had her. Cline knew McKinley—he had a dicey reputation, he told Minnie, for working on behalf of the underworld. But he said it would be worth her while to comply and put together some questions. She did and then promptly dismissed the incident along with the dozens of "crank letters" she was getting every day. On May 25, a week after Aimee's disappearance, Minnie Kennedy released a formal statement: "There is absolutely no hope on our part of Sister McPherson being alive on land or sea."[3]

But then, three days later, Minnie, who had been mourning her daughter's death and insisting that the search should end, did a strange thing: she offered a $25,000 reward for the return of her daughter, unharmed:

> Because of the many rumors that my daughter, Aimee Semple McPherson, has been seen here, there, and everywhere during the last ten days we have decided to offer a reward for her safe return. Never for one moment have we had the slightest hope or reason to hope that she is alive . . . But to set at rest the rumors and call the bluff of irresponsible persons and publications, we offer the reward . . . There is the offer, and until it is claimed, let silence reign.[4]

Amid the confusion, the Los Angeles coroner refused to sign the death certificate.

Minnie told the press in May that Aimee was a marked woman, saying that her daughter had feared for her life from the crime syndicates. She didn't name the reigning gangster kingpin Charlie Crawford, but the implication was that the underworld boss could be responsible. "Before the April 30th election, Aimee told me she was going to tell the truth about the Venice dance halls. When I sat and heard what she said, that she would rather see her own daughter dead than in a Venice dance hall, I realized she was taking her life in her hands," she continued. "Often last summer after evening service we would drive out to the beach, and my daughter would almost weep at the scenes there. We often talked about the young girls there, many younger than Roberta."

Reporters asked the evangelist's mother if there had been specific threats against Aimee. "No," said Minnie, "but the underworld never warns before it strikes."[5]

Despite her own offer for a reward, Minnie insisted they would have a memorial service on June 20 at the Temple—a month after Aimee's disappearance. The day before the service, the Temple staff was in a flurry of preparations. Someone handed Minnie an envelope, postmarked from El Paso. She removed the letter, which read:

> Dear Madam:
>
> Exactly one month has elapsed since we grabbed Aimee McPherson and now is time for action. We nearly bungled it once, but we've moved her to a safe place now and have doped out a plan of ransom payment that is absolutely safe to us. You won't be able to trap us if you act in bad faith. We doubt if you will attempt any funny business though when you are convinced this is no hoax or Sunday school picnic and that we really have your daughter . . . First, in order that you may know without doubt that Aimee is alive and, in our hands, we are enclosing a lock of her hair.

From the envelope, Minnie removed the gnarled lock of auburn hair. Minnie gasped as she touched it—it was dirty and oily, but it looked like Aimee's. She read on:

> We tried to get answers to your silly questions but because she knows about the half million ransom she won't answer them. Says she would rather die than cripple the church to such an

> extent. But before she knew what it was all about, we tricked her into a couple fool answers, something like "A woven wire one between two apple trees" and the hound was black and named Gyp. She shut up then realizing what we were after but you insist a lighted cigar against a barefoot often gets results. Her middle right-hand finger has a scar on it you aught to recognize, suppose we chop it off and send it along to kill your doubts?

The letter concluded with a threat to sell Aimee in Tijuana:

> But though we've treated her respectfully in fairness to her position and value to us, what the future holds for her is entirely up to you. Our alternative is to sell her to old Felipe of Mexico City. We are sick and tired of her infernal preaching, she spouts scripture in answer to everything.

The kidnappers said they were out to destroy that "damned Temple," and collect a "tidy sum" of money—the equivalent of close to $9 million in today's dollars.

> Now get busy. Have the $500,000 ready in big bills. Watch for the final letter of instructions which will reach you next Friday. That letter you must keep absolutely confidential, but you will alright when you read it. Follow the instructions exactly and on that same night you will have your Aimee back and we'll have the dough. If anything slips Felipe gets her.
>
> Till Friday,
>
> THE AVENGERS.[6]

The letter had disturbed Minnie. For all its melodrama, there were troubling truths within it: Aimee did have a scar on her middle finger; they did have a dog named Gyp. How could these people know those things? Minnie stroked the hair, and that night, she placed it under her pillow before she went to sleep. She tried to dismiss the "Avengers" note as just another piece of fanatical correspondence—an absurd and dramatic document that in no way could be legitimate. There'd been dozens of Aimee sightings in the previous weeks—reports of Aimee in Arizona, California, Colorado, and New York. On a single day, Aimee was reported to have been seen in sixteen different places from coast to coast.

Cline didn't think anything more of the blind lawyer's story until Minnie had handed him the Avengers letter on the train to Douglas. She had held on to it for five days, sleeping with the lock of hair under her pillow and proceeding with the memorial service for her daughter. Minnie would later say she had thought it was a hoax, but when Cline opened the envelope, he saw that the letter answered two of the questions that McKinley had been given.

That July, as Aimee's team cast about for evidence of the kidnappers for the grand jury, they soon turned to McKinley's story of the two men in Long Beach. Aimee's private detective drove down to Long Beach, and McKinley confirmed his account. It was those same men, McKinley said, who had sent the Avengers letter to Minnie just days before Aimee returned, with the single lock of oily hair. Because the blind man was the only one—besides Aimee—who said the kidnappers were real, McKinley suddenly became very important to her. And to Asa Keyes.

In his appearance before the grand jury that July, McKinley described how the two men had come to his office in downtown Long Beach on the morning of May 31, nearly two weeks after Aimee had disappeared. They were holding Aimee for ransom, they said, and they wanted McKinley to go to Aimee's mother and arrange a payment of $25,000 and a promise of immunity in exchange for her daughter. For his trouble, they would pay him $5,000. McKinley said he immediately called the Long Beach chief of detectives, who reached Captain Cline, who was reluctant to bother Minnie with another outlandish claim about Aimee's whereabouts. Still, Cline asked Minnie to write a set of questions that only Aimee would know the answers to, which he gave to McKinley:

1. Describe the hammock at our home in Canada and where the home was
2. Describe our dog and tell what his name was
3. Describe the stove in our dining-room
4. Who was Wallace and what was his relationship to our family?[7]

McKinley reported to police that the men hadn't shown up at the appointed hour but came between ten o'clock and ten-thirty. The building's elevator operator confirmed to authorities that two men had taken the elevator that night and gone to McKinley's office. McKinley reported the incident to the police and said that was the last he heard from them—until the letter arrived.

While newspaper photos showed Aimee in front of the grand jury with a twinkly-eyed, mischievous smile, her mother seemed to suffer. For Minnie, whose name was suddenly as well-known as her daughter's, with papers dubbing her "Ma Kennedy" or just "Ma," the public scrutiny had become an ordeal. The small woman was not as open with reporters. She appeared stone-faced and sad, her gray eyes staring out somewhere beyond the viewer.

On the morning of July 13, Minnie arrived at the Hall of Justice to give her testimony. Unlike with Aimee's appearance five days earlier, she had no interest in staging a spectacle; she entered through a side door.

Keyes began his questioning with the most basic premise of Minnie's narrative.

"You believed she was drowned?" he asked.

"I either believed that she was drowned or that God had taken her," she responded.

"What do you mean by that?" Keyes asked.

"I believe that God has taken people, according to the Bible, whose bodies have never been found."

Aimee had been chosen, she said. When Keyes expressed confusion, Minnie explained: "Of course, I don't want to bring any Bible chapters here, but we do believe that there have been times when God took people and that their bodies have never been found, such as Moses. Not that Sister would be compared with that, but when we couldn't find her body we knew not what to think."

Realizing he wasn't getting anywhere, Keyes pivoted to physical evidence. Had Minnie brought a watch to Aimee in Douglas? No, she said. When and how had she received the Avengers letter? She had been given the letter on the morning of June 22, by Aimee's secretary, Emma. She had turned the letter over to Cline the following day, and the detective noticed writing at the bottom of the envelope that asked for a special delivery fee—but the envelope did not have a special-delivery stamp. It had been mailed from Tucson on June 18. The prosecutor was suspicious that Minnie had tampered with the letter's envelope to make it seem as if she had received it after the memorial service.

"Did it strike you," Keyes asked, "that the general tone of this letter was—sounded like your daughter?"

"No," Minnie replied. "Something about the letter sounded to me like somebody was trying to impersonate somebody. It didn't sound . . . some of it sounded like the underworld, and some of it sounded like somebody had listened to our conversation, our mode of speaking, and was trying to imitate her; and I spoke to Mr. Cline about that, and I said, 'The letter doesn't sound entirely sincere.'"

Keyes asked her if she had any ideas or leads that would help the grand jury in apprehending those who took Aimee. She explained that with reporters inundating her and everything else going on, she hadn't been able to sleep and was in incredible distress. She didn't have any idea who might have kidnapped her daughter: "I think it is wonderful that I have even kept up as I have, but you . . . there are so many things come in that I have had no chance even to have them looked up. We are endeavoring to do that now."[8]

Keyes then turned to the testimony given by witnesses that Minnie and her daughter had been fighting before Aimee disappeared. A church employee had testified that he had heard the two bickering the day before Aimee disappeared, with the evangelist shouting to her mother: "Well, we'll see if you can run it any better than I can!"[9] Perhaps this was a simple case of an imaginative and unruly daughter wanting to escape an overbearing mother? Minnie scoffed at this. Their relationship was perfectly matched, she said: she supported Aimee, who had a special gift, and Aimee supported her, who kept everything in order. "I boss her around considerably and try to keep her from getting into trouble." The jury laughed; they understood her role as the mother/manager.

When Keyes began to circle around the church finances, Minnie's answers were more certain, more concrete. Was there an $85,000 mortgage on the Temple? he asked, testing his theory that the organization was struggling. No, she replied. She and Aimee had paid for the Temple in full and incorporated the property with no financial backing—all from hard work and perseverance and faith. "It was just from the love offerings and what we had saved and from people who believed in us. And the only thing that many of the people in our campaigns who gave us money asked me to see was that while Mrs. McPherson lived, I see that she never let any bunch of men get it in their hands—that she was to preach the Foursquare Gospel, and I have stood by that."[10] Power was centralized, she said, at Angelus Temple, with the executive board of directors consisting of only Minnie, Aimee, and their secretary, Emma Schaeffer.

How, Keyes asked, did Aimee make a living? Minnie explained that the offering from the first Sunday of each month was given entirely to Aimee. "We just let her use it at her own discretion," Minnie said. The rest of the money collected during the month went to pay the "expenses of the work." Minnie said that while she didn't handle the incoming money anymore, she handled all the outgoing. "I write the checks and watch the amounts." While the tax laws governing churches as nonprofits make the use of such donations limited to the maintenance and expense of the church itself, Aimee and Minnie had arranged things differently. The Echo Park Evangelistic Association was incorporated as a private entity, with Aimee and Minnie fully in control of the use of funds. This was Minnie's innovation—her genius. Every penny that was given in the collection plate at Angelus Temple was the private property of the two women. Minnie had bifurcated the structure of the Temple so that the Foursquare Church enjoyed all the freedoms of a religious organization, but it was run by this private entity. The land deed for the Temple and other property around town that they had acquired was held solely by the mother and daughter.[11]

"Mrs. Kennedy in Tears Before Grand Jurors," read the *Los Angeles Record* headline that evening, describing her grilling by the district attorney. But the photos of Minnie outside the courtroom show her grinning. Her time on the stand finished, she cheerfully ran an errand. She took an elevator to the top of the Hall of Justice, where the county jail was located. She was overseeing a new Temple welfare project to get radio receivers installed in the jails so inmates could listen to KFSG—a captive audience.

When Keyes left the courtroom, he gave a wry smile to the waiting photographers and said only that "the kidnappers are as elusive as ever." When reporters shouted questions about whether his office was any closer to finding Aimee's kidnappers, he smiled again and repeated his statement. "The kidnappers are as elusive as ever."[12]

Every day, the headlines seemed to shift the story—suspects in Arizona were arrested and then released with alibis; witnesses came forward saying they saw Aimee in Tucson and then retracted. Numerous confessions to various crimes were made by madmen, but all amounted to nothing. Mexican officials were accused of taking bribes. A cartoon in the *Los Angeles Times* depicted people on the street all saying Aimee's name over and over, except for one man who held a sign that said, "I am deaf, dumb and blind." "Four out of Five Have It," read the caption. Aimee's kidnapping—or non-kidnapping, depending on one's point of view—was the talk of Los Angeles. The *Times* published daily letters—hundreds were sent every day—that both attacked and defended the evangelist. "Every loyal citizen who wants to see Los Angeles grow must demand full facts," wrote one reader who saw Aimee as an existential threat to the city's growth and prosperity. But others saw her as a singular and heroic figure who was being treated unfairly. One reader wrote that Aimee had acted out "the greatest amount of religious work by any individual ever here."[13]

On the eve of the final day of hearings, Kenneth Ormiston sent a letter to the district attorney, denying his involvement in the episode. "I have not been in Riverside, Santa Barbara, San Luis Obispo, Salinas, Oakland . . . since I left Los Angeles," he wrote. "Furthermore, I know nothing of the disappearance of Mrs. McPherson."[14] The star witness in Keyes's case hadn't even bothered to show up. For his part, Keyes seemed to want to give Aimee a slap on the wrist, satisfy the power brokers, and move on.

That day, Keyes and Judge Keetch held a private conference in the district attorney's office. Keyes had told the judge he wanted the grand jury to issue a special report—a formal but toothless rebuke usually done only for corrupt public officials. Keetch said this was impossible. "Asa, you know as well as I know that no grand jury can bring in a report on anybody except an official," the judge told the prosecutor. Keyes admitted they did not have enough evidence to warrant an indictment against Aimee.

On July 20, Keyes asked the grand jury to vote on bringing indictments against Aimee's unnamed kidnappers. The answer came back quickly: no indictments. "The grand jury has had presented to it for consideration the evidence in the alleged kidnapping of Aimee Semple McPherson and finds there is insufficient evidence to warrant an indictment." The foreman gave a statement to the press that the grand jury would be available if Aimee wanted to submit any more details, "if Mrs. McPherson cares to continue her efforts to further substantiate her story." The grand jury had concluded that there was not enough evidence to issue an indictment against the kidnappers—known or unknown. It was an embarrassing resolution for Aimee and her followers. Reports quickly leaked that fourteen out of seventeen of the jurors had not believed her testimony.

Aimee's response was consistent: there was a plot to destroy her, and the grand jury's conclusion was just one more example. After she spent the afternoon with her lawyers, they issued a statement to reporters: "Following her appearance, many agencies, set to work, not to apprehend Mrs. McPherson's kidnappers, but with a powerful endeavor to disprove her story and 'show her up to the world.' Now that the end of the present official investigation is here, the efforts of these agencies are all in vain. Mrs. McPherson's story related, time and time again, to officials and others, remains as firm and unshaken as the first time it was told."[15]

Aimee wasn't the only one unhappy with the lack of charges: her rival minister Bob Shuler was furious Keyes had failed to get an indictment—only he had wanted one of Aimee. "Poor Asa Keyes had a hold of a hot potato and didn't know what to do with it," the pastor told a local reporter. "Keyes is the most helpless man in Los Angeles in a crisis. He's as helpless as a baby. I know him well and there's mighty little to him."[16] Shuler announced he would hold a mass protest that Sunday, implying that the grand jury had been part of a cover-up to hide Aimee's lies. Meanwhile, Keyes was just relieved for the whole thing to be over. He could devote his full attention to the County Board of Supervisors investigation that would keep his career on its ambitious, political course. But Ryan did not want to let the case go. He wasn't sure what Aimee had done or why, but he was convinced she was lying. He just lacked evidence.

22

CARMEL BY THE SEA

Just forty-eight hours after the grand jury closed the case on Aimee's kidnapping, on the evening of July 22, a woman walked into the police station in Monterey, California, the booming fishing town 320 miles north of Los Angeles, and asked to see Chief William Gabrielson. Once she had his attention, the woman boasted that she knew where Aimee Semple McPherson had been during the first ten days of her disappearance. The answer, she said, was Carmel by the Sea.

An insular seaside settlement, just south of Monterey, Carmel was known for picturesque cliffs, sandy streets, bucolic homes, and the well-to-do artists it attracted. It was a world unto itself—in theory a perfect place to hide in plain sight. Earlier that week, the woman told the police chief, she had gone to a speakeasy in Carmel to have a drink. A few chairs down, a barfly was slugging beer after beer and soon began to tell her the village gossip. Everyone in town, he crowed, knew that the world-famous lady evangelist had spent ten days in May in an oceanfront cottage with her lover.

Chief Gabrielson sprang into action. He found the drunk, who gave him the address where he claimed Aimee had hidden out with her companion. There, across the street from a romantic bay, the police chief found a squat stucco home bordered on two sides by a tall stone wall. The cottage's most defining aspect was its privacy. Gabrielson returned to the station and called Asa Keyes's office, offering to take the train to Los Angeles to report his findings. But Keyes cut him off—he didn't trust some yokel from a small town to do police work at the level needed, not on this case. Keyes called Joseph Ryan and told him to take the train north.

Ryan arrived in Monterey the next evening, with his wife in tow—Captain Cline's daughter insisted on joining her husband for the adventure. By the next morning, the prosecutor was knocking on the door of the small seaside cottage. Henry C. Benedict, a retired insurance adjuster, opened the door. Benedict told the attorney that a man named George McIntire had arrived at the office of Carmel Realty Company on May 14, four days before Aimee's disappearance. McIntire (or McIntyre—the man used both spellings in the documents he signed) said that he had a sick wife in San Diego. What she needed was seclusion and quiet, and he wanted to rent a cottage for three months. He was an amiable fellow, according to Benedict, bald and handsome in an unlikely way, with a pronounced limp—a bit of a dandy. McIntire told Benedict he'd just driven in from Seattle, which explained why he had Washington plates on the bright blue Chrysler coupe he was driving. The car was flashy. It had made an impression on Benedict, and others in the sedate village.

A woman from the rental office showed McIntire around Carmel. When he saw Benedict's cottage with its tall stone walls, he said it was exactly what he was looking for and took out a large roll of cash. He paid both the rent and the deposit on the spot—$550 (nearly $10,000 in today's money). He asked when the place could be ready, and the Benedicts said they could move out in a few days. McIntire could have the place on May 18: the day of Aimee's disappearance.

Benedict said that he'd encountered Mrs. McIntire just once. The cottage's owner arrived at his house on the morning of the 19th to make sure his new renters were well situated and, he said, to plant a few spring bulbs in the garden. McIntire came out to say hello;

accompanying him was a woman whom Benedict assumed to be Mrs. McIntire. "She was rigged up with a kind of afternoon tea outfit," he said to Ryan. "I mean by that she had on a silk waist and a silk skirt and white felt hat, one of those bucket or scuttle-shaped things, pulled well down over the back of her neck and eyes, and had on a pair of black goggles. All she said was, 'How do you do,' in a very subdued voice, and she didn't say a word beyond that. I noticed she had on satin slippers, and you know Carmel is a rough-and-ready place, and I said, 'Those slippers won't last long around here.' But she didn't answer, and she turned and went into the house."[1]

As he left, Benedict said he noticed a bright green women's bathing suit drying on the clothesline. He found the woman's costume and manner odd, but decided it was none of his business. Benedict didn't hear from the McIntires again until May 29, when he received a letter postmarked from Salinas, an agricultural city twenty-five miles away. Typewritten and signed "McIntyre," it was addressed to "My dear friends, Mr. and Mrs. Benedict" and explained that the couple had had to return quite suddenly to the East Coast because of a family emergency. Mr. McIntire could be reached at the Hotel Pennsylvania in New York City and encouraged the Benedicts to use the fresh groceries he and his wife had left behind. "Needless to say," he concluded, "we enjoyed every moment of our stay in your cottage."

After giving his account, Benedict showed Ryan the items the couple had left: a battery-operated portable radio, newspapers from Los Angeles and San Francisco, a dozen hairpins, spice cans, including a pepper can with what appeared to be a clean set of fingerprints. On the bookshelf, the couple had also left a few books: *Why I Am a Christian*, *Unmasking Our Minds*, *History of France*, and *Science Remaking the World*.[2] Inside the front cover of each, someone had drawn a small cross.

When shown a photograph of Kenneth Ormiston, Benedict said that without a doubt George McIntire was the same person. But he refused to positively identify the woman as Aimee. Given the heavy driving-style goggles and the hat, he couldn't say for sure who the woman was. Furthermore, the testy Benedict had once been the victim of a false identification, and he told the prosecutor he wouldn't even be able to identify his own sister if she wore the same outfit as Mrs. McIntire. "Ryan tried his damndest to get me to say I could identify her," he said later in the courtroom.

Undeterred, Ryan went next door and interviewed the neighbors. Jeanette Parks had just given birth that spring, she told him, and at 4:00 a.m. on May 19, she had awakened to feed her newborn. Outside her window, she heard a noise and looked to see a man and a woman standing in the kitchen of the cottage. They were drinking by the sink. She described the woman as having "very beautiful hair, piled on top of her head." As she watched, the couple quickly drew the curtains. The curtains remained closed for the rest of their stay—about ten days.

Ryan and his wife drove around Carmel, interviewing witnesses. The delivery boy, the grocery store owner, the real estate agent—when shown a photo of Ormiston, each confirmed that Ormiston was McIntire. But the identity of the woman was more of a mystery—her face had been mostly covered whenever anyone saw her, and many said they couldn't positively identify her. When presented with a photo of Aimee, the next-door neighbor said: "That is the woman." The delivery boy said the same. A few others, who had passed by the cottage, said they thought the woman was the evangelist but weren't sure. One described her as "five feet six or seven inches, with thick ankles."[3] The store owner said that the couple had tried desperately to buy a Los Angeles newspaper from May 19 but hadn't been able to find one.

As Ryan made his way through the small town, piecing together witness accounts of the McIntires' mysterious sojourn, reporters trailed him constantly. They had come from Los Angeles, San Francisco, and the national wire services. The boundary line between the law and the press was so blurred—and corrupt to the point of absurdity—that Ryan folded them into his investigation. Soon reporters were working as de facto detectives, searching the yard outside the cottage. One found a crumpled slip of paper, made out with a grocery list, written in a flowery "female" hand, according to news reports. It was entered into evidence. Each new clue that Ryan inventoried, each new positive photo identification he made, was promptly reported back to the newsrooms in cities around the country. By that Sunday evening, a few late-edition papers carried the first stories of Ryan's discovery: AIMEE LOVE NEST ALLEGED.

The next morning, Ryan made two phone calls. One was to his father-in-law, Captain Cline, who said he would head to Monterey right away. His other call was to Keyes, telling his boss he had the proof. "There no longer exists any doubt in my mind," he told reporters, "as to what became of Aimee McPherson after she disappeared on the beach at Ocean Park." He proclaimed definitively, "I am fully satisfied now that Kenneth Ormiston and Mrs. McPherson occupied the beach cottage for nearly ten days."[4] He sent the spice cans back to Los Angeles to be analyzed for fingerprints, which he was confident would belong to the preacher. He'd had doubts about Aimee's story from the beginning. But if she hadn't been kidnapped, why would she make up such a story, and where had she gone? Finally, he knew. He had found definitive proof that Aimee had made up the kidnapping to cover up an illicit affair.

"I believed parts of the story," he would later say. "I believed she walked from the fork of the road until she came into the Gonzalez house . . . I didn't believe first of all that there was any shack. I didn't believe that she was taken there by Rose and Steve, or anybody representing themselves as Rose and Steve. I didn't believe that she was incarcerated in any shack in Mexico or that she escaped from any shack in Mexico. I didn't believe that she was bound as she described herself as having been bound. I didn't believe she traveled the distance that she claimed she traveled over the region that she described through the territory she described. I didn't believe that she was incarcerated in any form or fashion in the manner she set forth in her statement. That is that."[5]

* * *

Once he joined his daughter and son-in-law in Carmel, Cline looked over the evidence and called the Temple. Aimee refused to speak to him; instead, Minnie came to the phone. "Things look bad here, Mrs. Kennedy," Cline told her, asking them to come up to Carmel by the Sea immediately. "These witnesses are positive in their identifications of Mrs. McPherson. We want to be absolutely fair in the matter, and we feel that Mrs. McPherson's place is here at this time. I am just as anxious to disprove these identifications if they are incorrect as I am to prove them if they are true."[6]

Alluding to the group of look-alike caped women whom Aimee had brought to the grand jury hearing, he added, "You tell her attorneys they can bring as many Temple workers as they desire who resemble Mrs. McPherson to take part in the identification."[7] Minnie told him that Aimee would consider Cline's request, and she'd have an answer for him by four o'clock. She hung up the phone.

Roland Woolley, Aimee's attorney, opened the *Los Angeles Times* that morning and must have felt a wave of anger and frustration at being blindsided by the sordid headlines. He called the Temple in a froth, but his client wouldn't even come to the phone. Woolley was increasingly frustrated with Aimee. She did not follow his advice, and when he had questions, she did not want to answer; she was often quick to shift the conversation or dismiss his question.[8] Woolley called a contact he knew in Salinas, a lawyer and former judge named J. A. Bardin. Woolley begged him to rush to Carmel that day and start talking to Ryan's witnesses—run interference, in effect, on the city investigators' efforts. They wanted someone local and well-respected to face these witnesses on Aimee's behalf. Woolley also decided he needed to get to Carmel himself. He called and urged Keyes to "go slow" with this newest development.

Also agitated, Carlos Hardy called J. William Buchanan, the head of the Burns Detective Agency, the most prominent private investigative agency in Los Angeles, and hired him to help. Buchanan met Hardy at the Temple, where they conferred with Aimee, Minnie, and Arthur Veitch, who had effectively replaced Woolley as lead counsel. Their new strategy, they decided, would be to depict Ormiston as a womanizer who was juggling a variety of female companions—none of whom was Aimee. Buchanan took the night train to Carmel, where he worked with Bardin, making sure that Ryan's witnesses understood that their shaky recollections would be ruining a prominent Christian woman's life—and could result in perjury charges. He then went to San Francisco, where he interviewed Ormiston's parents and dug into the radio operator's tumultuous love life.

Aimee's lawyers informed Cline that Aimee would not be coming to Carmel, would not let her fingerprints be taken, and would not submit her handwriting so it could be compared with the grocery slip left in the cottage. Woolley issued an indignant statement to the press, saying he would not subject Aimee to the police inquiries "just for the purpose of exposing another one of the wild and obviously concocted identifications." All the leaks, he said, amounted to "malpractice of so-called investigators."

For Cline, who until then had been inclined to believe Aimee, this refusal to come to Carmel was tantamount to an admission of guilt. The *Los Angeles Times* headline the next day made explicit his and Ryan's shared outlook: CLINE SAYS MYSTERY OF MCPHERSON CASE SOLVED.

23

LOVE SHACK

Kenneth Ormiston was the talk of the nation. Every detail of his life—his limp, his marital strife, his close relationship with Aimee, their shared passion for radio, their intimate conversations in the radio booth—was discussed and debated. Plastered on the front pages of newspapers were their photos, juxtaposed over pastoral images of Carmel's ocean cliffs, with curlicued hearts printed around their faces. Reporters continued to descend on the village, collecting trash, cornering residents, and piecing together their own storylines, some of which evaporated as soon as they were printed, others of which were handed over to the police and, literally, entered into evidence.

By that last week of July, every newspaper in America, it seemed, had a story about Ormiston and his enigmatic, "heavily veiled" companion appearing in this romantic seaside village in California. By this time, Aimee had become a first-name entity for readers from New York to Idaho to Oregon. Each day's paper carried a front-page, bold-type story, promising a new "Sensation" and "Startling Disclosures" about the lady evangelist. Photographs of Aimee were set up in triptychs above the fold, next to Ormiston and the "love shack."

When she'd returned from Douglas, Aimee said she was the most famous woman in the world—in the month since she walked out of the desert, it had certainly become true.

The tawdry details of the Carmel "love shack" fueled the fires of her critics. The journalist Louis Adamic wrote with scathing misogyny: "Of course, a female mystery without a man is like well, like boiled cabbage without corned beef, or like a Hearst newspaper without a few pictures of crossed female legs: a thing wellnigh inconceivable."[1]

Her rival Bob Shuler used the explosive scandal as a tool to expand his audience. Three thousand people packed his service at Trinity Methodist Church in Los Angeles that weekend, to hear what he advertised as a "formal protest" of not only Aimee, but also Asa Keyes and Judge Keetch for their failure to bring her to justice. "If McPherson's story is true then an infamous injustice has been done her, for she is the butt of derision and ridicule and every humorist in this country is busy concocting jokes and verses about her," he shouted from his pulpit that weekend. "If her story is false and she has fabricated the whole affair for purposes of her own, then an outrage has been committed against true Christianity." In her own pulpit, when her followers asked her to respond to Shuler's accusation, she aimed for dignity. "A dog may bark at a queen," she said. "But the queen doesn't necessarily have to bark back at the dog."[2]

Aimee gave a statement to the Associated Press, addressing Ormiston directly and insinuating that his behavior was all part of the elaborate conspiracy to shame her: "Many believe you are a party to the kidnapping and received large sums of money, being paid to drive around the country and be seen here and there with an unknown 'mystery woman' resembling myself—a woman whose part in the transaction it was to act mysteriously, wear veils and goggles, and act in such a secretive manner as would draw inevitable attention to you both."[3]

As Herman Cline and Joseph Ryan took the train south to present their evidence to Keyes, Aimee released an incendiary statement to the press, which every newspaper in Los Angeles ran in full. She was, she said, the victim of a "sequence of sinister events." Ryan and Cline were part of a shadowy vendetta against her, using "tin can" evidence and false allegations to ruin her reputation. Their invitation for her to come to Carmel to face the eyewitnesses was a trap. Once again, she was being taken like "a lamb to slaughter."

Then came her most stunning charge: "Always just Cline and Ryan, or Ryan and Cline. Both are Catholics, prosecuting a Protestant minister." The Vatican, she all but said, was behind her persecution, and Ryan and Cline, the prosecutor's office and the police department, were puppets of the Pope, hell-bent on destroying the one true gospel: hers.[4]

Until this statement, Aimee had presented herself as a lover, not a hater. Her message to her followers was one of a personal connection with Jesus, healing through touch, and the celestial delights of heaven on earth. But sensing that everything she built might collapse, she abandoned those fundamentals. As the scrutiny intensified, her vision of a conspiracy against her expanded. She'd already darkened her evangelical message with insinuations of devilish work, but pushed and under pressure she went further. She made an oblique reference to the Ku Klux Klan—whom she had previously wagged a finger at from the Temple stage—saying, "many organizations, one of them 100 per cent American guards," would come to her defense.[5] She evoked and weaponized the anti-Catholicism of her followers to bolster her defense. "Must I permit pastors who preach hate against my creed to lead the hordes of darkness against my church?" Aimee asked in her editorial. "Am I a woman to be deprived of the chivalrous protection with which Americans always have guarded a woman's name?"[6]

For those who believed in Aimee, the claims resonated, confirming deep biases many held toward Catholic Americans. For many of her congregants, the past thirty years had radically shifted the face of America. The period between 1890 and 1920 had been a time of seismic and historical immigration, with over twenty million immigrants arriving to the United States. The vast majority of those arrivals were Catholics, from poor countries in Europe and Latin America. Often with large families and a willingness to accept low wages, these working-class immigrants represented a threat to the entrenched

WASP power structure. Aimee knew this and was willfully activating that bias to protect herself from the aspersions cast by investigators.

When reporters caught up with Cline as he returned to Los Angeles, he responded with gruff misogyny. "My business is catching criminals," he said. "I'm not arguing with women."[7]

Though Temple membership had exploded since Aimee had stumbled out of the desert—she was conducting hundreds of new baptisms, and every service had overflow crowds—she had reached a frenzied state over the scandal. While she did not keep a diary, she expressed herself the way she knew best: she channeled her emotions into a stage production. That last week of July at the Temple, she put on a performance that climaxed with her standing at the center of the stage as actors dressed as devils surrounded her. A rudimentary smoke machine churned. The evangelist shouted out to her audience that these were the kidnappers, law enforcement officials, rival ministers, and politicians—agents of Satan: all of them out to get her. They were all evil incarnate on a mission to destroy her—and thus all Christians. In the short span of a month, she had recast herself from victor to martyr.

Ryan and Cline spent Thursday, July 29, huddled in conference with Keyes, reviewing all the evidence. The spice cans had become central to the case, and they waited for the fingerprint analysis. When Keyes left the Hall of Justice that evening, he made no comment to the reporters who had been camping out all day. Ryan was more forthcoming, announcing to the reporters who followed him that he'd found his "ace in the hole," incontrovertible evidence of Aimee's guilt.

Ryan was referring to new evidence: a telegram that had been sent by Ormiston on May 28 from Los Angeles to the cottage in Carmel. It had arrived in the evening of May 28, and it read, "Lease Expires Tonight." The message was sent just hours after Ormiston had raced to Los Angeles at Minnie's behest and allowed himself to be interviewed by Captain Cline. He told Cline he had no idea about

Aimee's whereabouts and was photographed with Minnie during the search on Venice Beach for her body. Then he vanished.

The boy who delivered the telegram in Carmel told Ryan that a partially disguised woman had signed for the message, and that he could positively identify that woman as Aimee. Ryan was sure Ormiston had sent it to let Aimee know that they'd soon be caught, and she needed to pack her bags. Hours after the telegram was received, a man and woman riding in a blue coupe were identified as Aimee and Ormiston by a parking attendant in Salinas.

Seeing the puzzle pieces fitting together at last, Ryan had a youthful indignation about the whole incident. He was outraged at what he saw as Aimee's calculated deception of the public. He was sure that the telegram, along with the handwriting on the grocery slip and the witnesses he had found, showed that Aimee had spent ten days in a seaside hideaway on a romantic tryst. Ryan was confident that the prosecutor's office would win a conviction against this woman who had the audacity to deceive the public, make a mockery of Los Angeles, and accuse him of being controlled by the Pope. Ryan told reporters outside the Hall of Justice that prosecutors had all they needed to convict Aimee Semple McPherson of perjury and reveal her for what he believed her to be: "a fake and a hypocrite."

Ryan was sure that Keyes shared his conviction, but when he showed up the next day to meet with his boss and plan their next move, he found something surprising: Keyes was missing. All day Friday, Ryan tried to reach him. Cline didn't have any luck either. On Saturday, Ryan received a call from an investigator at the district attorney's office working in Carmel. The man relayed a strange new development: Keyes wanted to cancel the subpoenas he had issued for Ryan's witnesses just hours earlier. Ryan was bewildered. He tried desperately to get ahold of his boss, but Keyes wouldn't call him back. Meanwhile the Carmel witnesses were being told they weren't needed. He gave a statement to reporters that evening expressing his confusion: "I do not know what it is all about. Keyes is my superior and since he has not informed me of what has transpired during the past two days, I can make no statement." Still, he said, the Carmel evidence was indisputable. "There is no guesswork about it—it speaks for itself." Cline agreed, saying to reporters that the evidence found in Carmel was "as near perfect as it is possible to get."[8]

But as confident as Ryan and Cline were, Keyes understood how dangerous Aimee's accusations of a Catholic conspiracy were to his office and his larger endeavors. At the turn of the century, Los Angeles was one of the whitest, most homogenous cities west of the Mississippi—its port city of Long Beach had even earned the moniker "Iowa by the Sea." There were small neighborhood enclaves of Mexicans, Italians, and Chinese, but these communities were relatively isolated and not as powerful as they were in places such as New York or Chicago at the time.

Even with an influx of new residents, by 1920, three-quarters of Los Angeles residents were still native-born Caucasians who largely belonged to mainline Protestant churches. This meant that Catholics represented a very small and not very powerful voting bloc to the powers that be. The politically savvy district attorney had likely concluded that there was no winning a fight with Aimee Semple McPherson. If voters saw him as a persecutor of a Christian woman—a preacher, no less—he would never get reelected.

There was more to it: even as the newspapers were filled with salacious details of Aimee's alleged love affair, Keyes was quietly piecing together what promised to be his career-changing case against the Board of Supervisors. Following a series of investigative articles by the *Los Angeles Record*, he had been able to expose the building of private, well-appointed cabins in a recreation area deep in the San Fernando Valley. Keyes posited that the plot dated back at least five years, with virtually every major county official conspiring together to defraud Los Angeles of hundreds of thousands of dollars. This was political dynamite for Keyes—he really did not want to deal with a lurid love story, or a mystery woman in goggles, or fingerprints on spice cans.

On KFSG's Sunday radio show, a new guest appeared: Mrs. Carlos Hardy. The judge's wife spoke at length about how hard her husband was working to help defend Aimee and called on all women of faith to rally to her cause, saying the evangelist was one of a long line of great women who had been persecuted. "You know, my husband speaks here very often," Mrs. Hardy said, "and he would be here tonight were it not that he is in conference and has been all day, relative to this case. Outside of his heavy judicial duties, he is devoting all his spare time to the unravelling of this case, that truth and justice may prevail."[9]

Meanwhile, Aimee used her stage to attack the prosecutor's office. For the musical interlude one evening, Aimee joined an all-male quartet in a new song titled, "Ly-in Ry-an Won't Get Her!"

Identifications may come,
Identifications may go;
Goggles may come,
Goggles may go;
But are we downhearted?

To which the congregation gleefully shouted back: "*No! No! No!*"[10]

Hours later, reporters finally tracked down the district attorney on the eighteenth hole of the Lakeside Country Club.[11] As the summer sun sank, Keyes told them nonchalantly that he was dropping all investigations into the kidnapping of Aimee Semple McPherson. It was over. The prosecutor said he had nothing to say on the matter. He refused to confirm or deny reporters' assertion that he'd been in conference at the Temple with Aimee and her advisors, including Judge Hardy. But then Keyes proceeded to say quite a lot. He told reporters that the LAPD's fingerprint expert had conducted an analysis over the weekend of the spice cans and the books—and there were no usable prints. Besides, he said, Ryan's eyewitnesses were far from certain it was Aimee they had seen. Reporters demanded to know how the very same evidence he was now deeming "shaky" had been the basis for the subpoenas issued in Carmel just forty-eight hours earlier. Keyes explained that he had new evidence that was "as yet not made public."

"The case has now reached the point," he said, "where it would cost the county thousands of dollars to carry it on, and after our evidence from the north collapsed, I can't see where anything is to be gained by continuing. I am going before the grand jury Tuesday morning and lay what evidence I have on the table, and it is up to them to decide whether they care to go into it further. But after that, I think it is doubtful the McPherson case will ever be heard of any more."[12]

To Aimee, Keyes's decision was an act of grace. To reporters that evening, she gave the briefest of statements: "I am so happy! That is all I care to say."

It should have been the end of the story. But it was only the middle.

24

THE IDES OF AUGUST

In early August, an affidavit arrived for Asa Keyes from Kenneth Ormiston, following Aimee's public plea to come forward. Ormiston denied that he had been with Aimee and admitted that he'd been with a woman, who was not his wife—but was also not Aimee! Signed by a well-regarded Chicago attorney, the affidavit gave a new account of Ormiston's travels in May. He claimed that during the time that Aimee said she had been imprisoned in a shack by slave traders, he'd been traveling the California coast with a woman in various disguises because of his marital situation. To protect the woman's reputation, he would be referring to her as "Miss X." He wanted to be clear: Miss X was not Aimee.

Ormiston confessed that he had lied to the police when he'd told them in May that he had been in Washington State at the time of Aimee's drowning. He had, in fact, rented a bungalow in Carmel under the name of George McIntire in early May. On May 19, Ormiston and Miss X drove from San Francisco to Carmel and arrived at the cottage around five in the morning. The next day, he drove by himself to Salinas to pay a fine for speeding, he explained. While there, he picked up a newspaper at a diner and learned that his boss, Mrs. McPherson, had drowned two days earlier. He called Minnie to find out whether the story was true and to express his sympathy. Early on in their stay in Carmel, he said he introduced Miss X to the Benedicts as Mrs. McIntire. She wore driving goggles and a heavy costume to conceal her identity.

After settling in at the cottage, he traded the Washington license plates on his car for California plates. This was because he'd been slapped with three speeding tickets, he said, and had decided his out-of-state plates were making him a target. On May 26, he wrote, he was shocked to hear his name on the radio—during a gossipy news account of his relationship with Aimee, full of untruths and innuendo—and he was mortified. He promptly drove to Salinas, parked his car in a garage with the attendant who later identified him, and caught a train for Los Angeles. When he came to Los Angeles on May 27 to dispel rumors and speak to the police—he now admitted in the affidavit—he had lied completely about his whereabouts.

He met with Minnie on the seashore in May, posing for photos in front of reporters with his arm around her. During this time, he left Miss X alone in Carmel. During his visit to Los Angeles, he realized he needed to shut down their love nest. "I had decided," he wrote, "that since my name had been dragged into the McPherson case, the Carmel incident had better terminate, since I and my car might be followed about. Such proved to be the case."[1] He then sent the infamous telegram to the cottage addressed to "Mrs. McIntyre" that read "Lease expires tonight."

Just after midnight, on May 29, Ormiston said he picked up Miss X and the two drove south, stopping in San Luis Obispo, a sleepy college town, where they checked in to a hotel under a new false name. They spent all day in their room and left only as night fell. Ormiston confirmed the account of another witness, saying that on the outskirts of Santa Barbara, he was stopped by Wallace Moore, a reporter from the *Santa Barbara News-Press*. An editor at the paper had received a tip that the evangelist was making her way through

California in the dark and suggested that the reporter head out to the highway and see if he could spot her. He gave the reporter Ormiston's license plate number.

According to Moore, the driver was indignant when he was pulled over. He said he was Frank Gibson, and he was a hardware salesman from Sacramento, traveling with his wife to Los Angeles, where they would be checking into the Alexandria Hotel. When the reporter told him that he had been told that this was the radio operator and the evangelist's car, the man responded, "My God, we hate to be mistaken for those two people!"[2] As he spoke, Moore leaned in to look at the female passenger. She wore a small red hat and goggles, sat stiffly, and stared straight ahead, and looked an awful lot like the evangelist, whom Moore had seen preach in Fresno a few years earlier. Without any legal authority to stop them or arrest them, the reporter let the couple go. He watched as the car made a U-turn in front of him on the dark road and drove back north, into the darkness.

Ormiston said he dropped off Miss X at a location he would not disclose and then went on to Oakland, where he stayed for a time. He concluded the affidavit by endorsing Aimee's innocence: "I have not seen Miss X since the night of May 29th, but I have corresponded with her. I know her true name and her present whereabouts. She has insisted that I make this statement. She is a trained nurse by profession . . . I have sufficient confidence in Miss X to state that I am of the opinion that before any great harm should befall Mrs. McPherson, who is entirely innocent of the matter and yet utterly unable to defend herself, that Miss X will make an affidavit supporting mine."[3]

To Joseph Ryan, the Miss X story was outlandish and insulting. But Ormiston's description of his movements confirmed much of what Ryan had dug up in Carmel, paired with the witness testimonies he'd taken in Salinas and Santa Barbara. Ryan felt that he finally had the full picture: Ormiston and Aimee drove to Carmel in the hours after her disappearance. Their love nest fell apart amid the public outcry over her disappearance, and she headed south, going to Arizona to hide out at H. D. Hallenback's ranch before emerging in the desert in Mexico.[4] There were the witnesses in Tucson, who said they'd seen her with Hallenbeck, and there was C. A. Pape, the car dealer, who said he'd seen her in Mexico. To cover up her disappearance, she'd invented this absurd adventure story, and the hoax had cost the city of Los Angeles two lives, tens of thousands of dollars, and hundreds of man hours. She had followed her passion at all costs. Or worse, she'd created a spectacle on purpose—to increase her fame.

Keyes, however, had reached the opposite conclusion. He went downtown to visit the grand jury, which was in session on another case, and told them he believed Ormiston's affidavit entirely. He maintained his intention to drop the investigation, but the push-back from the public to his decision was immediate and the appetite for getting to the bottom of Aimee's story insatiable. Daily leaks from Keyes's office, Aimee's legal team, and the police department had made armchair detectives out of the hundreds of thousands of newspaper subscribers who were well-versed in the intricacies of the telegram dates, the witnesses, the hair net, the bathing suit, the spice cans, the curl of the *e* on the grocery list. Keyes had been naive to think that the inquiry belonged solely to his office. Aimee's story now belonged to the public mind.

As soon as Keyes said he was dropping the case, the grand jury issued an unusual public statement to the press, asking to see all of Ryan's evidence from Carmel. The foreman met with the district attorney, afterward bragging to the newspapers that he demanded Keyes "place all the evidence in the case on the table and he agreed to do so and to permit any and all of his assistants or witnesses to be available for the grand jury questioning."[5]

"Keyes Bows to Grand Jury," read one headline on August 3. "We are through fooling with Keyes or anyone else!" said an unnamed juror to a reporter.

That week, Ryan appeared before the grand jury as a witness. He passed around the grocery slips that he'd found near the door of the Benedict cottage. A handwriting expert said that anyone could tell the script was written by the same person who had written the "Light and Darkness" sermon on the beach in May. As the grocery list was passed around, a female juror said she needed to use the ladies' room.

Later, when Ryan asked the jurors for his evidence back, the list was gone. It was quickly deduced that the female juror, sympathetic to Aimee's plight, had flushed the paper down the toilet. They were in "El Secundo," Ryan said sadly, making a pun about the seaside town where the city of Los Angeles offloaded its sewage.

Keyes was exhausted by the circus. He released a statement to the papers that same day, bemoaning the sensationalism that had surrounded the inquiry into Aimee's kidnapping. "The investigation of this matter has been one of the most difficult ever presented to a prosecutor," he moped. "Because of the prominence of the persons involved, the sensational features of Mrs. McPherson's disappearance and return and the unfortunate entanglement of the religion, this case has been investigated in the full flare of publicity."[6] The grand jurors were reprimanded by the judge. They quickly announced they would take two weeks off and reconvene after Labor Day. When they did so, they would move on to considering other cases.

Aimee should have been relieved by the grand jury's decision—officially her case was over; she could ignore the rumors, step away from the scandal, and return to her dignified role as the founder of the Foursquare Church and the head of Angelus Temple. She could use her new level of fame to amplify her preaching and to help her connect to their growing membership. It was time to move on.

But Aimee could not let the story go. During her thirty-five years of life, she had carefully crafted her own mythology, bending and interpreting her personal turmoil into a meaningful narrative. That summer, her own story had taken on a life of its own, had jumped beyond her control. The version of events published in the newspapers was ugly and depraved; her image and words were distorted into something she did not recognize as herself.

Aimee continued to use every opportunity to speak about how she was being persecuted. The August edition of *The Bridal Call*—which Aimee always had final edits on—compared Los Angeles law enforcement to Pontius Pilate and Aimee to Christ on the Cross. She wrote a long first-person account of her abduction entitled "Kidnapped!" that read like pulp fiction: "One moment, sunlit skies, singing, preaching, thronging thousands of the dearest friends, bright plans for immediate extension of the Master's work. The next—horror, wild fear, rough hands, the roar of a car, and I, prone upon the floor of that car."[7]

Meanwhile, the intangible dread that Minnie had felt after her daughter's memorial service in June had exploded into a nightmare. By August, Minnie was living crisis to crisis as she fielded constant visits, calls, letters, and telegrams from people purporting to have information for or against her daughter. She did not know who she could believe or trust.

Aimee's inner circle had stood by her throughout the drama, shouting alongside her that this was a felonious plot. "We are under the persecution of certain interests," Minnie told the press, "bent upon our destruction and they would stop at nothing to put us out of the way."[8] But internally, according to later interviews, the crisis had taken its toll. "Sister did not confide in me," Minnie told a reporter, two years later. "And many people think I know a lot more than I really do."[9]

In mid-August, Judge Hardy intimated to Minnie that he was exhausted by the ordeal. He needed a vacation. He reiterated that he had been an integral part of their defense—he'd hired private detectives, suggested lawyers, and even tried to drum up witnesses who supported Aimee's version of events. In turn, Minnie wrote him a $2,500 check, made out from the Angelus Temple account. It wasn't a payment, she would later insist, but simply a "love offering" for all his work in trying to help Aimee prove her story. Hardy cashed the check and headed north, stopping in Santa Barbara to see the reporter who had claimed he had spotted Ormiston and Aimee together at the end of May. According to the journalist Wallace Moore, Hardy intentionally intimidated him during the visit, telling the reporter that he could go to jail if he was wrong about the identification. Leaving Moore sufficiently scared and ready to recant, Hardy drove on to San Francisco with his wife to unwind.

Meanwhile, downtown at the district attorney's office, Keyes was hopeful that the investigation into Aimee's kidnapping was over.

Quietly, he cleaned house. He transferred the disgruntled Ryan to a post in Long Beach, a humiliating demotion for the ambitious twenty-six-year-old. Ryan had become a liability, openly critical of his boss, and, in Keyes's words inside the DA's office, the kid needed to take a "prominent backseat," according to later testimony.[10] A journalist wrote a few years afterward that the staff of the district attorney's office "still groans at the lack of foresight which, in placing Ryan in charge of the case, [Keyes] considered only his legal talents and not his private religion."[11]

Things were even worse for Ryan's father-in-law. On the night of Sunday, August 22, Captain Cline rear-ended a car on the eastern outskirts of Los Angeles. Despite reportedly shouting, "I'm Captain Cline of Los Angeles, you can't arrest me,"[12] he was booked into the local drunk tank overnight in Azusa. His arrest made the next day's front pages, a humiliating exposure for one of the city's leading law enforcement officers. He was temporarily relieved of command, pending investigation.

His son-in-law saw it as part of a plot against them both—engineered by Angelus Temple. Ryan told the newspapers that Cline had been framed—although he refused to directly accuse Aimee. "For the past week or so private detectives, whose employers are so far unknown, have been following both Captain Cline and myself," Ryan said. "Captain Cline had only two drinks, which was not strong enough to make him as ill as he was unless they had been doped."[13]

The day after Ryan gave his statement to the press, events took an even stranger turn.

In the dawn hours of August 26, Russell A. McKinley, the blind lawyer, was found dead, drowned in a muck-filled ditch after a car accident in Long Beach. McKinley was the one person besides Aimee who said they'd encountered the kidnappers. He was vital to her case. His body was found submerged in water, along with those of two other men, identified as close friends and painters. In his pockets, investigators found a note that read, "I am starting on my vacation tomorrow, driving north to Canada. I expect to be at the Palace Hotel at San Francisco Thursday, Friday and Saturday. If your friends communicate with you and if it is necessary for you to reach me, you will know how to do it."[14] It was signed by Judge Hardy. McKinley had drowned in just a few feet of water; investigators found the note suspicious. Keyes was alerted. Aimee and her mother rushed to Long Beach. But the dead lawyer was soon to be the least of Aimee's problems.

25

MISS X

No one could have imagined that the strangest character in Aimee's saga was yet to be introduced. The Associated Press printed a small story in early August, one of many that claimed to have uncovered the latest "clew" in the Aimee saga. A telegram had been sent to Asa Keyes's office, asserting that "my sister, Mrs. George McIntyre, was in the house at Carmel. Mrs. McPherson was not the party there. My sister will proceed immediately to Los Angeles from the East." The telegram was signed "Mrs. Belle Owens."[1]

Just hours after the story appeared in print, a woman knocked on the door of the parsonage. Vibrating with a manic energy, her expression intense, the woman told the Temple receptionist that she had to see Sister Aimee right away. When she was told Aimee was busy, she asked to speak with the receptionist privately: she said she had a secret. It wasn't unusual for women to come to the Temple late in the night, when they had nowhere else to go. Pregnant, beaten, turned away by their families, they often came to Sister Aimee hoping to be saved. The secretary had a protocol for such women. But this woman had a different story.

"This has weighed on me for some time," the woman explained. "It was my sister that was at Carmel."[2]

Immediately, the receptionist ran upstairs to find Minnie, who said to bring the woman to her. Arthur Veitch, the lawyer, happened to be in their upstairs office, strategizing with Minnie. The woman introduced herself as Mrs. Lorraine Wiseman-Sielaff, but, more importantly, she said she was known also as Belle Owens. With finely drawn eyebrows and deep-set eyes, Lorraine was a striking and strange-looking woman. Minnie was so desperate for evidence that supported her daughter's story, she would later say on the stand, that she was quick to ignore the woman's jumpiness and odd manners. Instead, she felt as if she was seeing an angel, an answer to her prayers. Veitch found Lorraine suspicious and began to interrogate her; she ignored him and focused her attention on Minnie. Aimee came to join them in the parlor, and in front of an eager audience, the mysterious lady laid out her wild, seedy story.

On May 19, Lorraine told them, she had driven with a doctor to a cottage in Carmel, where her sister was staying with a man. Lorraine had never met the man before, and he gave the name of McIntire, but Lorraine said after reading the news reports from Carmel, she knew this man was Kenneth Ormiston. According to Lorraine, her sister was not "well" and in a "delicate condition." At the time she merely made hints, but later she would tell Keyes under oath that this sister's condition was an unwanted pregnancy, and that the doctor was there to perform an abortion.

The plan, Lorraine explained to the riveted group in the parsonage, was for her sister to marry Ormiston when she was "better." The doctor tended to the sister while Lorraine was in and out of the cottage.

Of course, it was illegal and wrong. Her sister, Lorraine explained, was exceedingly private and didn't want to come forward, but she was willing to do so to clear the evangelist's name. As she explained these events, the women in the room said they couldn't help but notice something shocking about her: Lorraine looked an awful lot like Aimee. It could all be a terrible case of mistaken identity! Quickly, the group came up with a plan to together clear Aimee's name.

Within days, Lorraine called Keyes's office, saying her sister was the mystery woman of Carmel. Keyes didn't want to hear it—he'd been inundated with screwball stories, and the case was closed—but Aimee's lawyers pressured him to grant the woman an audience. Keyes took the meeting and was struck by how unstable and secretive she was. "You don't want to tell me where you live. You don't want to tell me where you work. You won't tell me your sister's name," he said. "Those are three very important factors and things for me to know before your story holds good at all."[3]

Still, with Veitch and Roland Woolley nagging him, Keyes arranged to have Lorraine taken to visit Henry Benedict, the owner of the Carmel cottage. Benedict was spending the month in a sanitarium in Glendale after having a mental breakdown—he'd checked himself in when his home had been overrun by people chipping pieces off the walls and the roof to take as Love Shack souvenirs. Sitting in a car with Keyes and Lorraine, as well as a stenographer, Benedict applied his years as an insurance inspector to grill her about the cottage. What color was the bedspread? What about the color of the dress she wore when she met him in the yard?"

Lorraine failed to answer any of his questions correctly. "I know you feel you recognize me in some way," she said, trying to entrance him into her version of events.

"I cannot say that I do," Benedict responded huffily. "I don't see that we are getting anywhere sitting here chewing this thing over," he said, unconvinced. "I think there is no use sitting here frying in this car any longer."[4] The interview over, Keyes told Aimee's lawyers to drop it.

But instead of letting it alone, Woolley—on Aimee's demands—served Lorraine up to reporters. Journalists from the *Los Angeles Times* and *Los Angeles Examiner* as well as the wire services crowded into Woolley's office as Lorraine paced the floor and told them, "I have been unable to sleep since this thing happened, and although I know it means that I will lose the position I have held three years and also may ruin my name, I can't stand by and see another woman suffer for an indiscretion in which she was not connected in any way."

She explained that she had revealed herself to Aimee weeks before but that the evangelist had heroically told her she needn't come forward, for "her shoulders were broad and inasmuch as her people had confidence in her, that there was no use in me giving up all. However, I just can't stand back and see her persecuted for something she didn't do, and I am not going to."[5]

Lorraine told the reporters that she had tried several times to tell her story to the district attorney's office, insinuating to the papers that Keyes and his prosecutors were not interested in evidence that would absolve Aimee. Now that the newspapers had ahold of this sordid twist on the Carmel story, there was a renewed demand from Aimee to give interviews. Despite the advice of her counsel, Aimee would not stop talking to the press. At the end of August in an interview with the *Times*, Aimee seemed to have internalized the scandal, putting the skepticism of her over the previous two months in the starkest possible terms: "Either I am a good woman, or I am the most terrible, unspeakable person in the whole world. There is no half-way ground in a situation like this. And I am not afraid of the judgement."[6]

Despite these bellicose sound bites, there was evidence that Aimee was deeply frightened by the idea of being seen as a fraud; it threatened everything she had built. Perhaps worse, she could not bear her mother thinking that she had done this awful thing. She had been her mother's prophecy, but the newspapers were depicting some new version of her, one as a temptress, a liar, and a fake.

"Aimee Laughs Heartily at Ormiston Clew," read the *Herald Examiner* headline. In the story, Aimee said, "I am through commenting on these wild rumors. I am always glad to see them, however. They amuse me and I am very grateful for a good laugh now and then." The story ended with a quote from Aimee about how well she was feeling physically. "I have gained nine pounds a day," she bragged, hyperbolically. "That doesn't seem to indicate worry, does it?" But as the weeks wore on, the tone was changing, increasingly self-important and strident. "If they indict me, it will split open the country," she proclaimed. In the early days of September, her desire to be absolved by the masses would drive her to desperate and strange acts and unreliable alliances.

In a peculiar coda to a very strange summer, Lorraine spent more and more time with Aimee. They went to a wealthy congregant's beach house together for the Labor Day weekend. Aimee brought Roberta and Rolf, and Lorraine brought her adult son. At the home, they reenacted witness accounts of the Carmel mystery woman. Aimee dressed Lorraine up in heavy clothing that matched witness descriptions, had her wear thick goggles, and then photographed her. Aimee had Lorraine practice writing out the words that were on the grocery list. Lorraine slept in the guest bed while Aimee slept on the sofa. The strange woman embedded herself in Aimee's inner circle, although many of those loyal to Aimee did not trust her. Mrs. Elizabeth Frame, whose home they stayed in over the holiday weekend, did not understand why the "eccentric and peculiar" woman was being given so much access. "I didn't believe her from the first to tell you the truth," Frame later told the district attorney. "Mrs. Wiseman always acted very nervous and peculiar. She said something about being a detective and a reporter—she said so many different things that I just got so I didn't put much stock in what she did say. I said to Mother, 'Be careful; I don't like the way that woman acts. She has got a limpy handshake for one thing.' Mother says: 'She is all right, darling. She is sincere. She has gone and got all those witnesses and everything.'"[7] As unstable as Lorraine was, Aimee acted as if the woman were her only hope. She wanted the public—and her mother—to believe in her again.

26

HOAX WOMAN

The newspapers were like sharks circling the Temple. Everything about Aimee's story was increasingly, mouthwateringly scandalous. On September 10, a reporter from the *Los Angeles Times* called Lorraine, who was staying downtown at the Continental Hotel on well-to-do Hill Street. He asked if she could come to the newsroom, just a few blocks away. "We have not been very nice to you," he told her. "We have acted as if we did not quite believe your story. But we are no longer skeptical. We are ready now to reverse our position and back the truth to the limit." Further, he told her, the *Times* wanted to pay for a series of articles that she could write herself. Lorraine showed up that night to find that the paper had assembled eleven witnesses, all of whom said that she was a derelict scam artist and that she had lied about everything she'd told the papers—about herself and about Carmel. She was not, in fact, a legal secretary in San Francisco but an occasional seamstress, a deadbeat mother, and a petty criminal who had been living in downtown Los Angeles for months. There were even bank records showing that she'd cashed checks at a bank on Beverly and Western in Los Angeles when she purported to have been in Carmel with Ormiston.

The paper had also invited officers from the LAPD. They had been pursuing a woman named Villa May McDonald Wiseman-Sielaff who been writing dummy checks across Southern California. They searched the contents of Lorraine's bag, where they found she had kept an expense account ledger with Aimee's and Minnie's names and different dollar amounts written—along with the name of A. M. Waters. As she screamed that it was all a "frame-up," the policemen dragged her off to the county jail. Reporters called Waters, who said he was a retired physician and denied any connection to the McPherson case. But the next day, when police arrived to question the man, he had committed suicide by swallowing poison. In a wastebasket, investigators found both correspondence from Carlos Hardy and a series of letters to Kenneth Ormiston's parents, all, it seemed, seeking the doctor's help in producing a "Miss X."[1] Newspapers trumpeted it as the "Fourth Death" in the McPherson case.

That night, from her jail cell, Lorraine wrote Aimee, assuring her that she needn't worry; she had a new plan—if she could have some cash: "Oh, what a terrible thing they have done to me. They said they would get me, and they think they have. But wait, I have got a card to spring they don't know of yet. Now, dear, if you will send down $3,000 for bond in cash . . . I will get out long enough to come back. Believe me, I only want about four hours; I will get them then."[2] There were other notes that night, which Minnie would later describe as increasingly threatening.

For Minnie, the shrill demands for money from this unstable woman from the county jail were the limit. For months since Aimee's return, Minnie had written dozens of checks for the "expenses" of various witnesses who had claimed they could help—the vegetable-monger who declared he'd seen Aimee being taken away, the preacher in Texas who said he'd found her shack. The judge who needed a "love offering" check. But Minnie was done; she would not pay. Lorraine's jailhouse pleas were met with silence that night.

As the *Times* went to print with its story that Aimee's primary witness was a wanted felon, the *Examiner* moved in to get its own scoop. Its journalists bailed the desperate Lorraine out of jail on the condition that she come directly to the paper's offices. When she arrived at the building on South Broadway, *Examiner* reporters had arranged their own confrontation: they had found Lorraine's identical twin sister. Surrounded by the reporters, Virla Kimbell of Oakland bemoaned her sister's mental deterioration following a railroad accident fifteen years earlier: "She has done such terrible things since her head was hurt," Lorraine's sister said. "Each time, after she got herself into trouble, and we have had to get out of it, she has cried and cried and cried—just like a child who doesn't realize what it is doing." As her sister spoke, Lorraine cried. Kimbell explained that her sister had a "mania for passing worthless checks and borrowing money," but that it was the grift itself that she seemed to hunger for, never spending the money on anything of substance, often just throwing it away. A decade earlier, in Utah, Lorraine had left behind a normal home life with her two children, along with her husband, a geologist who worked for the Southern Pacific railroad.[3]

Lorraine broke down. She admitted that Aimee had coached her over the past few weeks, that she had practiced her handwriting so it matched the grocery list. She had dressed up with Aimee in matching clothes and been photographed face-to-face. Indeed, the two women had grown so close, Lorraine said, that she had taken to sleeping at the Temple, sometimes in the same bed as Aimee. They'd even vacationed with their families together, just the week before, riding the roller coaster at the beach and touring the local "fun house." They'd shared a room over Labor Day and awakened together at dawn, to go swim at Venice Beach—right where Aimee had disappeared four months earlier. They had both worn red swimsuits. She said Aimee and Minnie had paid all her "expenses," of which she'd kept a careful ledger. In six weeks, she'd received $750 for those expenses—at a time when receptionists in California were making less than $1,000 annually. Thrilled with all these details of the peculiar relationship between the pastor and the con artist, the *Examiner* gallantly hired a lawyer for Lorraine. The scoops from the *Times* and the *Examiner* trumpeting "Aimee's Hoax Woman" were reprinted around the country.

The *Times* had one last play. The next night, Bernice Morris,

Russell McKinley's legal secretary, sat down with a reporter. Morris dished on what she said was the real relationship between Aimee and the blind attorney. The young woman said that Aimee had hired McKinley, paying him more than $1,000, to find the shack where she'd been kept captive and to track down someone—anyone!—to play the part of the kidnappers.

As a stenographer took notes, Morris recounted how her boss had concluded that Aimee had never been kidnapped and that she would identify anyone as her captors. To prove this, he and Morris had dressed up a friend, darkened his face and hair, added a fedora, and taken photos. When McKinley brought the photograph to Aimee, Morris said that the evangelist had clutched Minnie and shrieked, "It's him!" Morris said that McKinley was convinced that all of Aimee's stories were for her mother alone. "I honestly believe," Morris said, "that Mother Kennedy doesn't know where Aimee was, and I believe that Aimee thinks more of fooling her mother than all the rest of the public. That is what Mr. McKinley thought. He said, 'Before tonight you could never have made me believe that that old lady didn't know what was going on. As honest as I am standing here, I believe she is an innocent party.'"[4]

The love shack, the "hoax woman" con artist, the blind lawyer drowned in a ditch, the pileup of deaths, the grim cast of grifters and the mentally unsound were a sordid tableau consisting of everything that Aimee's critics had accused her of from the beginning—that she was a woman who manipulated people and lied to further her own interests. That she herself was a hoax woman. It was as if the scandal had congealed into her accusers' worse depiction of her over the years.

Confronted with a slew of damning headlines, Aimee repeated her only defense: a "giant conspiracy." Lorraine and Morris were part of a vast plot to humiliate her—but more than that, they were part of "a worldwide movement against evangelism." She asked her followers over the evening radio program to let Asa Keyes know—by telephone, telegraph, letter—that the people would not stand for this abuse of their beloved Sister. Minnie made the same charges from the Temple stage. "We are under the persecution of certain interests bent upon our destruction," she declared, "and they would stop at nothing to put us out of the way." The conspiracy to destroy Aimee, she said, was because of her daughter's drive to stamp out vice—an effort that was "so great and so powerful that a movement was started to crush it by branding her as a sinner."

By eleven o'clock the night of September 15—five days since Lorraine's initial arrest—Keyes had received fifty-two telegrams from Aimee's supporters and so many telephone calls that he disconnected all the telephone lines at the DA's office. According to reported accounts, at this point all Keyes wanted was to be left out of Aimee's drama, but he found himself unable to back away from this outlandish abuse of the legal system and the public trust that was being serialized on the front pages every day. Aimee's language from the pulpit was even more hyperbolic. If God willed it, she would be a martyr for his cause: "I am not afraid to go to the electric chair if my persecution should be carried that far. They will not stop till they have me behind prison walls."[5]

The death penalty wasn't at play in California and certainly not for Aimee's level of crime. If she were ultimately convicted of perjury, the worst sentence she would face was four years in prison. Even that was unlikely. More important, Keyes was not a conspiring force of darkness—he was trying to get as far away from the case as he could. He didn't care if she was a saint or sinner. There were later accounts that Keyes had started to drink heavily during this time, exhausted and unmoored, sometimes showing up inebriated at the office. Rumors swirled about his ethics on other cases. Ryan told confidants that Keyes didn't "breathe a single sober breath" during the investigation into Aimee. The prosecutor was indisputably in over his head.

In a last effort to save himself from continued vilification by the press, and the wrath of taxpayers for wasting money, he asked Aimee and her mother to a private conference to see if they could find a resolution. They refused—Aimee said she was too sick; Minnie said she was too tired.

* * *

Aimee was like a sorceress, spinning up the feelings and emotions of those who followed her into a cauldron of energy and outrage. On the Temple stage that night in September, she renewed her accusations of an elaborate conspiracy among all the powers that be of Los Angeles to take her down—overseen by the devil himself. Aimee said that her arrest had been postponed to the morning so that the news cameras could better capture her image, implying an unholy alliance between the law and the press. She said that the worst murderers in the history of the United States had not been persecuted the way she had. "How many of you here, whether you believe my story or not, feel that I have had a raw deal?" she asked the packed audience. According to news accounts, the response was emotional and hysterical as people shouted and screamed their support. Aimee said she and her mother were just "two little women" who had been hunted by a corrupt press and a crooked district attorney's office. "What a silly goose I have been," she said to her congregants that night, with a sad smile. "I guess I was not diplomatic—that I was not afraid of the truth and did not hesitate to tell it."

Aimee described to her outraged followers the ways that she and her mother had so naively trusted the prosecutor's office and Lorraine. But now, she concluded, she was in some sort of hellscape. She gazed up at the American flag that she flew next to the platform and then turned to the audience. "Am I really in the United States?" she asked, her voice breaking. "I can't believe it. Some one pinch me please, and awaken me from this horrible dream."[6]

The next day, Minnie and Aimee refused to discuss a resolution. Under increasing pressure from the press, Keyes reluctantly asked to issue felony complaints against Aimee, Minnie, Ormiston, and Lorraine. The charges were significant: criminal conspiracy to suborn perjury, the preparing of false evidence, and conspiracy to "pervert or obstruct justice in the due administration of the law" by trying to "procure another to be charged with the crime of kidnapping."

Charges were filed, and Aimee and her codefendants were subpoenaed. *The People of the State of California against Aimee Semple McPherson, Minnie Kennedy, Lorraine Wiseman-Sielaff and Kenneth*

G. Ormiston was a preliminary hearing, a proceeding in advance of a criminal trial, and very different from the grand jury investigation that had taken place in July.

This time, Keyes would move the case to a single judge for a pretrial hearing. Instead of a group of jurors, the case would be heard before a Los Angeles municipal court judge. Aimee would be able to bring her own attorneys into the courtroom. After hearing evidence from both sides, if the judge found that the district attorney's evidence was compelling enough, then he would issue a ruling for Aimee, Minnie, and the others to stand trial.

Keyes's office sent out a statement:

> Mrs. McPherson is not and never has been a victim of persecution in so far as the law-enforcement agencies of this city are concerned. Every act of my office concerning her kidnaping story was weighed carefully and thoughtfully. We went over every shred of evidence before issuing the complaints against Mrs. McPherson and her mother in order that we would not be guilty of hasty or ill-considered conclusions. Mrs. McPherson returned home after a month's absence with a story that she had been kidnaped and held prisoner in a shack by a Steve and Rose whom we now know to be purely mythical.

Given all the accusations that Aimee had lobbed at his office over the past three months, Keyes concluded with an unusually conciliatory note—a likely effort to appease her many supporters. "This office has its duty to perform and must do it regardless of who is hurt. I am sorry for Mrs. McPherson, but that cannot influence my sworn duty."[7]

27

PERSECUTION

As newsboys' cries of "Extra! Extra!" reverberated across Echo Park Lake on a perfect seventy-two-degree day, announcing the warrant for her arrest, Aimee lay on her sickbed, giving an exclusive interview to a female journalist from the *Los Angeles Record*. The mood, Sadie Mossler wrote of Angelus Temple on September 17, was one of "infinite sadness." Despite doctor's orders to stay in bed—with a 102-degree fever—Aimee rose briefly to hear her Bible students singing at her window. Returning to bed, she said she was eager for the trial to begin and to receive justice. "I am anxious to see these witnesses go before a court of justice and perjure themselves," she said faintly. "Supposing I did come out and say to them, 'All these things you say about me are true.' What, then could they do to me? Nothing. I have reviewed the sections of the penal code upon which these charges are based, and there is not one chance of successful prosecution."[1]

It was Minnie who walked into the Hall of Justice that morning, alone, looking as if she were on her way to a funeral, in a black dress and a floppy hat. She was accompanied through the crowded hallways by W. I. Gilbert, a lawyer who had joined the team that morning.

Gilbert had built his reputation as a defense attorney among the moneyed echelons of Los Angeles, although mostly in divorce suits and high-stakes estate battles—including that of the recently deceased Rudolph Valentino. Gilbert took his client to the judge's chambers, and Minnie was arraigned on the charges. She pled not guilty and paid the $2,500 bail. Lorraine pled guilty. Having turned over evidence to the state, she had essentially become a prosecution witness. Ormiston remained missing and was officially a fugitive from justice. His mother gave an interview to the *San Francisco Examiner*, begging Kenneth to "tell the truth" and complaining that her son was under Aimee's spell.[2]

As for Aimee, Gilbert informed the judge that she'd suffered a nervous collapse at the Temple that morning and was too sick to appear. He would pay her bail in absentia. But just two days later, Aimee was preaching to a packed house for the Sunday service. Carrying a bouquet, she stood in front of the large American flag draped across the stage. She started with a passionate rendition of "The Star-Spangled Banner," backed by a choir, cloaking herself in the patriotism of her adopted nation as thousands inside the Temple wept with joy in their love of country and of Aimee.

She then excoriated the newspapers, calling on all those in attendance to storm the offices of the *Los Angeles Times* and the *Los Angeles Examiner*. Aimee's relationship with the press had become increasingly volatile as she attacked reporters from her stage at night and then joked with them gamely the next day as they waited outside the Temple, greeting them by name and giving them juicy quotes.

"Snap! Bang! Flash! Boom! Clouds of smoke rolling heaven-ward! Startled eyes and heads of worshipers lifted and turned in wonder toward the line of attack. The sacred precincts of the church had been invaded. Strange faces and forms were moving in our midst," Aimee wrote of the reporters and photographers who followed her everywhere. "There are strangers—and strangers. We were accustomed to new people coming constantly from the ends of the earth to Los Angeles, and of course, to Angelus Temple. But these were strange strangers. Their eyes looked, not with the hunger and thirst of people coming to the house of God solace bent but with a curious, roving restlessness, with narrowing, unsmiling inquiry. Theirs were the eyes of a hound on the scent or a dog on the trail."[3]

Despite Aimee's public condemnations onstage, the Temple gave reporters a warm reception that summer, so much so that the walkway between the Temple and the parsonage apartment became known as Reporter's Walk. Aimee held forth happily to the press as she traveled back and forth between services. She often didn't like the stories they wrote, but she still needed them. Reporters noted that she often stopped the service to pose for the photographers who sat in the front-row pews assigned to them by Temple staff.[4]

During the Sunday service, Aimee asked all those willing to donate a thousand dollars to her $100,000 "Fight the Devil" fund, to help pay for her defense. For all the love that Aimee's followers had for her, few raised their hands. A thousand dollars was a significant sum at a time when the annual average income was less than five thousand dollars. Aimee was losing sight of the day-to-day reality of her congregants. For more than a decade, she'd had a singular ability to connect with her audience, to speak to them plainly about the hardships of life and the promise of divine love. But this case consumed her; she was lost in the drama of her own martyrdom. The relatability that had made her everybody's sister was dimming.

As Aimee shook her fist onstage, behind the scenes Minnie made some radical changes to the financial and legal structure of Angelus Temple in anticipation of a potential trial. According to a forensic analysis later done by prosecutors, Minnie was preparing for a coming legal onslaught. She filed to move the ownership of the deed of trust that had been in the Echo Park Evangelistic Association's name—the one that legally belonged to Minnie and Aimee—into the official holdings of the International Church of the Foursquare Gospel. It was a move that would put the Temple out of reach of possible legal claims against Aimee.[5]

Minnie seemed to be inside her own nightmare. She was quoted as saying that week, "I started for Douglas, Arizona, knowing that my daughter was alive because I had heard her voice, but I went on that journey with a presentiment—something seemed to have told me, '*Perhaps it were better if the sea had claimed her, if she were dead as you had mourned her.*'"[6] There were signs of financial strain at Angelus Temple. Earlier in the summer, Aimee and Minnie had sold off a lot they owned in Venice. That September, Aimee's first home was put on the market—the one her followers had built her back in 1919. While donations to a church were obligated to go toward maintenance and expenses of the facility, all fundraising at the Temple was focused on Aimee's legal needs. By late September, both women openly admitted in court that the collection plate money was being largely funneled toward their legal defense fund as well as expenses related to trying to find Aimee's kidnappers. "Every available source of income was open and free to be used in whatever way it was necessary at that time,"[7] Minnie later testified as she described their "Fight the Devil" fund. The survival of Angelus Temple—one of the largest churches in America—was anchored to the fate of Aimee and this legal inquiry.

Aimee's legal team reshuffled, with Roland Woolley stepping down as lead counsel and Gilbert overseeing her defense. By the end of September, newspapers reported that Woolley had a guard placed outside his house, following death threats against him by those who felt he had not properly defended the evangelist.

The night before the hearing began, Aimee asked her followers not to come to the courtroom. It was a radical reversal from the grand jury hearing in July, when she asked her supporters to show up en masse. "No one who loves me—no one who cares for me—will go anywhere near the Hall of Justice tomorrow or any day I am there," she said from her stage, a statement that was carried out to her radio audience. "Only people who want to satiate their vulgar curiosity will be there. You would not want to be in such a mob. Mother and I are on trial alone—and Mother and I want to go through with it alone. We are going down there smiling and coming up shining! Hallelujah!"[8]

At dawn on Monday, September 27, crowds began to form around the Hall of Justice. People from all walks of life stood along the street, inside the lobby, on the lawn outside: fancily dressed men and women, weather-beaten ranchers, Angelenos from every corner of the city. This crowd—estimated to be five thousand—was, according to media accounts, mostly made up of spectators who wanted to glory in the drama of watching this famous woman be knocked off her moral high horse.

The downtown streets were thick with cars. On the seventh floor of the courthouse, carpenters constructed makeshift bleachers to increase the capacity of the courtroom by a hundred. To be admitted, one needed a signed pass from the judge, which scalpers were selling for twenty-five dollars per session.

At ten o'clock that morning, a new judge walked to the front of the courtroom and announced the opening of the preliminary hearing. Judge Samuel R. Blake was a handsome, baby-faced, thirty-one-year-old former prosecutor who had come into his position as a municipal court judge after his predecessor was fired for graft. He had fought in the Great War and then graduated from law school at the University of Southern California just nine years earlier.[9] Part of the new LA smart set, he and his wife were often listed in the society pages as they attended tea parties at the posh California Club. The newspapers reported that this was his first big case, and that women found him charming for his boyish manners.

With the Foursquare followers told to stay home, the bleachers were filled mostly with young women, who wore their hair and skirts short. For these nonreligious ladies, Aimee offered a model of independence. By some estimates, women spectators outnumbered men ninety-nine to one. Sadie Mossler, the metro reporter from the *Los Angeles Record*, described these stylish attendees: girls from well-off families with bobbed hair and sport coats, sharing boxes of candy.[10] Some were office workers from other floors of the Hall of Justice, who would pass through the seventh floor to get a glimpse of Aimee and her mother. The women said they were there for the thrill of the whole scandal, but some also felt sympathy for the evangelist, saying they didn't really care if she had run away with her lover. It wasn't a crime to fall in love, was it?

Aimee and her mother entered the Hall of Justice with confident smiles, slipping in from a back elevator, dressed all in black. Aimee wore no makeup, according to news reports, and her face looked lined and tired. Her clothes hung loosely on her frame. Barricades separated them from the crowd. There was applause and "sibilant hisses" as they passed through to the courtroom. Alma Whitaker, the female reporter from the *Times* who had interviewed Aimee years earlier, heard the evangelist muttering to herself as she left the courtroom: "It will never end; never till I die."[11]

Asa Keyes had replaced Joseph Ryan with E. J. Dennison, who was loud, midwestern, and most importantly not Catholic. While Aimee might have briefly celebrated Ryan's being pushed off the case, his replacement was by all accounts an even more zealous prosecutor. Known by the press as "old Hickory"—because he was so tough and so strong-willed—Dennison at fifty-five years old was a far more experienced prosecutor than Ryan. He sat together with Keyes, crammed behind a single table alongside Aimee's defense attorneys. Keyes was conscious of the global spotlight—the press began calling him "the best-dressed district attorney in California"—but his mind often seemed elsewhere. While he opened the prosecution's case, he soon sat down and left Dennison to do the majority of witness examinations. It quickly became clear that Dennison would supply the intensity and righteous conviction that Keyes seemed to lack.

On that gloomy morning in late September, the courtroom packed, the prosecution laid out the case for Judge Blake. Aimee was the mastermind of a cover-up of her illicit entanglement with her married employee Ormiston. While an affair was no crime, Aimee's cover-up had been devious, dangerous—and criminal: she had solicited false evidence and suborned perjury. Keyes described the events of the past four months, beginning in May with her disappearance and culminating in the hiring of the deranged Lorraine to hide Aimee's amorous escape to Carmel.

The story began even earlier, though, he alleged, in hotel rooms around Los Angeles as Aimee conducted an amorous relationship with Ormiston starting the previous year, an illicit liaison that climaxed in her plan to disappear with her lover (perhaps for good!) to Carmel by the Sea. The prosecutors posited that tempestuous Aimee had wanted to escape life under her controlling mother's thumb and had thought she could start over with her lover in a place where she thought no one would find her. But she'd changed her mind—likely missing the limelight too much. She'd invented a wild story and ensnared dubious characters such as Lorraine as well as A. M. Waters and Russell A. McKinley to lie and create evidence and false testimony. This version of events would be bolstered by evidence such as hotel registrations and witnesses, the prosecutor said, that would confirm that Aimee and Ormiston had been meeting frequently for months before her disappearance. The people's first exhibit was a photograph of Kenneth G. Ormiston—the indicted coconspirator at the center of the fraud.

The prosecution commenced with witnesses from Carmel. Five identified Aimee as the woman in thick driving goggles, leaning on Ormiston's arm. One witness, who saw her on a Carmel street corner on May 25, remarked upon her "large, open, brilliant, and deep-set" eyes and her "large mouth." Three people who lived near the Benedicts' cottage all said they'd seen the evangelist, also noting her luxurious auburn hair and the intensity of her gaze. The young boy who delivered the groceries and the specially requested Los Angeles newspapers said the woman in the cottage had made a strong impression on him. He confirmed that she was sitting before him at that very moment in the courtroom. When asked how he could be so sure, he was quick with his reply. "Her eyes. They were large. They seemed to draw me to her." He had also noticed the woman's large ankles.[12]

Henry Benedict, the cottage owner, however, was not certain that it was Aimee who had stayed in his cottage, but he conceded that the woman's ankles were "very similar" to those of the evangelist. Alma Whitaker, the *Los Angeles Times* columnist who had profiled Aimee so insightfully years earlier, attended the proceedings and took note of the prosecution's deep interest in the shape and size of ankles that arose during the interrogation of witnesses. "We discovered that all males," she wrote, "any grade, observe feminine ankles—truck drivers, messenger boys, grocers, contractors, and gentleman property owners. Silk clad ankles in court became self-conscious. The plump matronish flapper with red bobbed hair glanced down self-confidently. So did the brunette flapper in red. The two ladies from the Ebell Club drew in theirs under their chairs."[13] As much as the prosecution was focused on Aimee's lies, the proceedings had quickly become about the bounds of faith and the limits of what women were allowed to do and be.

While the prosecution's case was centered on perjury, the district attorney's office's contempt for Aimee was on full display. In the first week, Dennison referred to Aimee's nightly radio program as her chanting "garbled statements over the radio to the entire world."[14] The prosecutors continually deviated from the facts of the case to interrogate Aimee's persona. Her appearance and any sign of vanity or sexuality were continually raised as evidence that she was a hypocrite. In particular the prosecutors asked dozens of questions—of Aimee and those who worked for her—about Aimee's hair. What kind of hairnet did she wear? Did she wear a "switch"—a sort of extension? Did she supplement with fake hair? How long did it take for Aimee to do her hair? The courtroom filled with snickers as these questions were asked.

But Aimee refused to be embarrassed. Instead, she nudged Gilbert and whispered in his ear. He rose and offered that Aimee could give a demonstration of how she styled her hair. At first the prosecutors waved the idea off, but when her hair came up again, Gilbert restated the offer. The sunlit courtroom fell silent as Aimee stood up, smiling, and began to loosen her hair. There was a bit of a vengeful striptease to it—the men from the prosecutor's office had tried to expose the evangelist as an immoral fraud, with fake hair no less, and she was offering to reveal herself to them.

She unpinned her bun, and the courtroom gasped as her thick hair fell just past her shoulders. Her hair was natural—it had a faint auburn tint and was not excessively long, or secretly short, or filled in with "switches." Grinning, she expertly put her hair back up in seconds. Photographs of her taking down her hair ran in the newspapers the next day, Aimee smiling triumphantly. It was a small victory: she had evidence that she was the real thing.

28

DOUBLE LIFE

Sitting at the long wooden defense table, Aimee found the proceeding filled with dreamlike absurdity, she would later write. "Up with the curtain! On with the show! The droning of voices reading some stereotyped phrases. The winning smile from the bench as its occupant turned to be photographed."[1] Aimee experienced a constellation of emotions—indignation, disorientation, astonishment, fear. But from the outside, she presented herself as comfortable, smiling happily when people guessed her age at twenty-five or mentioned her alluring eyes. She sat still for the cameras. She laughed along with everyone else when her allegedly thick ankles came up. She chatted with reporters during recesses, making jokes. She offered no evidence of the persecuted rage she had exhibited in her sermons.

"A dreadful ordeal for you," commented a female reporter to Aimee in the hall one afternoon.

"Not as bad as I expected," Aimee responded. "I am rather enjoying it. I feel I am listening to the unfolding of a story about someone else altogether. They are not really talking about me."[2] Reporters who were able to steal glances at the notepad she kept in front of her saw that she worked on her sermons.

As the days passed, the crowds thinned. The district attorney's mounting evidence became more damning. Although Joseph Ryan had been removed from the case, the district attorney's office had plenty of evidence from his work in Carmel. Perhaps most upsetting to Aimee were witnesses who testified that Aimee and Ormiston had been meeting at the bustling Ambassador Hotel in the final months of 1925. The lavish resort was the home of the world-famous nightclub the Cocoanut Grove, and it was known as a place where the newly minted class of Hollywood celebrities could let loose, privately. A maid there testified that she saw Aimee at least six times and that always when the evangelist was there, she would see Ormiston "ducking" out of sight in the corridors. She said she'd seen Ormiston enter Aimee's room twice.

Ormiston's movements over the previous year certainly seemed like the actions of a man with something to hide. When Aimee had flown to Europe at the beginning of 1926, he had left his job at the Temple and vanished. When he reappeared, he had used different aliases as he traveled up and down the Pacific Northwest in the spring of 1926. There was also the visit from Mrs. Ormiston to the Temple, after which Minnie hired a chaperone for Aimee's travels. A month before Aimee's disappearance, Ormiston had purchased a car with funds wired to him from Venice by someone named James Wallace. He told investigators this was his brother—a blatant lie. It was, however, the name of Aimee's deceased half-brother from her father's first marriage. Ormiston had rented the cottage in Carmel ten days before Aimee's "drowning," giving his move-in date as May 18: the day Aimee vanished from Venice.

After Aimee's return to Los Angeles in April, there were more sightings of them together. On May 9 and 10, they were both registered guests at the luxurious Alexandria Hotel on Spring Street. Ormiston registered under a pseudonym: Frank Gibson. Three days before Aimee disappeared, witnesses said Ormiston checked in to the bustling downtown Clark Hotel. On the day she vanished, May 18, the doorman at the hotel, who had often attended Aimee's services, said he'd seen the evangelist walk into the lobby carrying a briefcase and rendezvous with Ormiston. "If I said it was not her, I would be lying to my own conscience," the doorman said. "I hope you can prove I am mistaken."[3] Ormiston checked out of the Clark Hotel at noon on May 18, just as Aimee and her secretary were driving down to Venice Beach.

Lorraine took the stand for the prosecution. With a sanguine smile and a fashionable hat, she said she had been hired by agents of Aimee's to pass herself off as the evangelist's doppelgänger. "I came to L.A. to help Mrs. McPherson out and receive compensation for it. I knew neither my sister nor I had ever been in Carmel. I came down and entered into an agreement to tell this fake story and be well paid. I would produce a fake woman and fake witnesses."[4]

She described meeting with Aimee and her mother and then going north to Carmel to do "detective work." There she tried to meet as many of the witnesses for the district attorney as possible and confuse them with her close resemblance to the evangelist. Repeating the account she'd given to the *Times*, she said she'd spent several nights at the parsonage, sleeping in Aimee's bed, while the evangelist slept on a "swing" outside. She said Aimee had coached her, rehearsing the details of the interior of the cottage, the color and print of the bedspread and wallpaper, so that she could fool Henry Benedict, Asa Keyes, and reporters. She also said the evangelist arranged for a photographer to take pictures of the two of them together, in identical dress, their hair combed back and styled the same, their faces meant to be mirror images of each other. For all this, Lorraine said, so far, she had been paid only expenses. But there had been the promise of thousands more.

One witness after another presented a picture of the evangelist living a clandestine life. To be sure, there were contradictions and holes in the stories. For every two witnesses who saw her sneaking into hotels, the defense had someone say the opposite or that they were there with her. Keyes was distracted. Dennison did his best. Aimee's cheerful demeanor chipped away, and she increasingly seemed exhausted by the whole thing, the papers describing her as looking "aged and grey." Minnie often wept.

For the prosecution, there was plenty of evidence of a criminal conspiracy to commit fraud and the production of false evidence. The accounts by both Lorraine and Bernice Morris that they were being paid to produce their dubious evidence of Aimee's kidnapping story—as if cast members in one of Aimee's legendary sermons—were textbook. Add to that the use of disguises in Carmel, Aimee's dramatic reappearance in the desert—all presented to police investigators as truth. Further, her decision to go in front of the grand jury in July and give her entire story under oath was clearly perjury, they alleged. Not to mention the multiple lives lost in the search for her in Venice. And to the prosecutors, Minnie was clearly a coconspirator, working with her daughter as she drove to McKinley's office to create an account of the kidnappers, and giving Lorraine money to produce witnesses.

The case wasn't airtight—they relied heavily on Lorraine's testimony, which Aimee's lawyers undermined by pointing out the time she'd spent in a Utah insane asylum and the repeated changes she'd made to her story. While more than a dozen witnesses positively identified Aimee in Carmel, there were a handful of others who said that it hadn't been her. And there was the underlying question that the prosecutor's office never gave an answer to: Why in the world would such a famous and successful woman do something so brazenly stupid? Beyond the facts of the case, the prosecutors stumbled over their constant criticism of Aimee's appearance, her sexuality, her financial prowess.

As the witnesses piled up, Aimee sensed public opinion was turning against her. From the stage and on the airwaves, she painted her prosecution as a biblical tragedy. "It has ever been in history that anyone who has stood staunchly for the cause of Christ has suffered for the sake of the Gospel. The apostles were imprisoned, beheaded, stoned, crucified. The Christians in Rome were tortured and killed. The martyrs were burned at the stake." She was a prophet, whom the forces of evil were trying to destroy. Yes, the tools were different, but was she not suffering on the same scale? "Men used to fight with sticks and stones and clubs. Today they fight with printer's ink. Is not the former the more merciful?"[5]

She decided to stage an illustrated sermon of her experience. The two-thirty service on Sunday, October 3, was entitled "March of the Martyrs," and the details of it were covered on the front pages, from Des Moines to Sacramento. Aimee stood onstage in front of a large cross, her body shaking. "I have been forced to endure the most exquisite cruelty and suffering that a human mind could conjure up. I am the victim of a vile persecution—the most brutal attacks ever made on a woman in the knowledge of man . . ." Aimee detailed the torture that true believers had endured throughout time, placing herself firmly in the arc of history. It was a solipsistic take, less than a decade after the end of World War I, with its loss of twenty million lives. Aimee seemed to be in a bubble of her own suffering, lost in the fragmented mirror of her own scandal. The newspapers loved the self-importance, snidely reporting: "Aimee Stages Pageant Based on Martyrdom." In the *New York Times* article, headlined "Martyr Show Given by Mrs. M'Pherson," the paper dryly reported that Aimee had presented her own suffering as the final slide in a show that began with the crucifixion of Jesus.[6] Aimee had become a spectacle inside her own spectacle.

Meanwhile Aimee's prosecutor was busy with other matters. On the night of Monday, October 4, a week into the proceeding, Keyes filed felony charges against all five members of the County Board of Supervisors, along with three other high-ranking county officials. A twenty-page indictment accused the eight elected representatives of using public money to build private cabins for themselves in a remote and beautiful county camp called Big Pines. The fraud ran into the hundreds of thousands of dollars, with the Board of Supervisors ostensibly having created a private resort for themselves on public lands. It was the largest case of corruption ever alleged in the City of Angels.

The Board of Supervisors reciprocated by bringing criminal charges against the district attorney, alleging he used public money improperly by financing the investigation. On a Tuesday morning, as Aimee and Minnie took their seats, Judge Blake turned to the prosecutor's table and asked where Keyes was. "He's being arraigned downstairs," responded one of the court officers casually.

In an editorial, the *Los Angeles Times* wrote that Keyes's charges against the supervisors were fraudulent, evidence of "a powerful organization that dispenses patronage and controls public officers for private gain. It has ramifications all through the invisible government of Los Angeles."[7]

Keyes didn't speak to reporters about the charges against him that day. Three weeks into Aimee's hearing, the prosecution closed its case with one of their key witnesses: a handwriting expert—fiercely opposed by Aimee's legal team—who said that it was definitively Aimee's handwriting on the grocery slips from the Carmel cottage. "The pencil writing on the grocery slips was written by one and the same person that wrote the Light and Darkness sermon,"[8] the expert concluded.

Late in the afternoon of October 19, Aimee's team opened their defense to Judge Blake. W. I. Gilbert said his strategy would be to call everybody that the prosecution had not. For their first witness, they summoned a longtime Arizona cowboy, who said that he—like Aimee—had walked twenty miles through the desert and had not needed water nor broken a sweat. The cowboy, who had joined the search team, said he'd observed Ryan, and that the investigator hadn't put any effort into looking for tracks during the hunt in the desert. "He got out of the car once and had his picture taken."[9]

The courtroom laughed, and for a moment there was a sense that Aimee's team could push back on the weeks of testimony and hundreds of articles of evidence. But then Aimee looked faint, collapsing. Her lawyer asked to adjourn. She was carried out of the courtroom by four private guards on a wicker chair. The reason given was gangrene developing on her leg—someone had placed a "poison pin" on her courtroom chair, and the wound had grown into an infected abscess, her lawyer said. Aimee returned in the coming days, although she was carried in on the wicker chair and was said to have a fever of over one hundred degrees. Gilbert called a number of witnesses from Agua Prieta and Douglas, those who had first seen her when she emerged from the desert. They testified that Aimee was exhausted, that she had fainted, that she had stuck to her story precisely. Over a series of days, the defense called more witnesses who tried to cast doubt on the state's case. A woman who worked at the hotel where Aimee often stayed said her door was always open and the woman had walked in often and found the evangelist alone, working.

The defense called numerous witnesses from Carmel who said it wasn't Aimee they'd seen at the house but another woman—a blonde. But their key witnesses were Judge Carlos Hardy and Aimee's own attorney Roland Rich Woolley, who attested to Aimee's character. The one witness they didn't call: Aimee. She sat at the defense table silently, battling her fever and infection.

The evidence and witnesses that Gilbert called made little impact in the newspapers. Much ink was spilled on the hunt for Ormiston. Clues of his presence popped up in California, Illinois, North Carolina, Florida, and New York City. The last week of October, investigators tracked the radio operator down to a seedy hotel in New York, where he had been staying for over a month under the name Ralph Stringer. Ormiston—likely tipped off—had checked out just before the police arrived. But in his rush, he left behind a trunk filled with women's clothing: silk gowns, lingerie, all in Aimee's size: thirty-eight. The trunk held a dress from Aimee's favorite dress shop; a flannel sports blouse, tagged by a Carmel dry cleaner; and a pair of black slippers from a small Los Angeles boutique, where Aimee maintained an account.

On October 29, as news of the trunk made headlines, Aimee was attending the hearing. During a break, she took the elevator down to the lobby. As the metal cage jangled to a stop and the doors opened, she faced a horde of reporters, shouting questions at her. She smiled and kept walking. But then a reporter from the *Los Angeles Examiner* yelled, "Mrs. McPherson, who is Ralph Stringer?" The reporter would later describe the shock that spread across Aimee's face—she did not know yet that Ormiston had been tracked down or that the trunk had been found. "I saw her hands slowly clench together until the knuckles stood out white and the blood showed in little red drops on her hands where her fingernails dug into the skin," the reporter recounted. "She looked at me, her face staring and white, as if I were a ghost. Then her head came up with a little jerk and she smiled."[10]

The discovery of the trunk was national news. *The New York Times* printed its contents, regaling readers with details, such as "silk evangelist's robe," and "a black evening dress, covered with black jet scales."[11] Keyes paid for the trunk to be shipped to a crime detection lab at University of California, Berkeley, accompanied by two armed guards. Some papers claimed that the trunk contained a boudoir cap, a silky lingerie hat worn at night, with strands of auburn hair stuck to the lace—hair just like Aimee's. What was not in dispute was that investigators had found love letters. One began: "Dear Darling Man: This is from a girl who loves you with all her heart! Wuff! Putting up noble fight here. Now, for any sakes, keep cool." The letter was signed, "Your Own Darling Woman That's Always Yours!"[12] It was postmarked from Los Angeles.

29

THE LESSER OF TWO EVILS

Aimee awoke on November 3, the day of the verdict, to the *Los Angeles Examiner* running an exclusive interview with her ex-husband, Harold McPherson. Running a car dealership in Florida, Harold hadn't seen her in eight years. He said that Aimee had written him a letter a year before, asking if he would take Rolf, as she planned on going away for a long time. He said that Aimee had changed over the years. "Ever since Mrs. McPherson has made her fight for prominence in the world, she has used her friends for all she could get out of them and they no longer could be of any use to her. She has had a habit of dropping them and forgetting them altogether." He said Aimee was "an angel in the pulpit, but a wild-cat at home" and that he was sure that she would drop Ormiston "like a hot penny"—just as she had him.[1] Harold was a damning witness from her past, voicing a criticism that even her worst enemies couldn't make: that Aimee had changed, and been corrupted by fame and power.

Inside the courtroom, on November 3, the lawyers made their closing statements, arguing for and against the charges of criminal conspiracy to suborn perjury, the preparing of false evidence, and conspiracy to "pervert or obstruct justice in the due administration of the law" by trying to "procure another to be charged with the crime of kidnapping."

Asa Keyes chose to make the closing statement himself, channeling his frustration with the whole mess. He described Aimee as a hypocrite. "I cannot forget," he exclaimed, "the impressive manner in which Mrs. McPherson swore to tell the truth with the oath, 'So help me God' and the impressive way she uttered those words 'So help me God!'" He described Ormiston as "a coward, hiding and slinking, afraid to come before this court, his co-defendants, and the world." Then he pointed his finger at Aimee and shouted that she was a "perjurer."

"It outrages human intelligence," he continued, "to believe that Mrs. McPherson was kidnaped! Mrs. McPherson and Mrs. Kennedy committed perjury and then coached Mrs. Wiseman, and now we have subornation of perjury!"

The defense attorney W. I. Gilbert kept his closing statements short and tried to avoid the larger question of Aimee's truthfulness. He reviewed what he called "undisputed facts": that Aimee had been kidnapped and that she had returned in a "sensational" manner. He quickly became technical, saying that the charge of manufacturing evidence should be thrown out, since Aimee had asked Lorraine and McKinley for their "reports" on events only for "publicity purposes to clear up the public mind."[2]

Judge Blake adjourned for ten short minutes before he returned with his findings: Aimee, her mother, and Ormiston would stand trial in January on charges of perjury. A new warrant was issued for Ormiston's arrest. Aimee stood and turned toward the court gallery and announced, "As God is my judge, I am innocent of these charges!" Then she pushed her way through the crowd toward the elevator. "This is enough to make one shiver" was the only thing she was overheard saying as she pushed her way past reporters.

* * *

Shortly after Judge Blake released his ruling, Aimee announced that her next Sunday sermon would be entitled "The Biggest Liar in Los Angeles." It was classic Aimee—she baited reporters and the curious with the possibility of a long-awaited confession. But instead, when Sunday came and the Temple was packed with congregants and press, she took aim at her old enemy: Bob Shuler. "There is one man in Los Angeles," she cried, "who is at the fountainhead of this thing." She railed against his accusations and implied that he had set her up—engineering her abduction but then also making the kidnapping appear fake so she would look a fool. But the real enemy, she announced piously, with a forgiving sigh, wasn't Shuler. No, the biggest liar in Los Angeles was the devil himself, who had been working around the clock to foment lies and distrust in her.[3] Beneath the Temple's sparkling sky-blue ceiling, Aimee's face hardened as she described her war with Satan.

A month passed, and the stories about Aimee and Ormiston continued to fill papers around the country. In mid-December, reporters for the *Examiner* at last found Ormiston in a small two-room apartment in Harrisburg, Pennsylvania. Sitting on a foldout bed, he was cordial, saying he didn't have much money and was mostly making a living by writing technical articles for radio magazines under a pseudonym. Ormiston had a small suitcase and a handmade radio. He said he'd spent the past few months on the run, living in the Midwest and New England under a series of false names. He told reporters that he would fight extradition. "This is only the beginning," he said mysteriously. "There will be a long hard fight before I go back to California. Also, I feel very certain that District Attorney Asa Keyes is not very anxious to have me go back for trial."[4]

Facing a trial in the new year, with Los Angeles's newspapers in a blood match to expose her, Aimee felt trapped. She had spent a decade building an exceptional life as a religious pioneer. She'd achieved things that no woman had done and few men could claim. She had brought Jesus to life for hundreds of thousands, built her massive and magnificent Temple, and used the newest technology of the radio to expand her fellowship with Jesus across the western United States. She had healed thousands from disease, saved marriages, helped addicts, and sent ministers around the world to preach the word of God. Her life story had been part of this process, a lens through which she explained the world and her gospel to others. She had written two memoirs, along with countless columns and sermons and songs and lectures. All along the way, her mother had been by her side, whispering to her that she was chosen.

Her life had been miraculous, but the district attorney's office and the press had popularized a version of her life that was the opposite: tawdry, mortifying, and scandalous. Through witnesses, evidence, and on-the-record testimony, they had composed a very public story that showed Aimee Semple McPherson to be a sinner, a hypocrite, a liar, and a fraud. Aimee did not recognize herself in the image that the world now held of her. Perhaps even more important, she couldn't bear her mother's disappointment.

For relief, she looked to the most important relationship in her life: a divine one. At the end of the court proceedings, Aimee later said, she knew there were only two ways out of her predicament: "thru the lawyers or thru the newspapers." She said she chose the lesser of the two evils, the one she understood best. While her lawyers had been perpetually frustrated by Aimee, the journalists had loved all of her theatrical doings. And so, God had "showed her the way," according to a cryptic statement she made the following year to the department leaders at Angelus Temple.[5]

In the last weeks of the grand jury proceedings, Aimee had hired three reporters who had been covering the case to be on her staff. The bright line between subject and reporter was not as clear during these early days of tabloid journalism, and so it was not so unusual for reporters to go back and forth between covering subjects and working for them. Her most important hire was Ralph Jordan, a curly-haired metro section reporter from the *Los Angeles Examiner*. He was officially Aimee's "press agent" but quickly took on the role of consigliere. Jordan was joined by James Kendrick of the *Los Angeles Times*, who continued to write stories for the paper while collecting a paycheck from Aimee. The entourage was rounded out by a man named Reginald Taviner, who also had worked for the *Times* and who, Aimee bragged to her mother and her lawyers, had the political connections they hadn't been able to give her. Aimee called these men her "deliverers," invoking a divine power to explain the presence of these worldly characters at the Temple. They roamed the halls of the Temple as if they owned the place—smoking cigars and talking loudly.[6] By the end of 1926, Aimee's mother and her legal team—Gilbert, Roland Woolley, and Arthur Veitch—could no longer get Aimee to listen to their counsel. Instead, Aimee assured them that these men would take care of her—they would handle things differently. They would save her.

FBI records released decades after Aimee's death suggest that she personally worked with the cadre of hired journalists to commit blackmail. Pushed into a corner, these documents allege, she decided to use the very corrupt tactics of the Los Angeles underworld she had spent years criticizing. Los Angeles was a city that ran on bribes and blackmail, and power belonged to those who took it by any means possible. Sometime around December 1, the files report, Aimee reached out to William Randolph Hearst, the publisher of the *Examiner*, which even more than the *Times* seemed intent on exposing Aimee.

Numerous witnesses later told the FBI that Aimee demanded Hearst apply his influence and get rid of the charges against her and that he change the way his newspaper syndicate covered her. If he didn't, Aimee would tell her hundreds of thousands of followers about Hearst's darkest secrets—with knowledge that she had perhaps been privileged with as a minister. She said she would share the fact that Hearst was conducting an affair with the actress Marion Davies and evidence that supported the allegation that he had murdered the Hollywood director Thomas Ince two years earlier. Hearst's relationship with Davies was well-known; exposing it did not amount to a serious threat. But a public accusation that Hearst had killed Ince was something else entirely; it had the potential of seriously damaging the magnate's reputation. According to one account, Hearst and Ince were on the publisher's yacht off Los Angeles when Hearst confronted the married and successful Hollywood director and accused him of sleeping with Davies, and then shot him. Eyewitnesses reported that Ince was carried off the boat at Long Beach harbor, with a bullet hole in the chest. (An alternate version went that Ince had died from ulcers that were aggravated by the huge amounts of bootleg booze he had consumed on Hearst's boat. In any case, Hearst had allegedly gone to great lengths to hide the death.)

The FBI records are conjecture, but within weeks of Judge Blake's ruling to send Aimee to trial, the charges against her were abruptly dismissed entirely. On January 10, 1927, the day that Keyes was supposed to file for a new trial, he told the judge that he was dismissing the case. The reason, he said, was that Lorraine had changed her story one too many times, and she could no longer be considered a credible witness against Aimee. But he took one last shot at Aimee when he made his announcement to reporters. "The fact that this defendant fabricated a kidnaping story, or that she spent a time at Carmel, are not, in themselves, offenses of which this court can entertain jurisdiction. Reputable witnesses have testified sufficiently concerning both the Carmel incident and the return of Mrs. McPherson from her so-called kidnaping adventure to enable her to be judged in the only court of her jurisdiction—the court of public opinion."[7]

For the remaining years of Aimee's life, Hearst newspapers gave fatuous coverage of the evangelist, allowing her countless column inches to sound off.

The two investigations into Aimee's kidnapping had shattered all local records for a case in their breadth, duration, and cost—a record not broken till the trials against Charles Manson and his followers. The case had taken twenty-three court days, involved eighty-three witnesses, and produced a transcript with 3,600 pages to be bound into five volumes (and, decades later, lost). It cost Keyes's office approximately fifty thousand dollars—close to a million in today's dollars. It would also mark the beginning of a dark turn for the prosecutor, and all those caught up in the case against Aimee.

PART III

LIGHT AND DARKNESS

If you want a happy ending, that depends, of course, on where you stop your story.

—Orson Welles, *The Big Brass Ring*

30

VINDICATION TOUR

Just before the start of Aimee's evening service, a whisper rippled through the crowd inside Angelus Temple. It spread down the halls and onto the sidewalks teeming with admirers outside the building: the charges against their beloved Sister had been dismissed. Aimee had been vindicated. Virtue had triumphed over evil. God was on their side.

Aimee entered Angelus Temple on January 10, 1927, aglow. She walked slowly down the center aisle, hands in the air like a prize-fighter. As she stepped onto the stage, the thousands of parishioners in attendance jumped to their feet, clapping and shouting out to the heavens. The scandal had raised her profile exponentially and doubled the congregation to fifteen thousand over the past year.[1] For a dozen minutes, the chorus of praises shook the building as Aimee gazed out at her followers, her mouth spread into a toothy grin.

The dismissal was "the greatest victory of her life," she said.[2] "The whole structure of this case against me was built like the Tower of Babel," she shouted, her voice sharp and indignant. "Rotten from the bottom. Each block, built one upon another, reached just so high, and then, like the Tower of Babel, God looked down and confused the tongues of the builders. Each told a different story. One confused the other, and thus it has ended, leaving standing only the true facts as told by me."[3]

The phrase hung in the air. What was the truth in Angelus Temple? Not just the facts, but "the true facts as told by me." Aimee's story—of her abduction, of her escape, of her persecution in the media—had ballooned beyond her control. In and out of the courtroom, every aspect of her being had been questioned—and derided. But when Asa Keyes dropped the charges against her, her version of her life could be reestablished. She could control her story—not the gossipmongers at the newspapers, not the corrupt district attorney's office, not the papally guided police investigators, not the envious male pastors.

Something had shifted in Aimee after having charges dropped. On the platform, she was like an animal after a long winter: her eyes glittering, filled with high-strung yearning. When Aimee had arrived in Los Angeles eight years earlier, she had presented herself as a country girl with a special connection to the divine. Physically, she had resembled a farm matron—a powerfully built, athletic woman, even though she stood just five foot three. She had enchanted audiences with her old-fashioned puritanism, her can-do attitude, and her conjuring of divine miracles.

In her milkmaid and nurse uniforms, with her high-collared Victorian dresses, she'd made herself symbolic and accessible. She'd worn capes, clutching a Bible to her chest like a shield as she conducted miraculous healings. She'd piled her hair high in just such a way that the midwestern émigrés who came to her in droves had recognized her from their own memories of long-lost mothers and grandmothers.

For the past six months, Aimee had defended every aspect of her life. She had battled for the world to believe her, selling herself as virtue made flesh. As the details of her private life were parsed in a courtroom and in the newspapers—the fabric of her undergarments, the price of her shoes, the width of her ankles, the length of her hair, the shape of her corset—she had frozen her innocence in a sort of psychic amber. Day after day, she'd donned her matronly uniform to affirm her virtue. Being photographed in these old-fashioned and modest dresses had helped her build her case in the newspapers. She had to cast herself as a victim, blinking and wide-eyed, held hostage and at the mercy of dark forces.

In the final months of the inquiry, Aimee had boiled her defense into a binary, populist vision of believers versus nonbelievers. As Aimee had raged about her persecution on her radio station, she was defending not just her version of her disappearance but faith itself: by coming after her, by calling her a fraud, prosecutors were trying to destroy all people of faith. According to Aimee, the stakes of the inquiry couldn't be more dire or more elemental: to believe Aimee was to believe in God; to believe the prosecutors was to believe in Satan.

Victory had transformed her. Any trace of her earlier softness, her sweet, maternal intimacy, her old-timey charm—it had evaporated by the time she stood on that stage on that January night. The figure on that dais was thinner, harder, angrier. Phoenix-like, Aimee declared that she would leave the next day on what the press called her "Vindication Tour." Twenty-two cities were scheduled.

Minnie disapproved. She had spent the previous six months defending her daughter and herself from the most sordid accusations, protecting Aimee from the menace of a hostile and secular society. She had been forced to deal with tabloid reporters, grifters, con artists, and the mentally unwell. She'd spent so much of God's money to make it all go away; all those dollars placed into the offering basket each Sunday—wasted on the state's unfair prosecution of Aimee instead of spreading the gospel. Minnie would later estimate the cost of the trial to her and Aimee—paid for by the Echo Park Evangelistic Association—as more than $100,000 (more than $1.7 million in today's dollars).

Minnie saw the future very differently than Aimee. Minnie wanted to hunker down; Aimee wanted to reach the world. Her happiest memories were her early days as an itinerant preacher, living hand to mouth, directed solely by divine messages. Besides, Aimee told her mother it was time to capitalize on all the attention—time to make the Foursquare Church a global entity. "I'd like to turn my face toward every port," she told her mother.

There was more to the tension than just strategy. Relations between mother and daughter had frayed during that last year of scandal. They had lived crisis to crisis, salacious headline to salacious headline. After years of itinerant living and endless travel, they had then been squeezed together in the close quarters of the parsonage apartment. For the past six months, the two women had been the focus of intense scrutiny, the constant focus of the public eye. Minnie had doubts about what had happened with her daughter, questions that she would turn over in her mind for years and yet find no answer. "I have lain awake many nights trying to solve some particular circumstance, only to find myself utterly baffled," Minnie said in a later interview. After her return from Europe in April 1926, before Aimee's disappearance, Minnie saw Aimee as a changed woman, both mentally and physically. "She was sarcastic in her talks with me and seemed an entirely different person."[4]

Aimee was more circumspect in how she spoke about her mother, saying to the press only that they were as deeply in love as ever. But she was increasingly interested in terrestrial pleasures. She was thirty-six years old, single, self-made, and wealthy. Her peers were shortening their skirts, foxtrotting with men, chugging bathtub gin. American women were chopping their hair off into modish bobs. "I consider getting rid of our long hair one of the many little shackles that women have cast aside in their passage to freedom," singer Mary Garden famously said that year. "Whatever helps their emancipation, however small it may seem, is well worthwhile."[5]

Aimee was one of the most famous women in the country, with a sex scandal behind her, and in 1927 she received invitations from movie stars, prizefighters, aviators, and stock traders to be a part of the whirlwind of fun being had by all. She couldn't help but dabble. She was part of a new social strata, a form of modern royalty that hadn't existed before radio and film: she was a celebrity. The scandal had made Aimee a mass-media icon, and she wanted to enjoy all the privileges and pleasures that came with being in this exalted group.

Aimee was beginning to look and act more like a woman from Hollywood, wearing makeup for every photo, her hair artfully done in the latest fashion. A few years earlier, Aimee had made damning remarks about women who cut their hair short, but suddenly she had a striking bob herself. She appeared in theaters around the country as a frequent face on the newsreels. Although Aimee appeared in the newsmaker section, she resembled more the Hollywood starlets whose glamorous faces filled the feature attractions.

"Mrs. M'Pherson Plans Movies," read a headline in the *Los Angeles Record* on January 17. The article reported that Aimee was considering becoming the star, director, and producer of films centered around her life. Aimee, always savvy about the power of new technology to spread her gospel, saw that the "talkies" were becoming the center of popular culture. The center was always where she wanted to be. "I believe the story of the Bible is as essential to the motion picture fans as it is to the constant church-goer," she told the newspaper. "I believe that by entering the field, the benefits derived would be mutual."[6] She denied that the movies would revolve only around her kidnapping and insisted they would plumb her entire biography and all the biblical importance it held. "The only motion picture I would consent to is my life." Aimee had one passion, one story, she said: that of her lifetime service to Jesus. She'd been offered movie contracts from MGM and other studios, she told the interviewer. But she was planning to start her own studio—once again, she would use modern technology which she controlled to produce her own stories.

For her Vindication Tour, she decided to charge her audiences admission for the first time—ranging from 50 cents to $1.10, based on proximity to the stage. (This was a pricey ticket in a time when tickets to the movie theater cost 25 cents.) She titled her show "The Story of My Life" and built it around many of the same themes she had relied on early in her ministry—her journey from an apple orchard in Canada to typhoid-stricken Hong Kong—but with a second act that focused on her abduction and trial. Audiences, though, seemed confused. Was this a show or a Christian revival? And if it was a revival, why should they pay?

Ninety minutes before she took the stage in Kansas City—a week into the tour—Aimee learned she would be telling her story to an almost empty house. She quickly reversed course, announcing that all could enter for free. But instead of worrying this misstep signaled a break with her followers, Aimee said her main concern was that her mother would find out. "From now on," she told her attendants, "we are going to hire a hall and fling open the doors, even in New York. I don't want it to get back home that I am commercializing myself in any way on this tour."[7]

It was too late. In Los Angeles, Foursquare church leaders were growing concerned about Aimee's comportment on the road. Minnie read about Aimee's fancy clothes and ticket prices and was displeased. Newspapers described her as a showwoman, a "weaver of fantastic tales" and the "Houdini of the Pulpit."[8] Her stylish clothes and her cosmopolitan behavior—not to mention the previous year's scandal—induced a change of tone in those reporting on her. It was more about the show, and less about the faith. Minnie, who was caring for Aimee's two children—now sixteen and thirteen—had one demand of her daughter: *Get off the front pages.*[9] Minnie was having to apologize constantly to staff members for Aimee's behavior and appearance. On January 25, the Temple's twenty-seven-member board of managers, made up of department heads and branch leaders and headed by Minnie, telegraphed Aimee in Omaha—a transcript of which immediately made it into the newspapers—urging Sister McPherson to abandon her tour on the grounds that "the cold weather and the strain" might injure her health. Echoing the telegram that Minnie had sent Aimee when she was traveling in Europe and Palestine the year before, the message may have felt like déjà vu to Aimee. And what was left unsaid was the same: without Minnie by her side, Aimee was untethered and likely to get into trouble. Aimee replied that her health was excellent, and she continued her tour.

Minnie only grew more concerned. Aimee was traveling with a

new entourage, the group of former journalists who had become her press agents and handlers during the district attorney's inquiry. Minnie heard from several longtime parishioners, congregants who had known Aimee from her tent revival days, that they had shown up to see her during the tour only to be turned away by her new press man, Ralph Jordan. The followers described these men lounging outside Aimee's hotel room, playing cards, smoking, and drinking whiskey while they caroused with reporters who were covering the show. There were also rumors of large piles of cash—presumably from the end-of-show love offerings—strewn about carelessly. Aimee's life on tour was resembling the kind of existence she had long preached against. But the power of these men in the world appealed to Aimee. "They were both worldly men making no Christian profession, and they offended some of my friends," Aimee later wrote. "Mother especially resented them, as they took matters into their own hands at times—both before and after I was vindicated."[10]

Minnie sent Emma Schaeffer, Aimee's devoted secretary, and Mae Waldron, a stenographer who had become part of the inner circle at the Temple, to accompany Aimee on tour. But privately, Minnie had concerns about Waldron. Waldron had worked with the two women for years. Waldron was more stylish than the dour Schaeffer; she wore her hair bobbed and favored modern, fashionable clothing. Waldron soon began to serve Aimee in ways that Emma could not—shopping for the latest dresses, making reservations at the buzziest restaurants.

With this expanded and divided entourage, Aimee plowed forward that January, every night giving a ribald and glamorous rendition of where divine destiny had guided her. Gone were the Victorian collars and corsets; gone was the séance-like atmosphere of her early revivals and healing services. She still wrote all her own material, regaling her audiences with knowing jokes about divorce and kidnappings and money. "I was always interested in radio. I can reach so many souls broadcasting," she told audiences at the beginning of her appearances. "I was interested in its mechanical end, its batteries, its tubes and antennae and wavelength but I never was interested in radio operators."[11] Her antagonists ranged from the district attorney to Darwin, and her humor included self-deprecating jokes about the sparkling green bathing suit she wore when she'd vanished. But vindication always came at the end, when she triumphed over the devil and returned to the only thing that mattered: saving souls.

Proof of that vindication, she said, was how Angelus Temple had grown the previous year. Membership had doubled; the Sunday school averaged three thousand attendees a week, and the six-story Bible College had hit its maximum enrollment. The Foursquare International organization had fifty-five churches with more than sixty-five thousand congregants. The monthly *Bridal Call* and the *Foursquare Crusader* had rapidly expanded their circulations, and dozens of stations around the country were now carrying Aimee's show, reaching hundreds of thousands of listeners every week.

The national crowds—worldlier than in years past—loved this new version of Aimee, cheering and shouting triumphant "Amens" and filling the collection plate with a thousand dollars or more a night (nearly twenty thousand dollars in today's money). While she continued to wear her white nurse's uniform onstage, offstage she was photographed in expensive and stylish suits and dresses, complete with an ermine coat, perpetually clutching an enormous bouquet of roses like a beauty queen. Still, Minnie made sure that Aimee was always flanked by Waldron and Schaeffer in the photographs as a way to reassure the folks at the Temple that their Sister Aimee had not become too fancy or full of herself. When staff and congregants asked Minnie when Sister would return, she would tell them, "We have heard that she is finding work enough to do to keep her busy indefinitely."[12]

"Tell Mother what a good girl I am!" Aimee said on a radio address broadcast from Shenandoah, Iowa, at the end of January. "Send her letters, write her telegrams," she exhorted the estimated audience of a million.[13] Even as she embraced her newfound fame, she wanted Minnie to approve. But Aimee was connecting to a different audience from the one she and her mother had built together. She criticized "Old Mother Hubbard preachers" for their outdated methods and their musty and boring preaching style. Aimee's revivals in the early

1920s had drawn huge crowds with her miracle working; these 1927 shows didn't include healings but were bigger and more Hollywood. Chicago newspapers described Aimee tossing rose petals to the audience at the end of her show, crowds surging forward to touch her, and police officers lifting her off the stage and carrying her to a waiting limo. The Associated Press reported that Aimee had struck a fifty-thousand-dollar deal to pen "sermonettes" that engaged with "morals and current affairs" for a consortium of newspapers around the country—a remarkable mainstream distribution deal for a religious figure.

In Des Moines, Aimee held a series of seven meetings over the course of a week. More than forty thousand people attended. "The devil thought he could frame me with a little blue trunk filled with circus clothes!" she crowed, to the crowds' cheers. "She is a finished mistress in the art of reading the mind of the mobs," concluded a local editorial writer in Des Moines. "Once you come beneath the spell of her personality, you're lost."[14]

While in Iowa, Aimee met a preacher named John Goben, a plainspoken man with a growing congregation in Des Moines. Aimee asked him if he would come work for her in Los Angeles as an administrator and a part-time preacher. Perhaps seeing a chance to chip away at her mother's control over the Temple, Aimee explained to Goben that she needed help organizing the rapidly expanding number of Foursquare churches being incorporated around the country. She described a salary so generous, he would later write, that he felt compelled to accept. "She made her offer so tempting that I couldn't well afford to decline it, in that it would give me a much greater opportunity to accomplish the good I had set out to do in Des Moines."[15]

Initially, Goben was in awe of Aimee. He was impressed by the great crowds that gathered to see her and felt her gifts had been handed down from on high. "Since the days of Jesus Christ upon this earth, there never has been a religious leader who has been blessed as Mrs. McPherson has," he wrote. But he would later write that when he traveled with her around the country, her behavior should have given him pause. One day, while preparing for an evening revival in Oklahoma, she asked him to buy her a bouquet of flowers. He did so without asking why. That night, he watched as she told a crowd of thousands a saccharine story about how a dear friend had sent her the flowers, that they were an emblem of how adored she was everywhere she went. Goben came to realize that she did this nightly. The artifice shocked him. Nonetheless, he was dazzled and said nothing. Goben still felt her work was important, if her tactics a little showy and insincere. There was something otherworldly about the way she connected to an audience, he felt. As he wrote in a tell-all book, five years later, "She has had one of the greatest opportunities to do good put in her hands that was ever entrusted to a human to carry on the work of God."

As they traveled by train between shows, Aimee told Goben about her dreams of expanding her ministry. She was planning a Palestine Holy Land pilgrimage, a sort of religious education cruise, she told him, and she wanted Goben to organize it. She asked him to charter a ship and sell reservations for between six hundred and twelve hundred dollars per passenger, an exorbitant fee (the equivalent of roughly twenty-two thousand in today's dollars). "All the pilgrims were to be rebaptized in the River Jordan by the evangelist with a most elaborate and impressive ceremony," he wrote. "She also planned to hold Easter services at the Tomb of Christ. Altogether a marvelous plan and I praised it enthusiastically, promising my heartiest support . . ."[16] Goben saw Aimee's concept as visionary: she was expanding the Foursquare Church to be a global brand, complete with once-in-a-lifetime experiences. He happily helped sell packages.

Aimee arrived in New York in February, causing *The New York Times* to announce that she was there "to purge the city of some of its sin." She wore a full-length wool coat, which she removed dramatically in her hotel lobby in front of reporters, revealing a yellow suit dress with a white fur collar. She made the society pages in all the New York papers, which assigned reporters to follow her around town. She booked a weeklong stint at the Glad Tidings Tabernacle on West Thirty-Third Street, a large brick Pentecostal church led by a couple who had been supporters of Aimee and Minnie since Aimee had lived in New York after Robert's death. Overflow crowds lined the sidewalk outside the event every night.

Aimee had honed her repartee with the press. She was sly and self-effacing, making chummy jokes about the scandal. She appeared to enjoy putting on a show for them as she delivered zinging one-liners. Her confidence and ease—along with the behind-the-scenes schmoozing by her handlers—helped win her a place on New York's front pages almost daily.

At one point, she told reporters that when she wasn't preaching, she liked to examine New York's underbelly by visiting its nightclubs and studying "at close range the flicker of the lights that singe so many butterfly wings." She speculated about what Jesus would have done if he had found himself in the presence of such debauchery. "If you think Jesus would like to go to a dance and put His arm around a fluffy little thing, with her eyes and face all covered with powder and 'goo,' with short skirts and high heels, then you can go to dances." As one newspaper put it, "she attacked the devil, and did it with a smile." Aimee offered a knowing critique of the dangers of modern life—from a front-row seat.[17]

The papers loved the story of this virtuous Christian woman who had skirted a sex scandal and proclaimed she was there to see the devil's work up close. "Is New York a very wicked city? The answer is yes and no," she wrote in a front-page editorial. "I am inclined to laugh just a little at New Yorkers, as it seems to me they rather pride themselves like naughty boys, on how tough they are."[18] For her first foray into sin, she visited a spot in Greenwich Village called the Open Door Club. Aimee dodged a fistfight as she walked in. She took a seat near the entrance, where a young flapper approached her. "I can see it, dearie," the girl said mischievously. "You're from out of town. This ain't a place for you if yer want to see things. Come on with us, we'll show you a show that's a wow. They're bearcats down there. Come on. Bring your whole gang." Reporters following Aimee merrily transcribed the conversation, including the girl's hilarious slang for hot-blooded women. The evangelist declined the invitation, turning away from the merriment, and addressed the reporters instead. She preferred the megaphone that was the press, playing to her audience back home rather than to the people hamming it up around her. "This is degrading. They are all so young."

As the clock moved past midnight, Aimee walked into the city's most infamous speakeasy, the Three Hundred Club. Reporters, once again, surrounded her as she made her way through its doors on West Fifty-Fourth Street. The space was run by another woman who frequently made the front pages—the actress, hostess, and former chorus girl Texas "Tex" Guinan, a broad-faced blonde in bright red lipstick who hobnobbed with the city's fast and beautiful. The Three Hundred Club was the gathering spot for the "it" crowd. Late into the night, Clara Bow, Irving Berlin, and Gloria Swanson swilled bootleg cocktails and champagne alongside members of the Chrysler, Whitney, and Vanderbilt families. The address card of the speakeasy read, "The World's Most Famous Rendezvous of Stage, Screen, Society and Finance."

Like Aimee, Tex had suffered scrapes with the law. Just days before Aimee's arrival, the Feds had raided Tex's club. The tabloids published photos of Tex, glamorous and gorgeous, carted away in handcuffs. The meeting of these two powerful, scandal-tinged women was a feast for the press, and reporters transcribed their interaction as if it were statecraft.

"I admire you for coming here," Tex said to Aimee.

"I am very interested. It is a remarkable study," Aimee responded. Seated at one of the white-clothed tables in the tightly packed main room, she conspicuously sipped water. As the clock struck 1:00 a.m., Tex climbed up and straddled two chairs—a nightly tradition—and shouted out to the crowd, "Hello, suckers!"

Standing beside Tex was a scantily clad, very young woman. Tex urged her to walk into the spotlight as she intoned a sexy comic-tragedy narrative. "How'd you like to be dancing to pay off your mortgage on your old home?" Tex asked. "And then forget most of your clothes on a night like this?" The audience properly titillated, Tex walked off, cueing the band to start. The dance floor cleared, leaving just one figure alone at its center. "The little blond danced," reported the *Brooklyn Daily Eagle* the next day. "And it was a wild, woolly dance. She flung herself everywhere and anywhere. The diners and revelers clapped and yelled. The little blond pranced near the table occupied by the evangelist and then danced off the floor."[19]

Aimee seemed truly moved by the plight of the young woman. Although she knew that the debauchery of the performance was probably meant to embarrass her, Aimee was the master of making stories her own. After the dance was over, Aimee asked Tex if she could address the crowd. Tex said yes, and Aimee walked to the middle of the room and smiled, a slow, sad smile. She waited as the crowd took notice of her. Conversations ceased; the music stopped—the crowd captivated by her silence, just as they had been a dozen years earlier when she'd stood on a chair on a street corner in Canada.

When Aimee finally spoke, her voice was startling and simple. "Behind all these beautiful clothes, behind these good times, in the midst of your lovely buildings and shops and pleasures, there is another life," she said, gazing boldly into the eyes of the hushed revelers. "There is something on the other side. 'What shall it profit a man if he gains the whole world, and lose his own soul?'"

She didn't preach or lecture the crowd. She spoke for less than a minute. "With all your getting and playing and good times," she concluded, "do not forget you have a Lord. Take Him in to your hearts."

For a moment, no one spoke. The audience seemed to be lost in reflection, considering her words. Ever the ringmaster, Tex broke the spell by joining Aimee, and when she threw her arms around the evangelist to embrace her, the room exploded with applause and cheers. The party recommenced, and Aimee went back to her table. The press loved this version of the evangelist, a well-dressed doomsayer, crying out for lost souls amid the revelry.

The next day, as camera bulbs flashed, Tex and a boisterous pack of her dancers arrived in the glare of daylight for Aimee's service. They were given front-row seats. Their presence gave Aimee the benediction of New York City's cosmopolitan crowd. In front of reporters, Aimee asked Tex if she believed in the hereafter. The club owner quickly retorted: "Oh sure, I believe in getting what I'm here after!" The banter seemed rehearsed, a preplanned publicity bit to make the papers. Both women were skilled players when it came to the press and seemed to genuinely delight in each other.[20]

The big-name social commentators of the day—H. L. Mencken, Morrow Mayo, Carey McWilliams, and Upton Sinclair—wrote at length on Aimee after her trial. Dorothy Parker dubbed her "Our Lady of the Loudspeaker" in *The New Yorker*. Dispatched by highbrow magazines with a more sophisticated readership than the dailies, these writers—to varying degrees—depicted Aimee as the embodiment of the times, the zeitgeist made flesh, waving away her "kidnapping episode" as an amusing youthful folly. Even for her critics, she had emerged a sympathetic character. "It is unheard of, indeed, in any civilized community for a woman to be tried for perjury uttered in defense of her honor," H. L Mencken, the gimlet-eyed journalist, wrote for *The Baltimore Evening Sun*. "But in California, as everyone knows, the process of justice is so full of unpleasant novelties, and so poor Aimee, after a long and obscene hearing, has been held for trial."[21] While Aimee had been good for a women's pages feature before her kidnapping, she was now a delicious launching point for larger ideas about society and religion.

In all these pieces, there was a reoccurring dismissal of Aimee's audience as ill-educated bumpkins. The writers were more interested in her theatricality and commercial techniques. Aimee, in their view, was a wolf in sanctimonious sheep's clothing, adept at duping the masses with an artful smile and a great show. The social critic Louis Adamic wrote of Aimee and her followers in a scathing essay entitled "The Morons of Los Angeles." Adamic wrote of Aimee's followers: "They are the folks whom the Lord blessed with a lot of feelings and scant reasoning power, making them, thus, abnormally suggestible to dynamic personalities—spellbinders, demagogues, bunkshooters, bunco-steerers of all sorts."

Vanity Fair's Joseph Henry Steele called her "the most successful actress of our day" and declared that "future historians cannot neglect Aimee in their summation of this era's highlights. She belongs to the glittering galaxy that includes Phineas T. Barnum, William Jennings Bryan, Harry Houdini, and Greta Garbo. Her life and her character have been prismatic and kaleidoscopic." He concluded, "She is vulgar, colorful, stimulating, greedy, vibrant, willful, good-natured, tireless. She believes blindly in her own destiny." For Steele and elite audiences, Aimee was nothing more than a performer, her audience members duped. "Five thousand souls, panting for salvation and starved for life."[22]

Just over two months since the charges against her were dropped, Aimee returned home to Los Angeles on March 30, 1927, to find the Temple brewing with staff tension and threats of mutiny. Numerous branch churches—grouped under the umbrella of Foursquare International—expressed concern to headquarters at Angelus Temple about the new version of Sister they saw in the papers. In particular, the longtime music director, Gladwyn Nichols, was the spokesperson of a revolt, leading three hundred congregants away from Angelus Temple to form a new church in Los Angeles. His primary complaint was Aimee's worldliness, embodied by her bobbed hair and her fancy gowns. "The God of the Gospels is being replaced at Angelus Temple by the god of materialism," Nichols announced.[23]

Minnie supported her daughter in the face of criticism, but privately she agreed that Aimee had changed. She told the press she stood by Aimee, "four square." But tensions were rising. In April, Aimee met with her board. She submitted a three-page resignation letter, saying that perhaps it would be better to install another pastor full-time as she traveled. The board unanimously rejected her resignation. It appears to have been a power play by Aimee—if they didn't want her the way she was, well, she would simply leave. As the spring turned to summer, conflicts continued at the Temple. Minnie seemed to be the only one who could voice criticism to Aimee, and as the messenger, she became an irritant to her strong-minded daughter. In July, Aimee called a meeting of her twenty-one department heads and asked them to vote on three counts: "Did I do right in obtaining a dismissal of my case? Did I do right in making this tour and taking Ralph Jordan with me as a manager? Will it be right to go again and take him?" All twenty-one voted and gave her a "vote of confidence." For Aimee, this ought to have put an end to Minnie's concerns.[24]

It did not. Their breakup played out messily in the press, with leaked stories appearing throughout that July of 1927, detailing slights and innuendo. "Ma" Kennedy and Sister became a serial drama for Los Angeles readers. Aimee used the echo chamber of the public to wage a war against her mother. She announced from her stage that workers would not receive their paychecks because of an "oversight" by Minnie. That month, the wire services carried an anonymous list of future options for Minnie that were bullet-pointed in all the major papers—allegedly supplied by a "peace committee." These retirement plans included going on an extended missionary tour and finding work elsewhere. But it was option four that signaled how far Aimee was willing to go to push her mother away: "Mrs. Kennedy might return to her well-to-do husband, W. Whittebeck, of New York."[25]

Mr. Whittebeck was a boat engineer who lived in Hudson, New York, with his wife, children, and grandchildren and had never been married to Minnie. Furious, Minnie refused to say much to the press except: "I have kept Aimee's personal secrets for ten years and I don't see why they should air my personal affairs."[26] But a Temple worker, Letha Brooks, was quoted in the papers as having overheard Minnie say inside Angelus Temple that she would "break Sister, crush her, and drive her from every pulpit in America . . ."[27] Implicit was the threat of a potential tell-all by Minnie. In turn, Aimee said all of this was a result of her mother's "inflamed mind and tired brain." She told the papers her mother should "take a vacation before a complete mental and physical breakdown should bring other horrors on the church."[28]

That summer, after a decade of working as the head of Aimee's vast enterprise, Minnie was asked to step away. Aimee formed a new, eight-member board, led by the administrative heads of the Temple. When Aimee asked for her mother's removal, they supported

Aimee's wishes unanimously. It was the beginning of the end of the mother-daughter reign.

Minnie made clear that she and Aimee were still equal partners in the Echo Park Evangelistic Association, a legal entity that held all their real estate assets. Minnie gave a scathing statement to the press: "My daughter's like a fish on the beach when it comes to handling money. I don't believe if you put an ad in the newspapers you could find anybody dumber when it comes to business. All they got to do is let her have her way for a year, and she'll bankrupt the place, mark my words."[29]

Minnie's bitter words would soon become prophecy. In August 1927, Aimee packed up Rolf and Roberta and moved out of her church apartment. Minnie announced her retirement and moved to an apartment a block away from the Temple. Using a team of lawyers, the two women split their holdings equally: Minnie took all the valuable land holdings they'd acquired around Los Angeles, and Aimee held on to control of the Temple—and the organization's steadily growing pile of debts.

31

AFTERMATH

With her mother out of the Temple, a certain frenzied energy seemed to descend on Aimee. She redoubled her efforts to do good works following the dismissal of her case. The Foursquare Church archives detail her activities on nearly every single day of 1927 and 1928. Aimee gave sermons, wrote articles, made speeches, attended revivals, and offered baptismal offerings, weekly healings, and prayer services—for the sick, the broken, the young and the old. She traveled throughout the Northeast, the South, and the Midwest and up and down California. By the church's account, the weekly services were more crowded than ever, with over fifteen thousand regularly attending every week. "In this show devouring city," wrote a journalist in *Harper's Magazine*, "no entertainment compares in popularity with that of Angelus Temple."[1]

In August 1928, her congregants gathered to celebrate Aimee's "Twenty Years in the Service of the King." The event was tied to the publication of a new memoir, *In the Service of the King*, with an updated version of her life story that included a detailed account of her kidnapping, her escape, and the first-person drama of her persecution. With a celebration planned weeks in advance, staff went to work decorating the Temple in the most resplendent fashion—banners were draped from the balconies, streamers of gold and blue formed a canopy overhead, and four thousand yellow roses were affixed to a "huge loving cup that hung suspended over the platform and showered its golden rose buds over the head of Sister McPherson." The stage itself was a "vision of loveliness," bedecked in marigolds, roses, and bright-hued dahlias. Roberta—seventeen years old—dressed herself as her mother at that age; with ice skates thrown over her shoulder, she regaled the audience with the story of Aimee's conversion that began in that little church with Robert. Then the teenager introduced her mother, calling her "the most wonderful woman in the world."

Thundering applause from the crowd—more than five thousand strong—reverberated through the Temple, followed by a rousing chorus of "Onward Christian Soldiers." Accepting a huge bouquet of flowers, Aimee demurred, saying, "I know you love me because I love Jesus and I just take all the love and praise and tie it in a bundle and give it right back to Him."[2]

The flowers, the tears, the parades, and the songs demonstrated an indisputable truth: Aimee was a deeply transformative spiritual figure in a huge number of lives. She had ordained hundreds of ministers and franchised and inspired hundreds of churches throughout the United States. She was known nationally by her first name, an icon who made headlines for a new dress or a funny joke. But for the hundreds of thousands of people around the country who loved her, Sister Aimee was a heavenly figure on earth. She had become almost a way of life, with her own palette of heavenly symbols, bright colors, and insider language.

That event also marked the one-year anniversary of the commissary, a new Temple department devoted to aiding the poor. Initially located in the basement, the Foursquare Commissary gave away food, clothing, furniture, and blankets. Aimee said she wanted it to be a place where "persons really in need, without regard to their color or creed, can call for help of every kind and get it instantly without red tape."[3]

One of the best recorded examples of the personal impact of her outreach is a story from a young emigrant from Mexico named Antonio Rodolfo. Rodolfo's parents moved to the United States in 1918, amid the revolution. When Rodolfo was eleven years old, his father died in a car accident outside their home in East Los Angeles. Rodolfo took on odd jobs to support his sister, mother, and grandmother. Devout, the young boy dreamed of becoming a Catholic priest. One day he came home to find strangers praying over his gravely ill grandmother. He shouted at them to leave, accusing them of being "disciples of the devil." His grandmother groaned for him to stop, telling him that they were doing a healing and that they had come from Angelus Temple.

Soon, the Foursquare Crusaders became regulars in his home, bringing groceries and supplies. As the months passed, Rodolfo's grandmother said she had been healed, and they began to attend Angelus Temple in 1926. The congregation shocked Rodolfo with its boisterous friendliness and joy. "I had never seen five hundred people happy at the same time," Rodolfo later wrote. He and his grandmother became born again, accepting Jesus Christ into their lives, and he joined the Temple's jazz band, playing the saxophone.

When Rodolfo was fourteen years old, he saw Aimee preach for the first time. As he gazed up at her from the orchestra, Aimee lifted her arms and in a slow, melodious voice said, "Glory! Glory! Glory!" Her smile, he wrote, felt like a blessing on the congregation. She opened a passage from the Bible, "caressing each word," interweaving the scripture with shouts of "Hallelujah, brothers and sisters!" The orchestra began to play, and people began to scream and faint. Roldolfo was enchanted, and he felt his life transform; soon the Foursquare Church was the center of his whole life.

Three years later, Aimee approached Rodolfo when he was in the orchestra. "I know you," she said. "I like you." She indicated she knew his name and his family situation. "Tony," she said, using his nickname. "I have the feeling that the Lord has singled you out to become a great preacher. It's a wonderful calling and people need help. I want to work with you." Aimee drove him to a predominantly Mexican neighborhood that weekend, inviting him to ride in her car. She apologized to the crowd that awaited her for not speaking Spanish but introduced Rodolfo as someone who would soon be a great evangelist too. She asked him to translate for her. Rodolfo felt as if he was being asked to aid a "goddess," and when she put her hands on him, he felt an electrical charge.

Rodolfo continued to work for Aimee, helping to translate sermons—something Aimee had only dabbled in intermittently. Soon he took bit parts as an extra at the film studios around town, and his acting career took off. Using the screen name Anthony Quinn, Rodolfo would go on to become one of Hollywood's most beloved and celebrated Latin American actors, starring in such epics as *Zorba the Greek* and *Lawrence of Arabia* and winning two Academy Awards.

Aimee was the person who transformed his life, he wrote. "Years later, when I saw the great actresses at work I would compare them to her," he wrote. "As magnificent as I could find Anna Magnani, Ingrid Bergman, Laurette Taylor, Katherine Hepburn, Greta Garbo and Ethel Barrymore, they all fell short of that first electric shock Aimee Semple McPherson induced in me."[4]

But charisma didn't run an enterprise. The debts grew at the Temple in Minnie's absence. Under financial pressure, Aimee promoted one absurd money-making scheme after another. Vacation homes, real estate developments, hotels, summer camps, cruises—Aimee attached herself to all of these and more. There was even an Aimee-themed cemetery: Blessed Hope Memorial Park, a fourteen-acre site in Burbank, where Aimee promised followers that she would be buried. Those who paid to be entombed with her would rise together for the Second Coming from this convenient, affordable meeting point in Burbank. Plot prices increased in proximity to Aimee, with the closest costing almost a thousand dollars. Minnie was quoted in the press criticizing the endeavor as "Aimee's Boneyard." Ralph Jordan, the former newspaper reporter whom Aimee had hired at the end of 1926, became her business manager. In time, he had his own business propositions for Aimee—real estate schemes and investments—but none of them were realized. She seemed to have lost herself without Minnie. It was as if she had absorbed her accusers' criticisms into her being.

Roberta later observed that once Minnie was gone, "all hell broke." Minnie had served as a gatekeeper who controlled access to Aimee. Without her, all manner of grifters burst into Aimee's life, looking to take advantage. Roberta, who was seventeen, felt caught between her mother and grandmother, and watched, powerless, as Aimee fell victim again and again.

An up-and-coming real estate developer—looking to promote a project—gave her a waterfront lot in the then little-known town of Lake Elsinore, seventy miles southeast of Los Angeles. An hour's drive outside the city, Aimee built herself a fourteen-room, five-thousand-square foot Moorish confection, with turrets, a prayer tower, hand-painted murals of biblical scenes, mother-of-pearl-tiled bathrooms, and cut-glass floors. Gold leaf walls, a mirrored bedroom, and a one-ton Czechoslovakian crystal chandelier were all a sharp departure from the parsonage's relative simplicity. "Aimee's Castle," as the house became known in the area and in the press, was her Babylonian escape. She would spend weekends at this lakefront San Simeon before returning for her Sunday night shows at the Temple. She even built a tunnel from the garage to the main house so that she could avoid ever showing her face to the reporters who often waited outside.

She sought reprieve not just from the press but from her Temple, where management without Minnie quickly turned ugly. John Goben, who had worked for a year as Aimee's associate pastor, became increasingly disillusioned by Aimee's behavior and the way she ran the Temple finances. His concerns about the way church money was being used became so acute that he hired private investigators to follow Aimee whenever she left Angelus Temple. Late one night, in 1929, they observed her leaving the Temple in a pink evening gown and a gilded turban, stepping into a chauffeured limousine. The limo headed into a wealthy neighborhood in the Hollywood Hills, where she stayed deep into the night with Alexander and Lois Pantages.

Alexander Pantages owned most of the theaters and vaudeville houses west of the Mississippi in the 1920s. After Aimee's trial ended, she became friends with the high-flying couple, who socialized with the Hollywood elite. There was a rumor that Aimee and Lois had been frequent visitors to the illicit—and sometimes deadly—dance marathons held in Venice, where impoverished couples twisted and spun themselves into exhaustion for hours—and even days—on end just to win a few dollars. Someone, it was said, had seen Aimee give a "silver shower," tossing change onto the dance floor.[5]

But the Pantages were worse than an indicator that Aimee was leading a double life. They were in the headlines quite a bit that year—for murder and rape. Lois had been charged with second-degree murder for killing her Japanese gardener one night while driving home drunk. Two months later, Alexander had been charged with the rape of a seventeen-year-old dancer, who said he had attacked her in his office during an audition. Building a case against Aimee, Goben said Aimee was frequently at their house during Lois's trial, and he claimed that he had proof that this was just one of Aimee's many less-than-saintly nocturnal movements. Her bad behavior and more were detailed in his tell-all volume, published in 1932, entitled *"Aimee": The Gospel Gold Digger*, which reads like an evangelical burn book. "I was very happy in my work at the temple," Goben wrote, "until those things which I have disclosed in the following pages began to open my eyes to the lust of the flesh and the love of money that dominates the life of this famed religious leader. She is truly a gospel gold digger."[6]

Goben's hiring of private investigators seemed unnecessary: there was plenty of evidence out in the open that Aimee had lost touch with her fundamentalist roots. That year, she filed articles of incorporation for "Angelus Productions," a movie studio that was to be financed with a fund of $200,000, raised through $100 stock shares (more than $3.5 million in today's dollars). Aimee, her attorney, and her business manager were listed as the directors of the corporation. The project was set to produce "Clay in the Potter's Hand," a film about Aimee's kidnapping, as orchestrated by the vice kings of the underworld of Los Angeles. Working with a producer, Aimee ran screen tests of herself and commissioned an established screenwriter, Harvey Gates, who had already written more than fifty silent films for the major Hollywood studios. Gates, who specialized in sweeping adventure epics and Westerns, charged ten thousand dollars to write Aimee's story, with her to be cast in the starring role.[7]

Goben also alleged that Aimee had a secret bank account under a false name containing more than a hundred thousand dollars, which she used to funnel her own spending money directly out of the church coffers. He also alleged fraud in her bookkeeping and payroll. After two years of working for Aimee, in 1929, Goben turned over evidence to the district attorney's office that raised questions about Aimee's use of charitable funds. (The new district attorney ultimately dropped the investigation.)

In the face of criticism, Aimee focused on church expansion. In 1929, her L.I.F.E. Bible College had ordained four hundred ministers, many of them women. There were two hundred Foursquare churches around the United States. Aimee's vision of having tourists to Los Angeles take the seed of her church and bring it back to their hometowns had worked, and you could find Foursquare churches throughout the Midwest and the South. The Temple continued its seven-day-a-week programming, with a massive choir and huge theatrical productions every Sunday night. Angelus Temple had become a must-see for any visitor to the city. As young children, both Richard Nixon and Marilyn Monroe were visitors in the 1920s, with their families. And Hollywood stars of the era, such as Charlie Chaplin and Mary Pickford, would attend for the spectacle of it all. Angelus Temple was still considered the greatest show in town, and for a time, from the outside, it seemed that maybe Aimee could do it all without her mother.

* * *

Then the stock market crashed at the end of October 1929. Initially, the events on Wall Street registered as a distant episode in California. The *Los Angeles Times* reported the next day with a certain detachment as it recounted the drama of "the nation's greatest bankers" reacting to the economic losses in New York. But as the months passed, the financial impact began to ripple out, across the nation and down to Los Angeles's working class, as economic misery washed over the young city in the first years of what would become the Great Depression. Aimee's audience had always been made up of working-class and lower-middle-class believers—and in the coming years as businesses and factories closed, her congregation found itself under increasing economic duress. Waves of immigrants from the drought-stricken Midwest flooded the streets of Los Angeles, and the money that had so easily been given as love offerings in the earlier boom years of the 1920s grew lesser and lesser. In the coming years, the unemployment rate in California would rise to 29 percent.

Meanwhile the Temple payroll ballooned to more than eleven thousand dollars a month (almost two hundred thousand in today's dollars). The Temple was able to skate along for a while, with staff and congregants hoping that the economic distress was a short-term trial rather than a new way of life. More than ever, Aimee needed help with the financial side of her empire. All her post-vindication dreams of expansion had failed. She had concocted her vision inside the golden bubble of the Roaring Twenties, and all the affluence and excess that they promised. Following the stock market crash, Aimee's vacation home development failed to sell, her hotel lost its investors, the movie was never made, and the cruise to the Holy Land did not sell enough tickets.

Frightened by the Temple's ever-growing debts, Aimee begged Minnie to return and clean house. Preferring discretion, Minnie worked in semisecrecy for six weeks at the Temple, attempting to balance the books. But Aimee couldn't resist making a show out of their reunion. At a Sunday evening service in December, Angelus Temple held a lavish Christmas celebration, the interior festooned in silver and crimson. Down the center aisle four men carried a gigantic

Christmas box to Aimee, who gasped theatrically from the stage. As the audience watched, Aimee tore off the wrapping and bow.

Inside the present stood her mother.

The two women embraced and wept as the band played and the choir cheered. Summarizing the sentiment of the crowd, the church newsletter later reported: "No Christmas day could have brought a better gift, for where in all the world is there anything more precious than a Mother and a Mother's love?"[8]

The rapprochement was brief. Minnie found her power greatly reduced—she'd been replaced on the board by Harriet Jordan, another female minister whom Minnie saw as a rival. Aimee seemed distracted from the Temple—she had grown accustomed to seeing her image in the paper every day and became increasingly self-conscious of her body. The *San Francisco Examiner* reported that Aimee had sought surgery to have her legs slimmed down—perhaps still reeling from the ankle shaming she'd endured during her trial. She was told surgery wasn't an option so then proceeded to conduct an eighteen-day orange juice cleanse.[9]

Then, in the summer of 1930, the *Los Angeles Times* carried a shocking front-page story: Aimee and Minnie were recuperating in separate facilities after getting into a fistfight—a fight that had come just after getting simultaneous facelifts.

The ensuing front-page stories quickly became a macabre over-the-top drama that felt almost staged for the public. Aimee, it was reported, was recovering in a guarded Malibu cottage—their dispute had led to a nervous breakdown, which had caused temporary "near blindness." Meanwhile, Minnie, who said she had a broken nose—she said from being punched by Aimee—was convalescing in the Brentwood Sanitarium. Minnie, now sixty years old, gave an interview from her sanitarium bed, accusing Aimee of pressuring her into receiving the newfangled "rejuvenation process" from a Budapest surgeon.

Minnie said she had returned to work at the Temple with "nothing but love in her heart and a burning urge to grasp the tottering helm of the organization and put its affairs in order." But soon she felt "evil influences" at work that she was "powerless to combat." Just as Minnie began to discuss her departure, she alleged, Aimee proposed "we submit to a rejuvenation process." Minnie agreed to do the surgery together, but then they'd had a fistfight.

They'd argued, Minnie said, over a staffing issue at the Temple. Aimee would later say that her mother accused her of coming "under the influence" of three other women in Temple leadership (the associate pastor Harriet Jordan, along with the two women Minnie had just a few years before sent to babysit Aimee on tour—Emma Schaeffer and Mae Waldron). As for the fight, Aimee would say it did not happen. Minnie had simply fallen. "The press reported—erroneously—that I had inflicted the injury," she later wrote. "I watched with distress again how degrading a disagreement or misunderstanding could look in print."[10] Regardless, Minnie resigned again, this time for good.

32

THE IRON FURNACE

Following the fight with Minnie, Aimee was bedridden for months, increasingly unwell. A parade of doctors visited, and she was diagnosed with a host of ailments: dysentery, intestinal blights, shingles, nervous breakdowns, exhaustion. That summer of 1930, she spent a month alone in a cottage in Malibu, overseen by church elders. But even the seashore felt harsh, according to an update published in the church weekly, which described the noise of cars and trucks on the Pacific Coast Highway with the "thunderous roars day and night" of the waves, all which made Aimee miserable. "Even broths and orange juice were distasteful to her."[1]

As Aimee grew weaker, a succession plan for the Temple was put in order. Aimee had always spoken of Roberta as the future leader of the church, calling her the "Star of Hope" and envisioning a matriarchal dynasty of female evangelism. At the age of twenty, Roberta was precociously comfortable in front of an audience after almost a decade leading the children's services. She even had a recurring column in *The Bridal Call*, with jokes and puzzles. While Rolf had been shipped off to live on a farm, Roberta had been kept close, groomed for a public life. Roberta lacked her mother's star power—she was reserved, with a slight lisp. But she had Robert's deep-set eyes, a wide, sparkling smile, and a steady poise onstage.

She understood that her life would be lived according to her mother's vision. "You did whatever was expected of you," she later told an interviewer. "You did not ask why, you did immediately the thing required."[2] Aimee's instructions from her sickbed were for Roberta to be the face of the Temple, and for Rolf to handle the administration. Soon, Roberta would be promoted to vice president—the second in command, overseeing all the departments.

Just a few months shy of Aimee's fortieth birthday, there was real fear that she might die. Rolf, at seventeen years old, was called home from missionary work in Oklahoma, and Roberta, who was in Ireland with her grandparents, was messaged to be prepared for "sad news." Minnie stayed away. She had a cottage in Hermosa Beach but began to spend much of her time in Washington State, where she preached and did evangelistic work for a variety of other churches. She gave no statement to the press.

In the fall of 1930, Aimee ceased in-person preaching, although she gave occasional radio sermons, via a portable microphone, from her bed. Visiting evangelists and associate pastors took over her stage. Aimee's health became her sole focus, the severity of her medical issues exceptional. The once-athletic woman who had swum in the open seas and ridden horses regularly, who had staked her own tent and driven a car across the continent, weighed less than a hundred pounds and could barely walk. Part of the weight loss was due to poor health, but it was made worse by what appeared to be an extreme diet inspired by her celluloid dreams. Aimee had intentionally lost more than forty pounds in anticipation of appearing in "Clay in the Potter's Hands," largely through sheer starvation.

Doctors' orders came that coincided with her own desire to escape. In October 1930, she sailed on a United Fruit Company ship to the Caribbean, and then on to Costa Rica. She visited a group of missionaries, who described her as a sad and frail woman who confided her terrible loneliness and her desire to get married. She returned to the United States a month later and was taken from her train to the parsonage by ambulance. A Temple spokesperson predicted that she would recover quickly. "We hope that a few days' rest, at this lower altitude, will see an improvement." One of her doctors was quoted in the newspapers, explaining that it was "the accumulated stress of four terrible, tempestuous years."[3]

But returning to the Temple meant returning to the harsh realities of her life: lawsuits, betrayal, mutiny, power struggles, and an ever-growing payroll. One by one, the people she took into her confidence left her—and litigated. The screenwriter, the producer, the business manager, the press agent, the real estate partners; they all sued. In those years, Aimee was sued dozens of times. She was sued for nonpayment by her lawyers, by her screenwriter, by her architect. She was sued for fraud by the investors in the real estate schemes that never came to fruition. According to her family, Aimee was simply a fool when it came to money. All the qualities that made her charismatic and enchanting seemed to fail her when it came to making decisions about investments. "Mother was frankly starry-eyed and visionary," Roberta would later say. "Very gullible. She only saw the best in people, she never doubted anything."[4]

Aimee was burned out. She saw her continued health problems as a manifestation of overwork. "William Jennings Bryan had predicted I would have a bad nervous breakdown if I continued the pace he witnessed," Aimee wrote of the infamous lawyer, statesman, and anti-evolution crusader who had befriended her almost a decade before. Soon, she did.[5]

The answer, again, was escape. Roberta and Aimee set out on a three-month-long cruise at the end of January 1931. But instead of bringing mother and daughter closer, the voyage drove a wedge between them. After just a few weeks on board, Roberta fell in love with the ship's purser. The giddy young couple asked Aimee's permission to marry, and Aimee agreed, giving the bride away at a church in Singapore that March.

As the journey continued, Roberta and her new husband found more and more opportunities to slip away from her mother. Aimee felt abandoned and privately confided to anyone who would listen that she was lonely. They sailed to Hong Kong, where they visited Robert's grave. There she laid a wreath with a message attached. "To Robert James Semple—to whom I owe all that I am that is sincere and thoughtful."[6]

They sailed to the Philippines, India, and Egypt. Occasionally, Aimee would disembark to preach at missionary outposts. All the while, Roberta served as her mother's secretary and nurse—responding to correspondence, managing spending, and interacting with reporters, along with making sure her mother was well enough to leave her bed.

When they stopped in Marseille, Aimee decided to seek out Charlie Chaplin, who she had heard was residing in the Hotel Noailles.[7] Aimee knew that the most revered man in Hollywood had covertly attended services at Angelus Temple and was said to be an admirer of her stagecraft. She went to his hotel and knocked on the door, where she was met by Chaplin's butler, who went by the name Kono. He was stunned to see the infamous evangelist standing before him. Still, he asked if she had an appointment. Aimee insisted; she'd long wanted to meet Chaplin . . . so perhaps this was the appointed time? Kono told her Chaplin was out and could be gone for a while. Aimee insisted she would wait. She sat down to tea with the butler, who later wrote that he found her bewitching and deeply lonely.

When Chaplin arrived and saw Aimee sitting in his suite, he made it clear that he was angry at Kono for letting the evangelist in. Kono wrote a detailed account of the evening in a later memoir. Chaplin thought of Aimee as a "devil-pelter," someone who had "got a white nightie and started a new religion." Still, he invited her to join him for dinner. Chaplin began to tease Aimee about religion. He asked her what she thought the mental age of her audience might be. She retorted by asking him what the mental age of his film audiences might be. "I've been to your Temple to hear you," he said, "and half your success is due to your magnetic appeal, half due to the props and lights. Oh, yes, whether you like it or not, you're an actress." Instead of reacting, Aimee listened, perhaps delighting in the repartee after years of being surrounded by slavish devotees. Chaplin kept going. "Religion—Orthodox religion—is based on fear," he said. "Fear of doing something on earth which will keep them out of heaven. My God, they miss out on all the glorious freedom of life in order to reach a mythical heaven where they can walk on golden streets and play a harp—a bait of pure boredom if you ask me."

Aimee refused to debate Chaplin, although he goaded her on the validity of faith, the truth about Jesus or God, and even the sincerity of her work. "Our worlds are different," she told him wearily. "Vastly different." Instead of arguing about religion, Aimee redirected the conversation to their shared profession of entertainment. They talked about the stage at Angelus Temple, about the plays Aimee put together. They conversed for hours. When they said good night, they made plans to see each other the next day. Chaplin turned in for the night in high spirits. The evangelist seemed to have briefly jostled him out of a depression that, by his own account, had plagued him for years. That week, the two had dinner every night.[8]

The encounter was a brief bright spot for Aimee, when she could feel the thrill of her achievements and connect with a like-minded person, far away from the restrictions of the Temple. There were rumors that Aimee let loose on these trips abroad: in 1930 a Panama cabaret sent an announcement to the Temple that they were naming their latest drink the "hallelujah cocktail," honoring Aimee and her recent visit. Even though she and Aimee weren't speaking, the cocktail was a serious enough allegation that Minnie gave a quote to the press, saying she was tired of Aimee being picked on. "If she did visit the place, I'm sure no harm was done and it's nobody's business."[9]

When Aimee returned to Los Angeles in May 1931, it had been almost a year since she'd preached in her own church. She was welcomed by the usual crowds, speeches from local officials, and headlines. The service at the Temple had all the requisite floral offerings and music. But the city of Los Angeles had become a dramatically different place in the years since the stock market crash. Thousands of businesses had failed, hundreds of thousands had lost their jobs, and poverty had become a way of life for many. Refugees from the "Dust Bowl" flooded the city, looking for food and work. "Hoovervilles," encampments of the unemployed, now filled large stretches of city streets.

Aimee returned to preaching, intermittently, but while she had physically recovered, her feelings of alienation and isolation only intensified. "Few people know as I did what it is to be lonely in a crowd—to feel deserted in the midst of the multitudes," Aimee wrote of that time.[10] Roberta's new husband had been offered an administrative job at the Temple, but he'd refused. Instead, the young couple had moved into an apartment on Wilshire Boulevard, far from the emotional entanglements of Echo Park. Roberta continued to work for her mother, but she and her husband fought about how large of a role the church should play in their lives.

Rolf dutifully adhered to Aimee's wishes. He graduated from the L.I.F.E. Bible College and promptly went to work as a junior administrator in the Temple. When his mother was well enough, Rolf would carry Aimee from the parsonage through to the back entrance of the Temple, holding her in his arms like an infant. She would stand at the pulpit and preach for an hour. By the end of her sermon, her clothes would be soaked in sweat. When she finished, Rolf would pick her up in front of the congregation and carry her back to her kitchen, where the maid would prepare a large ice cream sundae for her. Mostly, she preferred to be alone, but for an exotic pet spider monkey who lived in a cage on her balcony. Aimee would sit there with the monkey, eating ice cream as quickly as possible, trying to cool down and satiate herself before her next sermon.

Her estrangement from Minnie had fissured her sense of connection to the world around her. Aimee wrote that she was alone for the first time in her life. She channeled her loneliness into her work. Over the decades, she had learned that the place for her emotions and her pain was in storytelling. With a burst of energy and improved health, she decided in the spring of 1931 to put on a series of major theatrical shows at the Temple. The pinnacle of her dramatic work was *The Iron Furnace*, an epic "sacred opera" that she had begun to write during her European cruise. It would tell the story of Moses and his exodus from Egypt to Israel, with an enormous cast of four hundred, intricate scenery that included Egyptian temples, and ornate costumes. She even had a bona fide star: David Hutton, a six-foot, three-hundred-pound baritone, would play the pharaoh. Hutton had all the swagger of a minor celebrity in the small world of evangelical theater—he had worked as a song director, a choir leader, and a soloist.

That summer, her energy levels fully restored, Aimee threw herself into staging her show. The band, orchestra, and organist worked together with a choir of 250 people to create a stereophonic effect. The "mammoth production" consumed her with its elaborate costuming and the latest in lighting technology. But amid the flurry of preparation, a series of events with her family destabilized her. In June, Roberta—who had remained close to her grandmother—told Aimee that Minnie had married a man in Las Vegas. Then, just weeks later, Rolf married a sweet-faced twenty-year-old woman named Lorna Dee Smith. The couple had fallen in love while attending Aimee's Bible College together.[11] In less than a year's time, Aimee had irrevocably split with her mother and then watched as both of her children fell in love and found life partners. "I am really not losing Rolf, you see," she told a reporter from the *Los Angeles Times*. "But I have that mother feeling—that sense of loss, to a certain degree of course."[12]

It was telling that all that love registered as loss for Aimee. She had spent the past fifteen years as the center of the show, and she felt abandoned. When asked by reporters if she was happy for all the nuptials in the family, she described watching "sweethearts" leave her services, while she went home alone each night. "I have been lonely, lonely," she said mournfully. She also seemed to want to remain in the spotlight—she didn't comment on her children's happiness or their new spouses, but rather on her own feelings. "At the end of each day," she later wrote. "After every wonderful service, our dear people and my children would go to their homes arm in arm, with their tender words and little caresses, while I would sit in silence, watching the last light extinguished in the big auditorium and the last happy couple disappear in the darkness."[13] Aimee felt alone in the Temple she had built.

The Iron Furnace debuted at the end of August, and it was a "gorgeous success" for Aimee. "Throngs sat spell-bound," reported the *Foursquare Crusader*. Ancient Egypt was alive inside the Temple—pyramids, camels, palm trees, and statuary. The press compared her to the actress Sarah Bernhardt, and the production was celebrated as a new milestone in Aimee's career, a new epoch in the spread of the gospel. Aimee's suffering and anxieties were assuaged by the wash of new success.

On September 12, 1931, a group of journalists were at the parsonage after Aimee's evening sermon, drinking coffee and telling jokes. Rolf was living there with his mother and his new wife. Hutton, the pharaoh, was also in attendance, basking in the glow of his stardom. According to an account given by Rolf, a journalist suggested that Aimee elope with Hutton. He even offered to supply a plane to Arizona, a state that allowed quickie marriages. Aimee and Hutton quickly agreed.

According to Aimee, she had fallen for the baritone months earlier. "At first glance I knew instinctively that I was going to like him. He sang marvelously and was so enthusiastic about the forthcoming production," she wrote. "Love was rapidly coming to the surface, and my poor lonely heart was throbbing as it did in years gone by and the soul of me was glad."

She said that Hutton had already asked her to marry him before that wild night in September. "Like a great river, rushing toward a waterfall, our love ripened," Aimee recalled. "It was not the girlish elemental emotion of youth; but rather the reawakening of a mature tired heart."[14] Aimee was forty years old.

Regardless, the madcap romance was allegedly set in motion by the reporter's suggestion, and at three o'clock that morning Aimee and Hutton flew to Yuma, Arizona, where they were married on the tarmac. Aimee wore a powder-blue three-piece suit, trimmed in blue fox fur. A light rain fell. After exchanging vows, they kissed, with newspaper reporters standing so close they transcribed events as if it were theater: "Two large glistening tears rolled down Aimee's pale cheeks." Aimee, weeping a little, said brightly, "Everything is just going to work out all right now."[15] The new couple then boarded the plane and flew home, where Aimee gave the regular morning sermon at eleven o'clock. That afternoon, they announced their marriage to the papers.

Aimee's long-held beliefs—which she preached often—were that a divorced woman could not remarry until her former spouse was dead. But she attempted to overcome her hypocrisy by making her marriage just one more publicity stunt. The idea, it seems, was to make her followers feel so involved in the emotional intimacy of her life that they would be less inclined to judge it as sinful. In Los Angeles that evening, the couple threw a wedding dinner attended largely by the press. Aimee lied about her age to reporters that night, saying she was thirty-eight to Hutton's twenty-nine, even though her true age—days from her forty-first birthday—was already very much a matter of public record. The *Los Angeles Times* was genial in their coverage, writing that she looked even younger as she "went up in the clouds and came down with a third husband."[16] They ran a photo of the newlyweds, Aimee looking petite and exuberant next to the large-boned, gap-toothed Hutton. The wedding gave an opportunity to reintroduce readers of the 1930s to Aimee, and this time they presented her as a pioneer whose career had been "marked frequently by conquests of disconcerting obstacles." But if Aimee had hopes of a fresh start in the public eye, it was short-lived.

During the press dinner, a reporter mentioned offhandedly to Aimee that Hutton had previously been married. Aimee dismissed the idea, and that night she and Hutton appeared onstage together, singing a duet inspired by the Old Testament entitled "Ruth and the

Gleaning," a not-so-subtle nod to biblical precedent for a second-marriage love story. The next morning, they allowed photographers into their parsonage bedroom, where Aimee was photographed spooning cake into the mouth of Hutton, who wore a silky Asian robe and slippers. Aimee, wearing a ruffled white peignoir, conducted her radio program from their honeymoon chamber. The romance felt like the concoction of a Hollywood studio press agent—reminiscent of the arranged marriages between stars to keep audiences coming back for more. But Aimee seemed to genuinely delight in it all.

Less than forty-eight hours after she said "I do," the newspapers reported that Hutton was already engaged to a masseuse named Myrtle Joan St. Pierre and that she was suing the newlyweds. Reporters were invited to be an audience at the parsonage that week as David Hutton received a manicure, presenting a calm face as a process server arrived at the front door and handed him the papers.[17] Aimee looked on as Hutton read the breach-of-promise suit that asked for $200,000. St. Pierre claimed she'd given Hutton a relaxation treatment and they'd fallen in love. "To consider settlement with this woman," Aimee told the newspapers, "would be to encourage every little girl with whom Mr. Hutton has eaten ice cream or treated to a soda pop to file similar suits. She's barking up the wrong tree."[18]

She and Hutton hammed it up together for reporters as he accompanied her to several revivals around the country, laughing about the lawsuits and flirting openly with each other. Aimee seemed to have a bit of routine, slinging the same one-liners about girls getting ice cream with Hutton and then suing for two dollars, joking that maybe the reporters were going to sue too because their hearts were broken by Hutton as well. Still, Aimee later said these were "dark days" for her, and even as she presented a brave face to the press, her mental reserves were drained. She described the humiliation of having to hear the details of the lawsuit against David, stories that included champagne, massages, knee kisses, and "love making."[19]

Despite the drama, Aimee seemed intent on making the marriage work. She repainted the two-story sign alongside her commissary so that it read "Aimee McPherson Hutton," and her name in the papers was printed as such. By the end of the year, Hutton's parents had been added to her payroll, helping to manage the busy soup kitchen. Aimee told Hutton he would be the business manager of the Temple. The choice of that role for him was bizarre and ominous. Once the position from which Minnie had ruled Angelus Temple, it was a role that Aimee continued to fill with men who betrayed her, swindled her, and then sued her for breach of contract.

Aimee wanted badly to be refashioned as a wife, as a woman in love. Alma Whitaker, the female correspondent from the *Los Angeles Times* who had profiled Aimee when she was on the rise nearly a decade before, ran into her at a dinner party in January 1932. Initially, she reported, she did not recognize the ethereal blond woman with bright blue eyes who dressed in a ruffled, full-skirted, ultra-feminine "colonial style" gown, with a bright red sash. Once she realized it was *that* Mrs. Hutton, Whitaker had a sense that the evangelist had lost her old spirit as she watched the woman stroke her husband's arm mutely like a "sweet miss proud in her new-found love." But at the dinner table, when the subject turned to unemployment relief, the old Aimee came to life. Whitaker described how suddenly Aimee spoke up, urgently, with great confidence and animation about a project she was organizing to feed the city's hungry. "She was at once the practical Aimee we all know."[20]

As much as Aimee longed to be remade in love, she soon returned to the erratic highs and lows of behavior that had marked the years since Minnie's departure. She found frequent excuses—usually health related—to leave Los Angeles and the demands of Angelus Temple. She spent time in a hospital in Paris and on a cruise to Havana, and later contracted typhoid in Guatemala. When Aimee was away, the staff complained to the press that Hutton had invited a male dancer to come live with him in the parsonage, although ostensibly as a secretary. A growing number of administrative heads of Angelus Temple complained about Hutton's theatrical behavior and bossiness, and he was soon demoted by the board to musical director.

The following year, in the summer of 1932, when the masseuse's "heart balm" suit against Hutton went to trial, it was a source of constant headline fodder, with details of the ways that Hutton liked to be massaged and his fetishes for undergarments. It was another blow to Aimee's reputation—once again, she was associated with something sordid—and soon thirty-two Iowa and Minnesota Foursquare churches decided to leave the organization. Aimee's behavior—or at least her husband's—they declared, was unbecoming of a Christian woman.

She was hiding out in her castle in Lake Elsinore when Hutton arrived in the Temple limousine with the news that he had been found liable in the masseuse's lawsuit. On hearing this, Aimee fainted, falling over a balcony balustrade and onto a concrete porch below, fracturing her skull and hemorrhaging blood from her ears and nose. She spent several weeks in the hospital. Newspapers reported she was, once again, near death. "My body was weak and my spirit was crushed," she wrote. "And yet they talk of humiliation! The fall months went by rapidly and I was getting worse. These were dark days indeed."[21]

By the end of 1932, she announced that her poor health would not allow her to continue her preaching schedule. She hired an assistant, Giles Knight, who initially worked as an administrator and bookkeeper. Aimee also began to rely heavily on a rotating crew of visiting pastors to cover for her. Chief among these was a rising evangelistic star named Rheba Crawford. Crawford had come from the Salvation Army in New York, where she had gained fame as the "Angel of Broadway," standing outside the theaters and shouting her sermons. (She was said to be the basis for the Salvation Army preacher made famous in *Guys & Dolls*.)

Crawford had first glimpsed Aimee in 1917 as the young evangelist was hammering the stakes of her tent into the ground in Florida. Crawford had made a donation to the struggling Aimee and had remained an admirer. Aimee and Crawford shared a common language through their background with the Salvation Army, and its emphasis on good works. They had their differences—Crawford had worked for the state of California and was outspokenly liberal on political issues. Crawford had even been accused of Communism, which deeply bothered Aimee. Still, they posed for photographs, and as Aimee traveled more, Rheba held down the hometown congregation with energy and flair. But Aimee had become more suspicious of those around her, and the contract with Crawford stipulated that she could preach only when Aimee was out of town.

Aimee seemed to be caught in a cycle of attempts to escape her public life and recover her health. There is little record of her thinking during this time, except a sense that she was run-down and feeling unlucky. It was later revealed that in 1933 she had signed over her power of attorney to her lawyer, bypassing her children. Again, she set sail. She cruised to Cairo, Jerusalem, Athens, Rome, Milan, Germany, and Paris, where she had emergency surgery for vague, never-defined intestinal issues. Hutton filed for divorce, citing mental cruelty. The newspapers quoted Aimee and "Dave," trading barbs and accusations at one another. He was soon booked as a vaudeville act at the Palace Theatre in New York as "Big Boy, the Baritone of Angelus Temple." Photographs show him smiling jazzily as he played a ukulele.

After six months away, Aimee returned to the States and undertook a tour of the country, speaking at revival services in small and midsize cities. Then she received a call from someone at the William Morris Agency. They offered the evangelist the opportunity to appear at the Capitol Theatre, on Broadway, and do her own extended act in a vaudeville show. Aimee justified it as a new way to get the gospel out. "Why not," Aimee said, according to her daughter. "We'll make money for the Lord and if I sign a contract I'm going to preach a sermon."[22]

Aimee was one of several acts, coming last on the ticket, following "two acrobats and a midget." She wore a floor-length white gown, her hair bleached blond. She told, as she always did, the story of her life, with knowing jokes for the New York audience, making fun of her public image. "I didn't even know how to take up a collection," she said in describing her first years as an evangelist. "But believe me, I've learned since." Aimee made headlines as usual and was given generous praise. *The Wall Street Journal* wrote, "Mrs. McPherson drew scant applause at her entrance . . . but she came close to being a wow 'ere she subsided . . . Hardly a soul walked out on her . . . Mrs. McPherson is a swell show. Perhaps the theater is her true forte."[23] But the novelty quickly ran out, and the producers shuttered the show within the first weeks. Aimee collected her guaranteed retainer of seventeen thousand dollars. She presented it back home as a success—all that money plus free publicity.

She kept going, keeping a breakneck schedule of appearances. By the end of 1933, she had preached in forty-six cities in twenty-one states, giving 332 sermons to more than 1.5 million people in the span of six months, according to Foursquare Church records.[24] Aimee agreed with her critics: she was "God's Best Publicity Agent." If crass commercialism was what it took to get her gospel out there, she was more than willing to do it.

But Aimee resisted easy categorizations by those who wanted to dismiss her as a fame-hungry huckster. As much as she sought publicity, she also channeled her energies into systematic efforts to help the poor. As the economic realities of the Depression began to touch greater numbers in Los Angeles, she badgered the Yellow Cab Company into lending her a 24,000-square-foot warehouse downtown. As soon as the warehouse opened, as a commissary, workers were giving away 2,100 meals a day.

In 1933, the Angelus Temple commissary was in full swing and expanding rapidly. It contained a dispensary, a laundry, an employment office, medical and dental care, a nursery school, and even-greater efforts for the hungry. There were rooms devoted to sewing and food storage, along with a large dining hall. Aimee hectored everyone to help, from society matrons to her poorest parishioners. The organization became the epicenter of service for Los Angeles in the hard years after the Depression, and the LA fire, police, and county sheriff's departments all donated to her efforts—a sign of how central the Temple had become for the city. Amid the Depression, Aimee estimated that the organization fed more than 1.5 million Angelenos.

Her social outreach brought new members into the congregation. While many churches contracted during the Depression, Pentecostal and Holiness churches in California grew. They were able to draw in the thousands of migrants from the prairies who had come to California to escape poverty and the drought and did not feel comfortable in the established, upper-middle-class Protestant churches. It went beyond economics: in 1933, as Hitler expanded power in Europe and opened concentration camps, Aimee and other Pentecostal leaders translated these ominous headlines into modern-day prophecy. Fascists and Communists in Europe were evidence of the Antichrist to Aimee. She explained her engagement with the world to a reporter: "Just as the mariner uses his compass and the gyroscope to determine his position at sea . . . so the 'Christian mariner' may use his prophetic instruments to determine the outlook of the world in relation to coming events."[25]

Aimee kept up a vigorous schedule, and by the end of 1934, Angelus Temple boasted that she had preached to more than two million people over the past year—one out of every fifty Americans had come to see her preach, and with her radio audience, her reach was even larger.

Aimee was a lightning rod at a time when the nation was struggling under crushing financial strain. For all her good works, Aimee couldn't keep the lawsuits and her health issues at bay. She tried to reduce her debts and focus on her work, but the troubles began to feel insurmountable. She was prolific in these years, writing hundreds of sermons, plays, and theater productions, all printed in one of the Temple's numerous publications. A few years later, in 1941, Aimee wrote a sacred opera, complete with script and songs, to be produced at the Temple, called *The Rich Man and Lazarus*. One song in particular seemed to reveal her sense of isolation and failure:

Do you live in a castle of broken dreams,
Where Giant despair and his dark horde teems?
Are thy fabrics of life torn and tattered;
Are your spirits now broken and battered;
Are your strongholds of love rudely shattered
In the castle of broken dreams?[26]

In her mid-forties, Aimee ran one of the largest and most successful churches in the country. She had traveled the world and ministered to millions; she had achieved so much at a time when a woman was allowed to achieve so little. And yet she felt broken. In those years, she wrote in a slender posthumously published memoir of her sadness and a sense of despair. The funhouse mirror of fame had been harsh to Aimee—she often did not recognize the woman described in the press, the absurd figure who had become a punch line. But her life was not over yet. "I must carry on," she wrote. " I am carrying on."[27]

33

"WOE UNTO THE ONE WHO BREAKS THE LINK"

Aimee and Minnie had built a religious institution over the course of fifteen years that defied all expectations. Together, these "two little women" had ignored the restrictions of their gender and their class, harnessed Aimee's incredible charisma, and manifested their divine ambition. The result was one of the largest and most influential religious movements the United States had seen in decades. But their internecine fighting and the subsequent years of financial mismanagement, coupled with the crush of the Depression, compounded the Temple's debt issues. All that had been built teetered on the edge of collapse.

In 1936, a brief story ran in the *Los Angeles Times* about discord at the Temple. There was a passing mention of a new name: Giles Knight.

Knight had been recently promoted, following the ouster of Harriet Jordan, a longtime associate pastor and board member. In the coming months, Knight would be called Aimee's secretary, lawyer, accountant, and business manager. But the truth was much more extreme.

Knight, an ambitious midwestern pastor with an accounting background, had lived and preached throughout Southern California's Inland Empire with his wife for years. But once he became Aimee's business manager he began to manage every aspect of her life. Over the course of the coming year, Aimee would cede more and more control to Knight, including over all her assets, which included Angelus Temple. Knight worked with a small team of lawyers and administrators to rein in the spending at the Temple. He put the payroll on a cash basis and dramatically reduced salaries. Though the full legal details of the agreement were never reported in the press, nor made public, the arrangement resembled that of a guardianship—the predecessor to California's present-day conservatorship system—in which Knight was given ultimate control over Aimee's finances and daily affairs.

She gave Knight total legal and financial authority over Angelus Temple and the Echo Park Evangelistic Association, which held all the institution's assets and property. Knight would end up exerting his dominion over the smallest details of Aimee's life, including who she spent time with. By the late 1930s, Aimee would need to check with him before socializing with Temple office staff. "Complaints as to one-man rule at the temple are ridiculous,"[1] Rolf told the *Los Angeles Times* in the fall of 1936 in response to questions about the specifics of Knight's role. But the denial only served as confirmation.

Still, even Knight's iron rule didn't seem to contain the damage that fractured every aspect of Aimee's life. In the spring of 1937, Aimee walked once again into a Los Angeles courthouse. In the previous fourteen years, she had been sued forty-five times. The charges and the damages against her ranged widely—broken motion picture contracts from her unrealized cinema dreams, unpaid legal bills, liability for when her car had struck and injured a child, and real estate deals gone awry. Over and over, people who had been close to Aimee, who had worked with her on her latest endeavors, had become enemies.

But this time, it was her daughter—one of only a few people in her life who had given her unconditional love and support. When Aimee had given Giles Knight power over her estate, Roberta, who was still working at the Temple at the time, had fought the move. Roberta had sent Knight a letter threatening legal action. A legal back-and-forth ensued, with Knight ultimately ignoring Roberta's concerns and cementing his control. He fired the guest pastor Rheba Crawford and accused Roberta of working with others to take over the Temple.

Roberta was suing one of Aimee's lawyers, Willedd Andrews, for slander, after he implied that she was blackmailing her mother. Roberta sought $150,000 in damages, alleging that Andrews had made a statement disparaging her. Andrews had pushed back, saying Roberta had been part of a larger conspiracy within the Temple to take control away from Aimee. (Crawford was also suing Aimee, for slander, asking for more than a million dollars.)

Aimee made a bizarre decision that would change the course of her life—she sided with her lawyer, and with Knight, against Roberta. Her lawyer gave a revealing statement to the press: "While she regrets the war will be sanguinary—with her own child—the only course ahead of her is protection of the organization which has consumed the best years of her life."[2] She turned away from her cherished daughter, who she had prophesied would be her legacy. Instead, she chose the institution of Angelus Temple—and the men she thought could save it. Minnie put a public statement out that she would support her granddaughter during the lawsuit. "Aimee has done the same thing to Roberta that she did to me ten years ago. Ever since she left home at the age of seventeen, she has never been able to hold anyone close to her,"[3] Minnie told the papers.

Roberta was incensed. What should have been a small act on the larger stage of Temple politics—something easily resolved—had become a tragic rift that was once again playing out in daily headlines.

The fact that Aimee chose to testify against her daughter on behalf of her lawyer and publicly air such a private family feud is evidence of how much she had ceded control—both financial and emotional—to Knight, her lawyers, and the new hard-line administration. In advance of the trial, Roberta had issued a statement to the press:

> When I was a very small child, I was told that I must prepare myself for membership on the board of directors of the Echo Park Evangelistic Association. I devoted my girlhood to the church and was elected by the board . . . Now my mother has seen fit to oust me from my lifework. I didn't believe she would allow herself to be so unfair.[4]

Roberta entered the courtroom with her grandmother at her side. Aimee—dressed flamboyantly in a sharkskin suit and a turban—hadn't seen Minnie in seven years. The three women exchanged awkward smiles but said nothing. Minnie had told the newspapers that she kept her own archive of material from Aimee's kidnapping episode under her bed—a veiled threat. On the second day in court, she made a show of bringing a huge box of these materials to Roberta's lawyers. In the hallway outside, the two women had an argument in front of reporters. "Well Aimee, this is some different than your kidnap case ten years ago," Minnie shouted within earshot of the *Los Angeles Times*. "Then I was nailed to the cross for you. Now you're doing your best to crucify Roberta."

"No I'm not!" Aimee screamed.[5] It was a slow-motion train wreck, a matriarchy imploding in front of a public audience.

As Aimee gave her testimony over three days, she delved into all that had gone wrong since Minnie had left. She spoke of jealous guest pastors, debts, threats, warring lawyers, contract disputes, and more. She described being bullied and harassed by Roberta's lawyer, by Rheba Crawford and the other employees who had wanted legal contracts for work. She alleged that in April 1936 she had been throttled and struck by Roberta's lawyer and that he had not allowed her to leave the hotel room where Roberta and Rheba were negotiating their contracts. The lawyer, she said, kept her awake for more than twenty-four hours. Aimee's testimony was described as meandering, and she made a show of her thirst—she downed two pitchers of water one morning on the stand. The thin, fashionable, broken-down woman was a stark contrast to the vigorous figure who had dominated the same courthouse a decade earlier.

Testimony during the trial gave a window into the internecine conflicts—mixed with some amount of Aimee's paranoia—that by this point defined the inner workings of the Temple. The Associated Press reported Roberta's testimony, recounting that her mother had told her in 1936 of a "plot to take the Temple away from her." The story quoted Roberta saying, "Mother said that Andrews told her every time Miss Fricke, the organist, played a certain piece, it was a signal for a secret meeting at the home of Dean Harriet Jordan," the longtime associate pastor. Roberta continued: "She said Andrews told her that Rheba Crawford had formed a secret society among the girls to help drive Mother out, and that the pass-phrase of this Temple group was, '*Woe unto the one who breaks the link.*'"[6]

After finishing her testimony, Aimee crossed the room and bowed down, nearly to her knees, in front of her daughter, grabbing her hand. The words they exchanged are not known, but a photographer from the *Los Angeles Times* captured the image. All that can be seen of Aimee's face, which is largely shielded by her hat, is the sharp line of her right cheekbone. But Roberta's face is in full view, and her expression is devastating. Although twenty-seven years old, Roberta has the look of a child—one who both fears and pities the gaunt, stylish creature who clutches her hand so tightly. Aimee was escorted out, supported by Giles Knight on one side and Rolf on the other.

On April 23, 1937, the Superior Court judge Clarence L. Kincaid announced he had come to a judgment in the case. Before he could issue it, however, Aimee broke down and was led outside, sobbing. Kincaid ruled in Roberta's favor but awarded her much less than she asked for: one thousand dollars for Andrews's initial statement accusing her of threatening, intimidating, coercing, and blackmailing Aimee and another thousand dollars for his repeating that statement to reporters.

By then, the press had tired of the lawsuits and the allegations that emerged with near-constant regularity. While the newspapers had once luxuriated in Aimee's dramas, this one felt too sad for anyone to bear. "The first time it was a sensation. The second it was still good. But now it is like the ninth life of a cat, about worn out,"[7] the *Times* opined after Roberta's lawsuit.

Aimee, in her very brief writing of that time, glossed over the pain caused by the lawsuit, writing that the divide "prostrated me physically for a time." She was heartbroken to lose Roberta, she wrote. "Roberta had withdrawn. In the past she had occasionally told me, 'Mother I don't want to work like you work. I have seen you come home wringing wet with perspiration from your meetings. I never want to have to do that.' And who is to say she should?"[8]

Aimee retreated from the world. In a deposition that year, Rheba Crawford described her former boss as afraid and defeated. "I tell you, she is the most tragic figure in America, living in mortal fear that the glories of her past will be taken away from her."[9] By the time Aimee turned forty-seven years old, Knight had total control of her life, and he used it. Described as stern and paternalistic, he effectively placed Aimee under house arrest. She sold her Lake Elsinore estate and moved into a modest Spanish-style home in Silver Lake—next door to Knight and his family. She was not allowed to see anyone without his approval, and she was not allowed to leave her house without his permission—apart from preaching or teaching classes at her L.I.F.E. Bible College. There was a short list of people allowed to see her, which included a team of nurses, Knight's family, Rolf, and few others. Roberta was not on the list, nor Minnie. Those who broke the rules were subject to Knight's temper, which had become legendary within the Temple.

Aimee's existence became very small, her schedule one of focused routine. Fewer details are known of those years, in part because she dropped out of the news. Aimee had spent her entire professional life, two decades, publishing thousands of pages that shared the intimate details of her life, her spirit. In between preaching the gospel, she spoke openly of her mental breakdowns, of her heartaches, of her family dramas, and even of her own tortured medical history. But in the final years of her life, she went quiet. There are rumors that the Los Angeles press agreed on a blackout after the trial with Roberta. A few notices show up in the papers of birthday celebrations for Aimee—always held at Knight's home. She preached on a regular schedule and published a few pages in her church publication on the power of prayer and her increasing concern about the wars in Europe.

"Dr. Knight was very much in charge then," recalled a former research secretary for the Temple. "Sister was never allowed or permitted to go down among the students or mingle. She would have liked to have done that but he restrained her. She would just walk up, teach, and then leave. She would definitely mingle with people at the altar though. Nobody could restrain her from doing that."[10]

She continued to have health issues, but under Knight's control, she avoided the dramatic breakdowns of the past. When she left home, she was accompanied by a group of women that the church called "Sister's Guards," a half dozen or so attendants who would escort her from her car into the auditorium. [11] When she wasn't onstage at the Temple, she avoided the public eye, and most social gatherings. She spent most of her time alone, or with a hired nurse. There is evidence that she was on a significant regimen of prescription drugs. She preached three days a week, for which she drew a salary of $180 a month, equivalent to about $3,800 today. This was a major pay cut from her prime years, when she was in control and taking the first Sunday collection for herself, what had often amounted to thousands of dollars. Knight was focused on paying off the church debts, even issuing a special collection card that asked attendees to join the "Old Debt Club" and "go give instead of go get." Knight extended the offering section of the services to forty-five minutes—dragging it on in the hopes of raising as much money as possible. On the last day of 1938, Aimee climbed atop the dome of Angelus Temple in a ruffly white dress, holding Knight's hand, and burned a pile of old debt papers, celebrating their solvency.

Aimee traveled rarely, and then mostly to Foursquare organizations, for conventions and church dedications. As she had fallen out with the women in her life, Rolf had become the last family member standing in Aimee's inner circle. Rolf, who worked as an assistant pastor in the church, was his mother's dedicated servant and her only remaining hope for a legacy.

When America joined the war, Aimee threw herself into the cause. She used her platform to sell war bonds, taught first-aid classes, and welcomed servicemen into the Temple. She promoted fuel rationing. With bomb threats to the West Coast, the windows of the Temple were covered, and the magnificent white dome was painted black. Aimee offered the Temple up as an air raid shelter.

Aimee did not keep a diary during this time; nor is there much correspondence to reflect her state of mind. Her sermons show a turning inward, a focus on teaching and preparing the next generation of ministers to spread the gospel. Of Knight, she said little. She wrote in her posthumously published memoir that while she appreciated his efforts to balance the books, muzzle the press, and slow the onslaught of lawsuits, she "chafed at the restrictions he insisted on putting on my activities" and "longed for closer contact with my people."[12]

At the beginning of 1944, Aimee tried to reassert control of her life. In early January, she stood on the Temple platform and announced that she would be returning to preaching four nights a week. Giles Knight walked up to the microphone after her and said Aimee would be preaching only on Sunday nights. She walked up to the microphone again and said no, she would do four. In a letter on January 12, she wrote to Knight that she was putting into writing for him her "deep desire for a closer spiritual tie between the Angelus Temple and myself." She enumerated a few small ways she would like to start to meet again with congregants, faculty, new members, and children at the Temple. "I would be able to enter their office, shake hands and talk with them a moment and then have a prayer with each group," she wrote. "Many I have not met personally for years and some have been employed since I have made any rounds—this lack, of course, was because of my limited strength and time." Her tone was pleading, almost supplicating, as she signed off that she was "hoping that this may meet with your pleasure."[13] The next time Knight appeared on the stage, a few weeks later, it was to announce his resignation. There is no record of what finally happened between them.[14]

Aimee had a new prophecy for the future, and it enlivened her: that spring she submitted an application to the FCC for a broadcasting license and bought "hilltop acreage" to build the first Christian television station. She had a vision of what this new medium could do to spread her message even further. She dreamed of pioneering this technology for people of faith just as she had with her groundbreaking radio program, twenty years earlier. The medium would make her illustrated sermons come to life in the homes of millions. It was a futuristic vision of a radical new idea: she would become a television evangelist.

In February 1944, Aimee invited reporters to her home in Silver Lake and introduced them all to the new vice president of the church: Rolf McPherson. The VP was the second most powerful role in the organization after Aimee, and he would have control over every department.

Aimee was ebullient, and when the reporters asked after her health, she was effusive. "I feel magnificent—good for the next fifty years!"

She teased the reporters, playfully suggesting that they wouldn't print the story on her return. "Aimee good—that's no news, but Aimee bad, oh boy!"[15]

Aimee's desires remained the same. "As a woman I would wish that I might have a happy Christian home, a devoted husband and family," she once said. "As an evangelist, I would wish that I might have a pulpit and a public address system mighty enough to reach every person in the whole world with the message that God so loved the world."[16] She wanted to be heard, and she wanted to be loved. Was that so much to ask?

That spring in the now-monthly *Foursquare Crusader*, Aimee posted a celebratory ad proclaiming that "Happy Days Are Here Again!" accompanied by a photograph of her—gaunt but in full makeup—and Rolf, smiling together over the text. "Sound Spiritual Leadership!" the announcement read. "This is now assured for Angelus Temple and the International Church of the Foursquare Gospel as AIMEE SEMPLE MCPHERSON and son, ROLF K. MCPHERSON, assume full control and responsibility of all the far-flung world-wide activities of this great organization."[17]

Aimee went to work, preaching again every Sunday for three months straight. The grand return was scheduled for a revival in Oakland on September 26. She was opening a new Foursquare church there, and the press called it a "magic carpet" crusade—because of her perceived ability to transform the everyday into magic. She flew into the city with her entourage, which included Rolf, her nurse, a group of musicians, and a press agent. She was chauffeured to a parade, where she drove through the streets in a horse and buggy. She beamed out at the crowd, a queen among her people, the embodiment of the enduring power of old-time religion. The unrestricted adoration of the crowds must have felt like a homecoming for a woman who had once lived for that feeling.

That night, she preached to an audience of ten thousand. Her energy was intense, her excitement kinetic. She was soaring from the freshness of it all, the return to the crowd, hyperstimulated, full of ideas and hopes for the future. She told the audience that the next night, she would return to give them her most famous and beloved sermon, "The Story of My Life."

Aimee dreamed of a comeback. When she'd been lost in the wilderness of fame, scandal, illness, and familial disputes, Aimee always returned to her story. She had new pages for another memoir not yet published. When she'd been blinded and confused by accusations and character assaults, she had found solace in her sense of herself and Jesus. That was the ultimate truth when everything else fell apart. Her ability to narrate her life was her greatest tool, a pathway for others to connect with a higher power in a revolutionary way: simply, intimately, personally. With love.

After the Oakland event finished, she returned late that evening to the Leamington, an opulent twelve-story hotel downtown. She chatted about the night with Rolf, her energy high. Inside her dark hotel room—a mandatory wartime blackout was in effect—she tried to unwind from the show. She stood at her window, watching the planes flying in and out of the airport. "I wonder, when we die, if we will be riding around in airplanes," she said to Rolf. She was in a funny sort of mood—contemplative and giddy. "Keyed up,"[18] as Rolf described her later, but still very much herself. She tried to get him to stay up with her, but it grew late, and finally he kissed his mother good night and went to his room, leaving her alone.

"Actually, I feel that I have done so very little," Aimee wrote in her last memoir. "Though I have preached around the world and seen thousands of people saved. I feel I've done virtually nothing. If I were a man, I could do a lot more."[19]

Aimee was alone. She had lost three husbands; she had lost her mother and then her daughter. At some point, as the hours passed, she took out a bottle from her handbag. She had been prescribed sedatives by her doctor, but the white pills she took on this evening were a "hypnotic sedative," with the name of her doctor, Dr. Wilburn Smith, on the label. According to the autopsy, she took an unknown quantity of pills, leaving the bottle half-full. The next morning, when Rolf came to awaken his mother, he found her unconscious, breathing heavily. Several capsules were strewn on the floor beside her bed. He called for help, and for an hour, efforts were made to revive her. Aimee was pronounced dead at eleven-fifteen in the morning on September 27, 1944.

EPILOGUE

Two weeks after her death, on what would have been Aimee's fifty-fourth birthday, a raucous official memorial service was held at Angelus Temple, attended by ten thousand devotees. Around Echo Park, cars double-parked for a half a mile in every direction. Mourners crammed the sidewalks. Lines formed outside the doors of the Temple at five-thirty in the morning as people waited to catch one last glimpse of Aimee. Over the course of the previous three days, an estimated sixty thousand people had come to see her lying at rest.

Inside the Temple, Aimee's 1,200-pound bronze casket was placed at the center of the stage, enshrined in flowers. The lid, open, revealed Aimee's small figure, clad in a close-fitting satin dress, her body wrapped in her shimmering blue cape. Her lips were bright with red lipstick, her nails matching. On her chest rested a blue shield, made of cloth, emblazoned with a white cross. Her hands clasped a white suede Bible. At the foot of the casket, staffers had placed a telephone—should Aimee need to issue any edicts from the great beyond.

That morning, folks—both famous and ordinary—stood next to

her body as they took to the microphone and testified to Aimee's power, both in their own lives and across the city of Los Angeles. Foursquare leaders later wrote in remembrance that "to watch the long line pass reverently by her casket and see the tears shed by all types of people regardless of class or color helped us all . . . to realize more than ever before the far-reaching influence of her life and ministry."[1] Obituaries in every American paper recounted the sweep of her life—the gender-norm shattering, the drama of her evangelism, the scale of her ambition, the impact of her outreach as well as the tragedy, the romance, the intrigue, and of course the kidnapping. She was heralded as both a pioneer who had brought the underground movement of Pentecostalism to the mainstream and a woman dogged by scandal.

Rolf, not scheduled to speak, finally approached the microphone, his voice breaking as he said his mother was one of the greatest evangelists ever known, and that she would be remembered in the same breath as America's religious forefathers George Whitefield and Jonathan Edwards.

By late afternoon, a motorcade brought Aimee's casket to Forest Lawn Cemetery, where three thousand members of her church swarmed on the grass. Her tomb was placed amid the fellow elite of the city. Even her family, as fractured as it was, tried to honor their Aimee. Minnie attended, her face lined with sorrow. Harold slipped in quietly, head bowed, and sat next to Rolf's family. Roberta missed her plane from New York. There was no mention in the press of the Burbank plots that Aimee had sold fifteen years earlier to her followers. Instead, Aimee's grave sits alone, along a sloping hillside, a long marble memorial that seems suited for a prophetess. Two massive white stone angels flank her grave, kneeling, and a delicate iron chain closes it off from outsiders. Forest Lawn reported the greatest number of flower deliveries since Will Rogers had been buried there, almost a decade earlier.

According to Aimee's will and the board structure of Angelus

Temple, Rolf immediately assumed the presidency and pastorship of the International Church of the Foursquare Gospel, of Angelus Temple, and of the church's 410 branches throughout the world.

Rolf presided for another forty-four years over the church his mother built, a steady and level-headed man who reverentially expanded his mother's vision. By the time he retired, in 1988, the Foursquare Church had 1.2 million members with nineteen thousand churches in sixty-three countries. Before she died, Aimee wrote in her posthumously published memoirs of the rupture with Roberta, whom she had wanted to be her successor. "For my dear little star of hope, my love is unchanged." Of Rolf, she wrote simply that he "was a wonderful comfort and strength."[2] In the end, he was the one who ensured her legacy.

Today, Aimee's organization—now known simply as Foursquare Church—counts 67,500 churches with more than eight million members in 150 countries. Foursquare never stopped growing. Aimee's legacy lives on at Angelus Temple and in Foursquare churches, but it is not a cult of personality. Aimee is presented as an upright religious pioneer, a revolutionary woman of historical importance, of the distant past.

Minnie died three years after her daughter. The Canadian orphan and teen bride had dedicated her newborn to Christian service more than a half century before, and she had succeeded to a degree that was beyond her imaginings. Minnie had given the world an evangelical superstar. But she had lost her daughter—again and again. "I love her," said Minnie in a 1928 interview. "As much as any mother ever loved a child. I have battled to protect her from the world."

Minnie gave two in-depth interviews after she and Aimee parted ways. In both, there is the sense that Minnie saw her daughter as a woman with a shadow self. "There is no one in the world who can equal her," Minnie said. "She is a changed woman when on the platform. She is wholly spiritual, magnetic and beautiful." But Minnie said, seeming to choose her words carefully, "Off the stand she has human traits, the same as others have."[3]

In those interviews, Minnie refused to answer direct questions regarding what she knew about her daughter's alleged kidnapping, acknowledging only that Aimee had changed after Ormiston came into the picture.

Roberta used her settlement money to move to New York a few months after the lawsuit in 1937. She took a job on a radio show, as a researcher on celebrity guests. Divorced from the purser, she married Harry Salter, a music director at NBC, in 1941. Over the years they worked together on early TV shows such as *Name That Tune*. Roberta later said that after the lawsuit, she had written and called her mother for years but never received an answer. Whether it was Knight's decision or Aimee's to cut off contact with her daughter is not recorded in her archive. Roberta had little involvement with Angelus Temple after Aimee's death, although she occasionally did interviews and press appearances with her brother. She did not discuss her own faith but rather emphasized her mother as an icon and a legend. "Though I realize the comparison is flamboyant, I can offer no other. To thousands of her ardent followers in the years to come, Aimee was exactly that—a Joan of Arc, in a gleaming white uniform, leading the armies of the Lord against the minions of sin and destruction," Roberta later said. "She was an inspired leader, a flaming torch lighting the way to heaven."[4]

Aimee's kidnapping scandal was a study in the modern alchemy of faith and celebrity. Almost everyone involved would see their fates upended. Two weeks after the charges were dismissed, Lorraine Wiseman-Sielaff opened a concession at an amusement park in Long Beach, where the sign above her head read "Hoax Woman."[5] She called her show "The Truth about the McPherson Case" and announced she would follow Aimee on her national Vindication Tour and provide a counternarrative to Aimee's from a tent outside wherever Aimee was preaching. But she didn't make good on that promise. A few years later, at the height of the Depression, Lorraine's sister filed a lawsuit against Aimee, claiming the evangelist had defamed her and demanding a million dollars in damages. Aimee settled the case out of court, the news buried in a one-sentence bulletin.

Captain Herman Cline served as the chief of detectives for the Los Angeles Police Department for several more years. In December 1927, he led the investigation of the sensational kidnapping of Marion Parker, the twelve-year-old daughter of a bank teller; the girl's body was recovered dismembered and disemboweled. After helping solve the case, Cline had had enough of Los Angeles noir and he retired, starting a farm in Van Nuys in 1931. He died six years later from a heart attack.

Joseph Ryan quit the district attorney's office within a year of Asa Keyes's dropping the charges against Aimee. He wrote a bitter resignation note suggesting that Keyes was corrupt, saying, "I was not cognizant of the conditions prevailing in the office until your dismissal of the Aimee Semple McPherson case." He confided in friends that Keyes was drunk for the entire duration of the proceedings. Ryan went into private practice and avoided the public eye thereafter. But his letter of resignation led to inquiries into Keyes's conduct that were the district attorney's undoing.

Of all involved, Asa Keyes fell the hardest. In 1928, he took on another high-profile case: the prosecution of executives from the Julian Petroleum Corporation, which had allegedly swindled shareholders out of $150 million. A year later, Keyes was indicted and convicted for accepting a hundred thousand dollars in bribes from principals of the oil company. There was ample evidence that Keyes had held back in prosecuting key players in that case, and potentially others—and an insinuation that his drinking habits had spiraled out of control. In Los Angeles, he quickly became a symbol of the excess and corruption of the 1920s.

He was sentenced to up to fourteen years at San Quentin. As he entered the prison gates, he is said to have grumbled, "What is life? We have an hour of consciousness and then we are gone."[6]

In September 1931, Aimee went to San Francisco and stopped at San Quentin to see her former nemesis. Keyes wasn't the only person connected to Aimee who was imprisoned there. Her former attorney and business manager Cromwell Ormsby had been convicted of jury tampering, and was serving time alongside Keyes. The three prayed together. Aimee later told reporters that she was happy to hear that Keyes would be released soon. He was freed later that year and for a time worked as a used car salesman. He died of a stroke, at the age of fifty-seven, in 1934.

Judge Carlos Hardy stood by Aimee and her mother to the end. He claimed that his involvement with the case was nothing more than an attempt to help a lady in need. Hardy was tried for impeachment in California, and the hearing in 1929 that investigated his actions in helping Aimee and accepting money essentially became a do-over of Aimee's grand jury hearings. Although Hardy admitted to taking Minnie's "love offering" that summer, a jury acquitted him on all four counts.

After leaving Angelus Temple, Giles Knight retreated to the far reaches of the San Fernando Valley, serving as a pastor in Glendale. He made local headlines again briefly in the 1960s when an elderly widow sued him, accusing him of tricking her into signing over ownership of her Nebraska oil wells. She said he told her it was simply giving him the power of attorney. A few years later, Knight agreed to settle the suit, giving half the land back.[7]

Texas Guinan intersected with Aimee's story again in the 1930s when she was hired to play the evangelist in a derisive play based on Aimee's life. Guinan said she and Aimee were birds of a feather, two of the greatest living exhibitionists of their time. "Aimee thinks I'm a great sinner," said Guinan. "Well, I think she's a great sinner too. Only I don't blame her for it. We have our separate rackets."[8]

Kenneth Ormiston had always been a great exception in Aimee's life. He wasn't a member of the church; he spoke to Aimee frankly as an equal. While others reverently called her Sister, he called her just plain Mrs. McPherson. They shared a passion for the radio, and they connected over their belief in the capacity of this new technology to change the world. But after the scandal, he vanished from her life; no further interaction between Ormiston and Aimee was ever documented. Ormiston took a job at a radio station in Pennsylvania, tinkered with his radios, and stayed out of the newspapers. He died during an appendectomy at the age of forty-one, ten years after the trial ended. A small obituary appeared in *The New York Times*, noting his role in Aimee's scandal, the allegations of their epic love story, but in the end his life was just a sad footnote to hers.

AUTHOR'S NOTE

On a warm night in February 2023, I stood under a white vinyl tent to celebrate the hundredth anniversary of the opening of Aimee's Angelus Temple. I watched as pastors from the Foursquare Church danced on the stage and filmed short segments for TikTok on their iPhones. Behind them, a seven-person band played Christian rock ballads, and around me the audience swayed and reached their hands toward the night sky. The four hundred people here were part of the ongoing centennial celebration of the founding of Aimee's Temple in early 1923. I had spent the last five years inside an archival rabbit hole, trying to understand Aimee's life and its significance. But we were in San Dimas, thirty miles from downtown Los Angeles, on the far western edges of the county, a long way from the stately vastness of the Temple. The tent felt plastic and contrived, a bit of a gimmick and a far cry from the rough canvas and wild woods that Aimee first preached in. The air was filled with the smells of a taco truck parked outside.

I had gone to catch a glimpse of what Aimee's legacy meant to some of today's more than eight million members of the Foursquare Church. But as the night passed, there was barely a mention of Aimee and her blockbuster life. A series of pastors took the stage, and they said few words about her achievement, the building of her Temple, the restrictions on her gender, her work in Key West with African Americans, and her desire to bring people to God. The focus was on the immediate—the desire to connect to the Holy Spirit in the here and now. "It's good to remember the past for all that we can do in the future," said a blond preacher in leather pants, before she turned to the band to dance and shouted, "Hallelujah!"

I had expected an evening dedicated to an icon, but I wonder if in some way, Aimee would have wanted it this way. In the final years of her life, she had turned away from the blaze of fame, the media, and the theatrics. Aimee saw herself as a messenger. She believed she was an ambassador from the kingdom of God, who had been divinely appointed to help enact an ancient and prophesied plan.

What brought me to Aimee's story was a lifelong fascination with the relationship between heaven and earth, and the intermediaries we choose to interpret those realms for us. I grew up in a far different religion than the people who stood around me in the tent—less salvation, more meditation. My parents were members of the Transcendental Meditation Movement and followers of Maharishi Mahesh Yogi, and our lives revolved around our guru's teaching. Given my childhood, I was fascinated by the way spiritual experiences translated into power. I became a student of religion.

I first learned about Aimee Semple McPherson while in divinity school. I remember thinking how odd it was that I had never heard of her—how did this important female religious pioneer not make it into my American history books? And then I promptly forgot about her—as so many others had. I went to work as a journalist, and part of that work included interviewing and writing about celebrities. Reporting on the very famous, I soon saw common ground between religion and fame. There was something about the way these exceptional people described the unknowable to the rest of us and the ways in which they derived power and fame from that role as messenger—whether through music and art, or through spiritual experiences. In short, I was obsessed with what happens when we treat people as gods on earth.

I also saw up close how fame so often became a sickness, almost a madness. Many of the celebrities I wrote about seemed caged by their renown. I spent an evening alone with Amy Winehouse a few years before her death. As she puttered around her London flat, in an altered state, she earnestly tried to explain the pieces of her life to me and how she had ended up so far from the ambitious young jazz singer from North London whose otherworldly talent had propelled her to global fame. I wrote about others—Prince, Michael Jackson, and even Justin Bieber—and in all of these artists I saw a through line—the love from the throngs of fans seemed to separate them from the world, from reality, and even, at times, from themselves. I often had a sense that being famous was like being in a cage.

In 2017, I was living in Venice, California, and I had become serious about ocean swimming. I felt brave in the cold waters, the Easter egg colors of the boardwalk receding into the distance as I tried to keep my thoughts of sharks tamped down. One morning after a swim, I went to a café, where I saw a large black-and-white photo from May 1926. In the image, a great swarm of people stood on the beach. The caption read that they were searching for Aimee Semple McPherson. I hadn't known anything about what had happened to Aimee—beyond her achievements as an evangelist. I read everything I could that was written about her over the decades, and found much of it bizarrely simplistic—she was depicted as either virtuous and misunderstood or a conniving huckster; a great spiritual paragon or a fame monster. With a reporter's suspicion that neither of those things was completely true, I began to research this book in earnest.

In the five years I've spent researching and writing about Aimee's life, I have been fascinated by the ambiguity in it. I became less interested in the particulars of her version of reality and more interested in how she navigated the world according to her sense of what was important. In the midst of that ambiguity, I have been struck over and over again by her diligence, by how hard she worked, despite so many obstacles, to create what she believed in. That has felt sacred to me, a century on—the impassioned efforts of this woman and all that they cost her.

Aimee's life story prefigures so much about the world we live in today in terms of belief, power, truth, and the corrosive nature of fame. Aimee lived with her extraordinary gifts, her sense of total exceptionalism, and her devastating failures. From her earliest days on earth, a voice whispered in Aimee's ear, telling her she was destined for greatness. She had a sense of herself as divinely chosen. That sense allowed her to ignore or bypass all the ways—large and small—that she was expected to hold herself back as a woman. She got to be big because she saw herself on a cosmic playing field. She believed so strongly in the importance of her voice, and that belief emboldened her to do remarkable and, at times, unbelievable things.

Her relationship to reality was different from that of those around her—it allowed her to spin and weave a new dimension of life. She had the ability to stand in front of a crowd and describe the world in such a way that people found themselves transported. She could move the ground beneath their feet, open their eyes, expand their hearts, take hold of their tongues, shake their bodies, shift their very being. This was her power. But it also exhausted her—the exertion of that power over the world drained her.

Others saw Aimee's power, and they wanted to harness it for themselves. When she stood in front of a crowd and dazzled them, she became an object of intense fascination. People loved her, adored her, obsessed over her. They also hated her, resented her, wanted to ruin her, kill her—and even kidnap her! She was one of the twentieth century's first celebrities.

For me, this is not a story about the sins or the spectacle. Instead, I see nested inside Aimee's story a cautionary tale about fame. About how poisonous the gaze of the public eye can be for those who live their lives in front of it. The expectations, the scrutiny, the demands, the funhouse mirror that life becomes. The appetite for all knowledge of a person that is so parasitic, unquenchable, and distorting. In her later years, Aimee was forced to be protected from it, caged.

Given all that, there was an unexpected logic to this simple evening in San Dimas, in the backyard of the local middle school. The people on the stage were effortlessly using technology and pop culture language as they wove together ideas about the divine and the sublime with the relatable truths of everyday life.

As I walked out, I passed a young mother lying on a blanket under the stars. She smiled at me as she blissfully sang along with the crowd, a refrain about Heavenly Father. Beside her a little girl was glued to the screen of her iPad, headphones on. While my background and beliefs were different from the people in the tent, I shared a sense of wonder and awe about what faith can bring to the human experience.

A NOTE ON SOURCES

While Aimee Semple McPherson may not be known to many today, she was a global media star at the inception of global media. McPherson was the pioneer of twentieth-century self-mythologizing. She used her self and the story of her life as a tool to engage and transform the world around her. In the fifty-four years that Aimee barreled through life, she created thousands of unique sermons, speeches, skits, and songs, as well as six published memoirs. She performed a Broadway show and drafted an autobiographical film script. In all that material, Aimee plumbed her own personality—her strengths and weaknesses—and used the events of her life to express and understand both heaven and earth. For Aimee, the goal was always transforming the world.

All of which is to say that this is a book about someone who has said so much about herself. More than that, she was a person who saw in the minute-to-minute of her life the miraculous manifestation of divinity. Moments large and small for Aimee were all plot points in God's plan. She saw her story as woven from the same fabric as those in the Bible passages she had memorized as soon as she could read.

To many Aimee was their Sister, to others a Saint, and to some, a Sinner. There is so much written about Aimee, by those who adored her and by those who despised and ridiculed her, that navigating the source material for her history is tricky. When I asked Steve Zeleny, the inscrutable head archivist at the Foursquare Church, which book he thought offered the most accurate picture of Aimee's life, he said it was her first memoir: *This Is That*. Originally published in 1919 and republished and revised by her several times, *This Is That* is Aimee's enchanted and prophetic interpretation of her life as a young evangelist. It serves as a touchstone in this book, as does her later autobiography *In the Service of the King*, published in 1927, shortly after her charges were dismissed. I was fortunate enough to be the first researcher given access to the court records of Aimee's pretrial hearing from the Foursquare Archives. Los Angeles County has lost all but twenty pages of the file, but the Foursquare Church possesses the only known complete copy. For more than a century, they've refused to share it with the outside world. They gave me a redacted transcript, for which I am very grateful.

In addition to those important primary sources, I used hundreds of news articles written about Aimee during her lifetime. There are also significant biographies written about Aimee. I relied most heavily on *Sister Aimee*, the well-reported 1931 biography by the journalist Nancy Barr Mavity. Mavity's contempt for Aimee's self-promotion is more judgmental than I'd prefer, but her fact finding is unmatched. Other important sources include *Sister Aimee*, by Daniel Mark Epstein (1993); *Aimee Semple McPherson: Everybody's Sister*, by Edith L. Blumhofer (also 1993); and Matthew Avery Sutton's excellent academic analysis of her work, *Aimee Semple McPherson and the Resurrection of Christian America* (2007). For understanding Los Angeles at the time, *A Bright and Guilty Place* by Richard Rayner, *City of Quartz* by Mike Davis, and *Material Dreams* by Kevin Starr were vital. For a sense of Aimee's larger religious context, I leaned on the work of religious historians and scholars, most importantly Ann Taves, Tanya Luhrmann, Diane Winston, and my own brilliant professor at divinity school, Catherine Brekus.

NOTES

PROLOGUE: "AND SHE DID NOT COME BACK"

1. Aimee Semple McPherson, *In the Service of the King: The Story of My Life* (New York: Boni and Liveright, 1927), 263.
2. McPherson, *In the Service of the King*, 264.
3. This and the preceding five quotations are from Nancy Barr Mavity, *Sister Aimee* (Garden City, NY: Doubleday, Doran & Company, 1931), 80–84.
4. This and the preceding four quotations are from Otis Wiles, "Grief Stricken Kin Carry On," *Los Angeles Examiner*, May 19, 1926.
5. "Mother Reveals Divorce Suit Threats by Wife of Radio Operator Ormiston," *Los Angeles Evening Herald*, July 14, 1929.

1. PROPHETIC BEGINNING

1. Edith L. Blumhofer, *Aimee Semple McPherson: Everybody's Sister* (Grand Rapids, MI: William B. Eerdmans Publishing Company, 1993), 38.
2. Blumhofer, *Aimee Semple McPherson*, 44.
3. Rolf McPherson and Roberta Salter, interview by Matthew A. Sutton, New York City, March 16, 2004, transcript.
4. Aimee Semple McPherson, *This Is That: Personal Experiences, Sermons and Writings of Aimee Semple McPherson, Evangelist* (Los Angeles: Echo Park Evangelistic Association, 1923), 21.
5. McPherson and Salter, interview, 6.
6. Aimee Semple McPherson, *The Personal Testimony of Aimee Semple McPherson*, rev. ed. (1928; repr. Los Angeles: Foursquare Missions Press, 1997), 2.
7. McPherson and Salter, interview, 6.
8. McPherson, *In the Service of the King: The Story of My Life* (New York: Boni and Liveright, 1927), 70–71.
9. McPherson, *In the Service of the King*, 16.
10. McPherson, *The Personal Testimony of Aimee Semple McPherson*, 4.
11. McPherson, *This Is That: Personal Experiences, Sermons and Writings of Aimee Semple McPherson, Evangelist* (Los Angeles: Echo Park Evangelistic Association, Inc., 1919), 37.
12. This and the preceding five quotations are from McPherson, *This Is That* (1919), 35–37.
13. Acts 2:1–4. Revised Standard Version.
14. *The Topeka Daily Herald*, October 8, 1901.
15. Grant Wacker, *Heaven Below: Early Pentecostals and American Culture* (Cambridge, MA: Harvard University Press, 2003), 231–33. Parham's views on race

devolved over time, and he would later rant that he was repulsed by Seymour's interracial and interdenominational congregation. He seemed to have had an initial connection with Seymour, and helped pay his way to Los Angeles. But later he would become instrumental in the racial divisions of the fellowship Seymour created in California.

16. "Pentecost Has Come," *Apostolic Faith*, 1, no. 1 (September 1906), 1.
17. "Weird Babel of Tongues," *Los Angeles Times*, April 18, 1906, 17.
18. McPherson, *In the Service of the King*, 77.

2. THIS IS THAT

1. Aimee Semple McPherson, *The Story of My Life* (Waco, TX: Word Books, 1973), 24.
2. Aimee Semple McPherson, *This Is That: Personal Experiences, Sermons and Writings of Aimee Semple McPherson, Evangelist* (Los Angeles: Echo Park Evangelistic Association, 1923), 44.
3. McPherson, *This Is That* (1923), 25–26.
4. McPherson, *This Is That: Personal Experiences, Sermons and Writings of Aimee Semple McPherson, Evangelist* (Los Angeles: Echo Park Evangelistic Association, 1919), 49.
5. McPherson, *This Is That* (1923), 44.
6. McPherson, *This Is That* (1919), 49.
7. McPherson, *This Is That* (1923), 45.
8. McPherson, *This Is That* (1923), 45.
9. McPherson, *This Is That* (1923), 50.
10. McPherson, *This Is That* (1923), 51.

3. FALLING IN LOVE WITH DESTINY

1. Aimee Semple McPherson, *In the Service of the King: The Story of My Life* (New York: Boni and Liveright, 1927), 95–96.
2. McPherson, *In the Service of the King*, 97–98.
3. Aimee Semple McPherson, *This Is That: Personal Experiences, Sermons and Writings of Aimee Semple McPherson, Evangelist* (Los Angeles: Echo Park Evangelistic Association, 1919), 68.
4. The ceremony and title opened opportunities for preaching, mission work, and general evangelistic efforts, but it did not give the minister specific powers or access to a larger authority or power structure. Edith L. Blumhofer, *Aimee Semple McPherson: Everybody's Sister* (Grand Rapids, MI: William B. Eerdmans Publishing Company, 1993), 80.
5. McPherson, *This Is That: Personal Experiences, Sermons and Writings of Aimee Semple McPherson, Evangelist* (Los Angeles: Echo Park Evangelistic Association, 1923), 60.
6. Ann Braude, *Sisters and Saints: Women in American Religion* (New York: Oxford University Press, 2007), 1–3.
7. Aimee Semple McPherson, *The Story of My Life* (Waco, TX: Word Books, 1973), 47.
8. Blumhofer, *Aimee Semple McPherson*, 96.
9. Daniel H. Bays, "From Foreign Mission to Chinese Church," *Christian History*,

issue 98, 2008, 3–4; and J. Gordon Melton, "Chinese Pentecostalism: The Birth and Growth of a Uniquely Chinese Version of Christianity," paper presented at Beijing Forum, Peking University, Beijing, 2012, 258.
10. McPherson, *In the Service of the King*, 114.
11. McPherson, *This Is That* (1919), 61.
12. McPherson, *This Is That* (1919), 88.
13. McPherson, *This Is That* (1919), 89.
14. McPherson, *In the Service of the King*, 137.

4. FLAMINGO IN A CHICKEN COOP

1. "Religion By Riot," *The New York Times*, March 22, 1885.
2. Aimee Semple McPherson, *In the Service of the King: The Story of My Life* (New York: Boni and Liveright, 1927), 138.
3. Aimee Semple McPherson, *This Is That: Personal Experiences, Sermons and Writings of Aimee Semple McPherson, Evangelist* (Los Angeles: Echo Park Evangelistic Association, 1923), 72.
4. McPherson, *In the Service of the King*, 139.
5. Rolf McPherson and Roberta Salter, interview by Matthew A. Sutton, New York City, March 16, 2004, transcript.
6. McPherson, *This Is That: Personal Experiences, Sermons and Writings of Aimee Semple McPherson, Evangelist* (Los Angeles: Echo Park Evangelistic Association, 1919), 96.
7. Edith L. Blumhofer, *Aimee Semple McPherson: Everybody's Sister* (Grand Rapids, MI: William B. Eerdmans Publishing Company, 1993), 101.
8. McPherson, *This Is That* (1923), 75.
9. Roberta Semple Collection, Folder 42, 34. Foursquare Archives, Los Angeles.
10. Harold S. McPherson v. Aimee E. McPherson, Judicial Records Center, State of Rhode Island and Providence Plantations, Div. No. 13849, April 12, 1921.
11. McPherson, *This Is That* (1919), 97.
12. This and the preceding three quotations from McPherson, *This Is That* (1923), 76–77.
13. McPherson, *This Is That* (1919), 101.
14. McPherson, *This Is That* (1923), 75.
15. Aimee Semple McPherson, "Life and Loves of Aimee McPherson," *San Francisco Examiner*, February 18, 1934, 8.

5. ESCAPE FROM PROVIDENCE

1. Aimee Semple McPherson, *This Is That: Personal Experiences, Sermons and Writings of Aimee Semple McPherson, Evangelist* (Los Angeles: Echo Park Evangelistic Association, 1923), 104.
2. This and the preceding three quotations are from McPherson, *This Is That* (1923), 82–83.
3. McPherson, *This Is That: Personal Experiences, Sermons and Writings of Aimee Semple McPherson, Evangelist* (Los Angeles: Echo Park Evangelistic Association, 1919), 84.
4. McPherson, *This Is That* (1919), 111.
5. McPherson, *This Is That* (1923), 86.

6. SLAIN UNDER THE POWER

1. This scene and quotations are taken from Aimee Semple McPherson, *In the Service of the King: The Story of My Life* (New York: Boni and Liveright, 1927), 149–51.
2. Aimee Semple McPherson, *This Is That: Personal Experiences, Sermons and Writings of Aimee Semple McPherson, Evangelist* (Los Angeles: Echo Park Evangelistic Association, 1919), 114.
3. McPherson, *This Is That* (1919), 114–15.
4. Rolf McPherson and Roberta Salter, interview by Matthew A. Sutton, New York City, March 16, 2004, transcript.
5. McPherson and Salter, interview.
6. McPherson, *This Is That* (1919), 121.
7. McPherson and Salter, interview.
8. McPherson, *In the Service of the King*, 176.

7. NEW ROAD REVIVAL

1. Aleister Crowley, *Confessions of Aleister Crowley* (New York: Penguin, 1989), 824.
2. Hampton Dunn, "When Bill Sunday, Sister Aimee and Babe Ruth All Shook Up Tampa at the Same Time in 1919," *Sunland Tribune* 2 (1975), 3.
3. Aimee Semple McPherson, *In the Service of the King: The Story of My Life* (New York: Boni and Liveright, 1927), 154.
4. McPherson, *In the Service of the King*, 189.
5. Prophecies of Aimee Semple McPherson 2, ASM Collection, Foursquare Archives, Los Angeles.
6. Aimee Semple McPherson, *This Is That: Personal Experiences, Sermons and Writings of Aimee Semple McPherson, Evangelist* (Los Angeles: Echo Park Evangelistic Association, 1923), 100.
7. Heather Curtis, *Faith in the Great Physician: Suffering and Divine Healing in American Culture, 1860–1900* (Baltimore: Johns Hopkins University Press, 2007), 9–19.
8. McPherson, *This Is That: Personal Experiences, Sermons and Writings of Aimee Semple McPherson, Evangelist* (Los Angeles: Echo Park Evangelistic Association, 1919), 136–37.
9. Curtis, *Faith in the Great Physician*, 113.
10. Kip Richardson, "Big Religion: The Cultural Origins of the American Megachurch," PhD dissertation, Harvard University, May 4, 2017, 49–50.
11. McPherson, *This Is That* (1919), 141.
12. *The Bridal Call*, vol. 1, no. 1, June 1917, 1.
13. "Sign of the Times," *The Bridal Call*, vol. 1, no. 1, June 1917, 1–2.
14. This and preceding quotation from McPherson, *This Is That* (1923), 116–19.
15. "Race Riots in St. Petersburg, Florida," *The Journal of Blacks in Higher Education*, no. 14 (Winter 1996–97): 35–37.
16. Paul Ortiz, *Emancipation Betrayed: The Hidden History of Black Organizing and White Violence in Florida from Reconstruction to the Bloody Election of 1920* (Berkeley: University of California Press, 2006), 112.
17. Rolf McPherson and Roberta Salter, interview by Matthew A. Sutton, New York City, March 16, 2004, transcript.

18. McPherson and Salter, interview.
19. Edith L. Blumhofer, *Aimee Semple McPherson: Everybody's Sister* (Grand Rapids, MI: William B. Eerdmans Publishing Company, 1993), 126.
20. McPherson and Salter, interview.
21. Daniel Mark Epstein, *Sister Aimee: The Life of Aimee Semple McPherson* (Boston: Mariner Books, 1993), 141–42.

8. CITY OF ANGELS

1. Aimee Semple McPherson, *This Is That: Personal Experiences, Sermons and Writings of Aimee Semple McPherson, Evangelist* (Los Angeles: Echo Park Evangelistic Association, 1923), 155.
2. Kevin Starr, *Material Dreams* (Oxford, UK: Oxford University Press, 1990), 69.
3. Aimee Semple McPherson, *The Story of My Life* (Waco, TX: Word Books, 1973), 104.
4. "Los Angeles Marches On," *Foursquare Crusader*, August 25, 1937, 5.
5. Louis Adamic, "Los Angeles! There She Blows!," *Outlook*, August 13, 1930, www.libcom.org/article/los-angeles-there-she-blows-louis-adamic.
6. Parham attempted to set up his own rival mission in Los Angeles, but it failed to attract the crowds that Seymour's did. He would later be arrested in Texas and charged with sodomy in San Antonio. Parham denied the charges, and they were dropped. He countered that the whole scandal was an attempt by a rival to take him down and steal congregants. Allegations of financial irregularities dogged him, and in his later years he was distanced from the religion he helped to found. Grant Wacker, *Heaven Below: Early Pentecostals and American Culture* (Cambridge, MA: Harvard University Press, 2003), 232–33; Michael Corocan, "When the Spirit Spoke," *Austin American-Statesman*, February 20, 2005, K1.
7. Sydney E. Ahlstrom, *A Religious History of the American People* (New Haven, CT: Yale University Press, 2004), 820–21.
8. Douglas Nelson, "For Such a Time as This: The Story of Bishop William J. Seymour and the Azusa Street Revival; A Search for Pentecostal/Charismatic Roots" (Thesis, University of Birmingham, 1981), 225.
9. Nelson, "For Such a Time as This," 290; *Thirty Years of Lynching in the United States 1889–1918* (New York: NAACP, 1919).
10. Nelson, "For Such a Time as This," 290.
11. Aimee Semple McPherson, *This Is That: Personal Experiences, Sermons and Writings of Aimee Semple McPherson, Evangelist* (Los Angeles: Echo Park Evangelistic Association, 1919), 232.
12. McPherson, *This Is That* (1919), 239.
13. Aimee Semple McPherson, *In the Service of the King: The Story of My Life* (New York: Boni and Liveright, 1927), 246.
14. Carey McWilliams, "The Cults of California," *The Atlantic Monthly*, March 1946, 105–10.
15. "'Undo Eve's Sin, Women's Duty,' Says Only Feminine Evangelist," *The Sheboygan Press*, February 8, 1919.
16. David Halberstam, *The Powers That Be* (New York: Open Road Media, 2012), 110–17.

17. "Let Women Right Wrong Says 'Woman Billy Sunday,'" *New Castle Herald*, August 15, 1919, 7.
18. McPherson, *This Is That* (1923), 202.

9. FAITH HEALING

1. Aimee Semple McPherson, *This Is That: Personal Experiences, Sermons and Writings of Aimee Semple McPherson, Evangelist* (Los Angeles: Echo Park Evangelistic Association, 1923), 175.
2. Dayton Revival Documentary, https://www.youtube.com/watch?v=R2fG_ch93-o.
3. This and the preceding quotations are from McPherson, *This Is That* (1923), 201–12.
4. This and the preceding quotations are from McPherson, *This Is That* (1923), 203–207.
5. Daniel Mark Epstein, *Sister Aimee: The Life of Aimee Semple McPherson* (Boston: Mariner Books, 1993), 187.
6. McPherson, *This Is That* (1923), 212.
7. This and the preceding three quotations are from McPherson, *This Is That* (1923), 201–12.

10. A LADY BUILDS A TEMPLE

1. Aimee Semple McPherson, *This Is That: Personal Experiences, Sermons and Writings of Aimee Semple McPherson, Evangelist* (Los Angeles: Echo Park Evangelistic Association, 1923), 530.
2. Aimee Semple McPherson, *The Story of My Life* (Waco, TX: Word Books, 1973), 118; Aimee Semple McPherson, *In the Service of the King: The Story of My Life* (New York: Boni and Liveright, 1927), 245–50.
3. "Pentecostal Faith-Healer Dedicates Lot for Tabernacle," *Los Angeles Times*, January 4, 1921.
4. *The Bridal Call*, February 1922, 14.
5. McPherson, *This Is That* (1923), 250.
6. Carey McWilliams, *Southern California: An Island on the Land* (first published as *Southern California Country*, 1946; Layton, UT: Gibbs Smith, 2010), 259.
7. This and the preceding seven quotations during the Dreamland event are from McPherson, *This Is That* (1923), 252–56.
8. This and the preceding two quotations are from McPherson, *This Is That* (1923), 280.
9. McPherson, *This Is That* (1923), 250–56.
10. "Do You Know?" *The Bridal Call*, September 1921, 11.
11. Divorce Filings, Certificate of Caption, State of Rhode Island, February 1, 1921, quoted in Court Cases, Foursquare Archive, Los Angeles, 90–91.
12. Edith L. Blumhofer, *Aimee Semple McPherson: Everybody's Sister* (Grand Rapids, MI: William B. Eerdmans Publishing Company, 1993), 147.
13. "Healer's Revival Opens Saturday," *San Francisco Examiner*, March 29, 1922, 3.
14. Aimee Semple McPherson, "Foursquare!," *Sunset Magazine*, February 1927, 15.
15. McPherson, "Foursquare!," 15.

16. Kip Richardson, "Big Religion: the Cultural Origins of the American Megachurch" (PhD dissertation, Harvard University, May 4, 2017).
17. McPherson, *This Is That: Personal Experiences, Sermons and Writings of Aimee Semple McPherson, Evangelist* (Los Angeles: Echo Park Evangelistic Association, 1919), 543.
18. McPherson, *This Is That* (1919), 541.

11. THE BEST SHOW IN TOWN

1. Edith L. Blumhofer, *Aimee Semple McPherson: Everybody's Sister* (Grand Rapids, MI: William B. Eerdmans Publishing Company, 1993), 248.
2. *Who's Who at Angelus Temple*, 2nd ed. (Los Angeles: Echo Park Evangelistic Association, 1925).
3. *Who's Who at Angelus Temple.*
4. Morrow Moyo, "Aimee Rises From the Sea," *The New Republic*, December 25, 1929.
5. Blumhofer, *Aimee Semple McPherson*, 249.
6. Blumhofer, *Aimee Semple McPherson*, 221–22.
7. Tona J. Hangen, *Redeeming the Dial: Radio, Religion and Popular Culture in America* (Chapel Hill: The University of North Carolina Press, 2003), 15–17.
8. Aimee Semple McPherson, "Foursquare!," *Sunset Magazine*, February 1927, 80.
9. This and the preceding quotations from the "Arrested for Speeding" sermon are from Roberta Semple Collection, Roberta memoir notes, Foursquare Archive, Los Angeles, 39–41, 84.
10. Roberta Semple Collection, Roberta memoir notes, 30.

12. RADIOLAND

1. Tona J. Hangen, *Redeeming the Dial: Radio, Religion and Popular Culture in America* (Chapel Hill: The University of North Carolina Press, 2003), 15–17.
2. This and the preceding two quotations are from Hangen, *Redeeming the Dial*, 66–69.
3. Hangen, *Redeeming the Dial*, 65.
4. Hangen, *Redeeming the Dial*, 74.
5. William Parker, "Mrs. Kennedy's Own Story Bares Row with Aimee," *Los Angeles Evening Herald*, July 16, 1928, 1.

13. POWER AND PUSHBACK

1. Kevin Starr, *Embattled Dreams* (Oxford, UK: Oxford University Press, 2002), 232.
2. Richard Rayner, *A Bright and Guilty Place: Murder, Corruption, and L.A.'s Scandalous Coming of Age* (New York: Anchor Books, 2009), 19.
3. Rayner, *A Bright and Guilty Place*, 83.
4. Jules Tygiel, *The Great Los Angeles Swindle: Oil, Stocks, and Scandal During the Roaring Twenties* (Berkeley: University of California Press, 1996), 177.
5. Rayner, *A Bright and Guilty Place*, 83.
6. Aimee Semple McPherson, *In the Service of the King: The Story of My Life* (New York: Boni and Liveright, 1927), 14.

7. *Bob Shuler's Magazine*, June 1922, 100.
8. R. P. (Bob) Shuler, "McPhersonism: A Study of Healing Cults and Modern Day 'Tongues' Movements" (Los Angeles: Trinity Methodist Church, 1924), 19, 48, 116.
9. Shuler, "McPhersonism," 7.
10. Daniel Mark Epstein, *Sister Aimee: The Life of Aimee Semple McPherson* (Boston: Mariner Books, 1993), 272.
11. Alma Whitaker, "Reveals Intimate Charm of Angelus Temple Head," *Los Angeles Times*, March 23, 1924, 37.

14. BURN OUT

1. This and the preceding quotation are from Aimee Semple McPherson, "Milk Pail and a Birthday," *The Bridal Call*, November 1925.
2. William Parker, "Mrs. Kennedy's Own Story Bares Row with Aimee," *Los Angeles Evening Herald*, July 16, 1928, 1.
3. This and the preceding quotation are from Nancy Barr Mavity, *Sister Aimee* (Garden City, NY: Doubleday, Doran & Company, 1931), 71.
4. Telegram from Aimee Semple McPherson to Minnie Kennedy, Folder 65, page 22, Roberta Salter Archive, Foursquare Archive, Los Angeles.
5. This and the preceding two quotations from Parker, "Mrs. Kennedy's Own Story Bares Row with Aimee," 1.

PART II: SCANDAL

1. Nancy Barr Mavity, *Sister Aimee* (Garden City, NY: Doubleday, Doran & Company, 1931), 42.

15. ABDUCTION

1. This entire chapter is taken from Aimee's accounts of what happened, primarily from *In the Service of the King*. Aimee Semple McPherson, *In the Service of the King: The Story of My Life* (New York: Boni and Liveright, 1927), 260–70.
2. "Pastor Repeats Story as Officials Question Her," *Los Angeles Times*, June 25, 1926, 3.
3. Reporter's Transcript of Preliminary Examination, The People of the State of California v. Aimee Semple McPherson, Minnie Kennedy, Lorraine Wiseman Sielaff, Kenneth G. Ormiston, John Doe, Richard Roe, Sarah Moe, Redacted Version courtesy of Foursquare Archives, Los Angeles.

16. RESURRECTION

1. Senate of the State of California Sitting as a High Court of Impeachment, *In the Matter of the Impeachment of Carlos S. Hardy*, Joseph Allen Beek, Secretary of the Senate, California State Printing Office, Sacramento, April 16, 1929, 129.
2. "Twelve Thousand at Memorial Services for Mrs. McPherson," *San Pedro Daily Pilot*, June 21, 1926, 1.

3. William Parker, "Mrs. Kennedy's Own Story Bares Row with Aimee," *Los Angeles Evening Herald*, July 16, 1928, 1.
4. This and the preceding three quotations from Reporter's Transcript of Preliminary Examination, The People of the State of California v. Aimee Semple McPherson, Minnie Kennedy, Lorraine Wiseman Sielaff, Kenneth G. Ormiston, John Doe, Richard Roe, Sarah Moe, Redacted Version courtesy of Foursquare Archives, Los Angeles; Nancy Barr Mavity, *Sister Aimee* (Garden City, NY: Doubleday, Doran & Company, 1931), 117–19; Aimee Semple McPherson, *In the Service of the King: The Story of My Life* (New York: Boni and Liveright, 1927), 297–300.
5. This and the preceding two quotations from Mavity, *Sister Aimee*, 119.
6. "Temple Congregation Joyful, Cheerful," *The Fresno Morning Republic*, June 24, 1926.
7. "Times Wins War in Air," *Los Angeles Times*, June 25, 1926.
8. "Examiner Ship Makes Record," *Los Angeles Examiner*, June 25, 1926.
9. Mavity, *Sister Aimee*, 153.
10. Thomas Lately, *Vanishing Evangelist: The Aimee Semple McPherson Kidnapping Affair* (New York: Viking Press, 1959), 60
11. This and preceding Keyes quotation from "Reward Offer Is Puzzle to Coast Officers," *The Arizona Republic*, June 24, 1926.

17. DESERT SEARCH

1. This and all the preceding quotations from McDonald's memo are from Nancy Barr Mavity, *Sister Aimee* (Garden City, NY: Doubleday Doran & Company Inc., 1931), 150–51.
2. This and the preceding quotations from Minnie are from "Ransom Tale Scoffed at by Mrs. Kennedy," *San Francisco Examiner*, June 25, 1926, 5.
3. Mavity, *Sister Aimee*, 131–32.
4. Mavity, *Sister Aimee*, 142.
5. "Two Governments Act to Solve Amazing Crime," *Los Angeles Examiner*, June 25, 1926.
6. Mavity, *Sister Aimee*, 146.
7. Read Kendall, "Pair Sob at Reunion," *Los Angeles Times*, June 25, 1926, 1.

18. SKEPTICISM

1. "Mighty Ovation Along Route Shows Devotion of Temple Followers," *Pomona Bulletin*, June 27, 1926, 2.
2. This and the preceding quotation are from Nancy Barr Mavity, *Sister Aimee* (Garden City, NY: Doubleday, Doran & Company, 1931), 155.
3. This and the preceding three quotes from Mavity, *Sister Aimee*, 154–55.
4. Aimee Semple McPherson, *The Story of My Life* (Waco, TX: Word Books, 1973), 176.
5. "Aimee Assails Critics Doubting Her Kidnap Tale," *The Sacramento Bee*, June 29, 1926.
6. Mavity, *Sister Aimee*, 94.

7. This and preceding quotation from "Evangelist Uses Recent Ordeal for Sermon Text," *Los Angeles Times*, June 28, 1926, 2.
8. "Conquering Host Sermon," June 27, 1926, ASM Collection, Foursquare Archives, Los Angeles.
9. "Evangelist Uses Recent Ordeal for Sermon Text," 2.
10. This and all the preceding quotes from the sermon come from Aimee's "Conquering Host" sermon, June 27, 1926, ASM Collection, Foursquare Archives, Los Angeles.

19. THE PUBLIC MIND

1. "Seeing Aimee in Mexico Related in New Story," *Los Angeles Times*, July 7, 1926.
2. "Mrs. McPherson Replies in Detail to Various Objections Raised to Kidnaping Story," *Los Angeles Times*, July 1, 1926, 2.
3. "Trackers Say Tale False," *Los Angeles Times*, July 3, 1926, 1.
4. "Grand Jury Calls Aimee," *Los Angeles Evening Post-Record*, July 6, 1926, 15.

20. GRAND JURY

1. "Constructor of Angelus Temple Can't Be Located," *Los Angeles Evening Post-Record*, July 7, 1926, 1.
2. Nancy Barr Mavity, *Sister Aimee* (Garden City, NY: Doubleday, Doran & Company, 1931), 177.
3. "Spurns Secrecy Oath," *Los Angeles Evening Express*, July 8, 1926, 1.
4. Reporter's Transcript of Preliminary Examination, The People of the State of California v. Aimee Semple McPherson, Minnie Kennedy, Lorraine Wiseman Sielaff, Kenneth G. Ormiston, John Doe, Richard Roe, Sarah Moe, Redacted Version courtesy of Foursquare Archives, Los Angeles.
5. Mavity, *Sister Aimee*, 144–45.
6. Reporter's Transcript of Preliminary Examination, The People of the State of California v. Aimee Semple McPherson, Minnie Kennedy, Lorraine Wiseman Sielaff, Kenneth G. Ormiston, John Doe, Richard Roe, Sarah Moe, Redacted Version courtesy of Foursquare Archives, Los Angeles.

21. SINISTER PLOTS

1. "Ormiston Search Leads to Atlantic," *Los Angeles Evening Post-Record*, July 16, 1926.
2. "Mother Slapped Aimee, Jury Told," *Los Angeles Examiner*, July 17, 1926, 1.
3. "Angelus Temple Leaders Accept Death Theory," *Hollywood Daily Citizen*, May 25, 1926, 1.
4. Nancy Barr Mavity, *Sister Aimee* (Garden City, NY: Doubleday, Doran & Company, 1931), 97.
5. Thomas Lately, *Vanishing Evangelist: The Aimee Semple McPherson Kidnapping Affair* (New York: Viking Press, 1959), 18.
6. "Ransom-Note Text Given," *Los Angeles Times*, July 2, 1926.
7. "L.A. Sleuth Links Cleric to Clue Found at Inn," *San Francsico Examiner*, June 3, 1926, 1.

8. This and the preceding quotations from Minnie's testimony from Reporter's Transcript of Preliminary Examination, The People of the State of California v. Aimee Semple McPherson, Minnie Kennedy, Lorraine Wiseman Sielaff, Kenneth G. Ormiston, John Doe, Richard Roe, Sarah Moe, Redacted Version courtesy of Foursquare Archives, Los Angeles; "Eight More Appear for Inquiry on Kidnaping," *Los Angeles Times*, July 14, 1926, 1.
9. "Evangelist Subjected to Grilling by Grand Jury," *Los Angeles Times*, July 9, 1926, 1.
10. Lately, *Vanishing Evangelist*, 145–49.
11. From Nancy Barr Mavity's contemporaneous interview with deputy district attorney Daniel Beecher. Mavity, *Sister Aimee*, 295.
12. Lately, *Vanishing Evangelist*, 149.
13. Quotations from letters from "Letters Reveal Public Sentiment," *Los Angeles Times*, July 12, 1926, 2.
14. "Here's Text of Ormiston Note," *Los Angeles Evening Post-Record*, July 20, 1926, 2.
15. This and the preceding three quotations are from "Jury Refuses to Indict in M'Pherson Inquiry," *Los Angeles Times*, July 21, 1926, 1.
16. "Judge Keetch Will Ignore Attack by Rev. 'Bob' Shuler," *Los Angeles Evening Express*, July 26, 1926, 2.

22. CARMEL BY THE SEA

1. From Benedict's statement to the district attorney in Nancy Barr Mavity, *Sister Aimee* (Garden City, NY: Doubleday, Doran & Company, 1931), 203–204.
2. According to Nancy Barr Mavity's 1931 biography, the books left in the Benedict cottage contained passages quoted in McPherson's sermons, although she provides no evidence for that conclusion. Mavity, *Sister Aimee*, 205.
3. This and the preceding quotation are from Mavity, *Sister Aimee*, 201.
4. This and the preceding quotation are from "Aimee Not Kidnapped Says Ryan; Was With Radio Man," *Battle Creek Moon-Journal*, July 28, 1926, 1.
5. Reporter's Transcript of Preliminary Examination, The People of the State of California v. Aimee Semple McPherson, Minnie Kennedy, Lorraine Wiseman Sielaff, Kenneth G. Ormiston, John Doe, Richard Roe, Sarah Moe, Redacted Version courtesy of Foursquare Archives, Los Angeles; Mavity, *Sister Aimee*, 209.
6. "New Witnesses Said to Have Seen Pair in Cottage, Hunted," *Los Angeles Herald Examiner*, July 28, 1926, 1.
7. Thomas Lately, *Vanishing Evangelist: The Aimee Semple McPherson Kidnapping Affair* (New York: Viking Press, 1959), 168.
8. Mavity, *Sister Aimee*, 207.

23. LOVE SHACK

1. Louis Adamic, *The Truth About Aimee Semple McPherson* (Girard, KS: Haldeman-Julius Company, 1926), 43.
2. "Blue Coupe Arrived About Dawn May 19," *Los Angeles Evening Post-Record*, July 26, 1926, 1.
3. "Ormiston, Come Back!" *Los Angeles Evening Post-Record*, July 27, 1926, 1.

4. "Floodgates of Ridicule and Anathema Loosed on Detractors by Evangelist," *Los Angeles Times*, July 29, 1926, 1.
5. "Huge Throng Hears Aimee Cry Denial," *Los Angeles Examiner*, July 31, 1926, 1.
6. "Time Has Come for Showdown, Says Aimee, Investigators Flayed by Evangelist," *San Francisco Examiner*, July 29, 1926, 1.
7. "Grand Jury to Probe Perjury Is New Rumor," *Los Angeles Daily News*, July 29, 1926, 1.
8. This and the preceding two quotations are from "Keyes Tells Assistant to Take Back Seat in Case," *San Francisco Examiner*, August 2, 1926, 1.
9. "Senate of the State of California Sitting as a High Court of Impeachment, in the Matter of the Impeachment of Carlos S. Hardy," Joseph Allen Beek, Secretary of the Senate, California State Printing Office, Sacramento, 1930.
10. Nancy Barr Mavity, *Sister Aimee* (Garden City, NY: Doubleday, Doran & Company, 1931), 212.
11. "Senate of the State of California Sitting as a High Court of Impeachment, in the Matter of the Impeachment of Carlos S. Hardy," Joseph Allen Beek, Secretary of the Senate, California State Printing Office, Sacramento, 1930.
12. "Aimee Probe May Continue," *Los Angeles Evening Express*, August 2, 1926, 2.

24. THE IDES OF AUGUST

1. "Text of Affidavit Given in Name of Kenneth Ormiston," *Los Angeles Times*, August 3, 1926, 18.
2. Nancy Barr Mavity, *Sister Aimee* (Garden City, NY: Doubleday, Doran & Company, 1931), 101.
3. "Text of Affidavit Given in Name of Kenneth Ormiston," 18.
4. Mavity, *Sister Aimee*, 179.
5. "Keyes Ordered to Keep Up Quiz," *Los Angeles Times*, August 4, 1926, 2.
6. "Grand Jurors Under Attack," *Los Angeles Times*, August 6, 1926, 19.
7. "Kidnapped!," *The Bridal Call*, August 1926, 9.
8. Mavity, *Sister Aimee*, 288.
9. William Parker, "Mrs. Kennedy's Own Story Bares Row with Aimee," *Los Angeles Evening Herald*, July 16, 1928, 1.
10. "Senate of the State of California Sitting as a High Court of Impeachment, in the Matter of the Impeachment of Carlos S. Hardy," Joseph Allen Beek, Secretary of the Senate, California State Printing Office, Sacramento, 1930, 1123–25.
11. Mavity, *Sister Aimee*, 219.
12. "Couldn't Arrest Capt. Cline, but They Did Anyway," *The Pomona Bulletin*, August 24, 1926, 2.
13. "LA Detective Chief Ousted," *San Francisco Examiner*, August 25, 1926, 9.
14. "Impeachment of Carlos S. Hardy," 43.

25. MISS X

1. "Keyes Sure Aimee Wrote Order List at Carmel," *Stockton Independent*, August 1, 1926, 1.

2. Nancy Barr Mavity, *Sister Aimee* (Garden City, NY: Doubleday, Doran & Company, 1931), 223.
3. Mavity, *Sister Aimee*, 248.
4. This and the preceding four quotations are from Mavity, *Sister Aimee*, 248–50.
5. This and the preceding quotation are from "Woman Reveals Kin as 'Miss X,'" *Los Angeles Times*, August 23, 1926, 1.
6. Caroline Walker, "I Am Either Good or Bad Says Aimee," *Los Angeles Evening Herald*, August 29, 1926, 1.
7. Mavity, *Sister Aimee*, 231.

26. HOAX WOMAN

1. "Suicide Doctors Papers Link Ormiston to Plot," *Los Angeles Times*, September 24, 1926, 23.
2. Reporter's Transcript of Preliminary Examination, The People of the State of California v. Aimee Semple McPherson, Minnie Kennedy, Lorraine Wiseman Sielaff, Kenneth G. Ormiston, John Doe, Richard Roe, Sarah Moe, Redacted Version courtesy of Foursquare Archives, Los Angeles.
3. Various stories from the *Los Angeles Times* and *Los Angeles Examiner* between September 12 and 15, 1926.
4. Nancy Barr Mavity, *Sister Aimee* (Garden City, NY: Doubleday, Doran & Company, 1931), 265–66.
5. This and the preceding five quotations are from Mavity, *Sister Aimee*, 288.
6. "Evangelist in Dramatic Plea," *Los Angeles Evening Express*, September 16, 1929, 2.
7. Thomas Lately, *Vanishing Evangelist: The Aimee Semple McPherson Kidnapping Affair* (New York: Viking Press, 1959), 233.

27. PERSECUTION

1. Sadie Mossler, "Sadness Rules in Home of Pastor," *Los Angeles Record*, September 17, 1926, 1.
2. "'Kenneth, Tell Truth' Mother of Ormiston Begs in Call to Son," *San Francisco Examiner*, July 18, 1926, 1.
3. Aimee Semple McPherson, *In the Service of the King: The Story of My Life* (New York: Boni and Liveright, 1927), 53.
4. Nancy Barr Mavity, *Sister Aimee* (Garden City, NY: Doubleday, Doran & Company, 1931), 293.
5. From Nancy Barr Mavity's contemporaneous interview with Deputy District Attorney Daniel Beecher. Mavity, *Sister Aimee*, 294–95.
6. Mavity, *Sister Aimee*, 114.
7. "Senate of the State of California Sitting as a High Court of Impeachment, in the Matter of the Impeachment of Carlos S. Hardy," Joseph Allen Beek, Secretary of the Senate, California State Printing Office, Sacramento, 1930, 733.
8. Thomas Lately, *Vanishing Evangelist: The Aimee Semple McPherson Kidnapping Affair* (New York: Viking Press, 1959), 240.

9. "Samuel R. Blake Dies; Judge for 41 Years," *Los Angeles Times*, March 8, 1974, 2.
10. Sadie Mossler, "Women Wait, Wait for Trial Thrills," *Los Angeles Record*, September 29, 1926, 1.
11. Alma Whitaker, "Hotel Secrets Liven Hearing," *Los Angeles Times*, October 2, 1929, 25.
12. "Saw Aimee at Carmel, State Witness Says," *Los Angeles Evening Express*, September 27, 1926, 1.
13. Alma Whitaker, "Trial Discovers Ankle Mania," *Los Angeles Times*, September 29, 1926, 31.
14. "Garbling Facts on Radio Laid to Mrs. M'Pherson," *Los Angeles Times*, September 30, 1926, 1.

28. DOUBLE LIFE

1. Aimee Semple McPherson, *In the Service of the King: The Story of My Life* (New York: Boni and Liveright, 1927), 283.
2. Thomas Lately, *Vanishing Evangelist: The Aimee Semple McPherson Kidnapping Affair* (New York: Viking Press, 1959), 245.
3. "Doorman Says Pastor Visited Clark Hotel 'Drowning' Day," *Los Angeles Times*, October 2, 1926, 24.
4. Reporter's Transcript of Preliminary Examination, The People of the State of California v. Aimee Semple McPherson, Minnie Kennedy, Lorraine Wiseman Sielaff, Kenneth G. Ormiston, John Doe, Richard Roe, Sarah Moe, Redacted Version courtesy of Foursquare Archives, Los Angeles.
5. This and the preceding quotation from "March of the Martyrs," *Angelus Temple Bulletin*, October 3, 1926, 3.
6. "Martyr Show Given Mrs. M'Pherson," *The New York Times*, October 4, 1926, 1.
7. Barry Siegel, *Dreamers and Schemers: How an Improbable Bid for the 1932 Olympics Transformed Los Angeles from Dusty Outpost to Global Metropolis* (Berkeley: University of California Press, 2019), 73.
8. "Handwriting Expert Asserts Aimee McPherson Wrote Grocery Lists at Carmel Cottage," *Los Angeles Times*, October 20, 1926, 28.
9. "Illness Halts Defense of Aimee M'Pherson," *Los Angeles Times*, October 20, 1926, 1.
10. Nancy Barr Mavity, *Sister Aimee* (Garden City, NY: Doubleday Doran & Company Inc., 1931), 305.
11. "Says Hair Is Clue in M'Pherson Case," *The New York Times*, October 30, 1926. The contents included: "1 green dress (dark cloth), 1 blue evening gown with pink and red roses around belt, with gold lace. 1 bright cerise gown lined with gray iridescent silk. 1 white silk dressing gown with blue silk flowers.1 gold beaded evening gown with tag 'Imported by Bullocks' [Los Angeles department store] at bottom. 1 black beaded evening gown. 1 black scarf with silver beads. 1 blue dressing robe with gold thread embroidery. 1 silver sash. 1 gold head band.1 embroidered Arabic table cover. 1 bath towel with blue crocheted lace. 1 pair pajamas, two-piece, chemise and bloomers, pink. 1 morning gown, peach color, with green crepe de Chine. 1 blue and gray ribbed silk dress. 1 purple dressing gown with embroidered gold thread. 2 rhinestone hair ornaments. 1 pink crepe de Chine dress

with rhinestones and pearls. 1 pair brown kid shoes with pair brown silk stockings. 1 pink nightgown, crepe de Chine, with lace. 1 pink silk slip. 1 purple sash with embroidery (Chinese). 1 small linen lace handkerchief. 1 gray coat with cape effect. 1 black silk cape lined with white. 1 purple Chinese or Japanese kimono embroidered. 1 dark blue serge dress with cape. 1 black velvet hoop-skirt dress with flowers. 1 pair black satin slippers with steel buckles. 1 pair brown patent slippers with snakeskin, trademarked 'Schober.' 1 pink evening dress beaded with gold and silver lace and thread embroidery with rose on shoulder. 1 pair pink satin slippers with gold braided strap. 1 white crepe de Chine dress. 1 pale green dress with lace over slip (filet lace). 1 pink nightgown. 1 burnt orange scarf, shaded. 1 light tan slip. 1 sport coat with fur collar. 1 dark blue silk umbrella with black tassel. 1 black velvet sleeveless gown with red inserts and red and white steel beads. 1 peach morning gown with lace trimming. 1 blue case containing two perfume bottles. 1 pair peach silk hose. 1 two-piece blue sport dress. 1 embroidered white slip. 1 flesh silk brassiere. 1 pair pink silk bloomers. 1 peach-colored nightgown. 1 pink nightgown. 1 pink boudoir cap. 1 pink panne velvet dress with salmon rose. 1 lace morning gown. 1 black silk slip and black overdress. 12 water-wave combs. 1 orchid slip. 1 small black lace shawl. 1 dress slip, flesh colored, plaited. 1 lace boudoir cap, trimmed with little flowers and ribbon. 1 lavender embroidered nightgown. 1 lace hair band with pink ostrich feathers. 1 pair silver slippers with buckles. 1 pair green hose. 1 salmon chemise. 1 fur jabot trimmed with black crepe de Chine. 1 pair white shoe covers, cotton."

12. "Code Love Letter Laid to Aimee by Prosecutor," *San Francisco Examiner*, October 31, 1926, 2.

29. THE LESSER OF TWO EVILS

1. Nancy Barr Mavity, *Sister Aimee* (Garden City, NY: Doubleday, Doran & Company, 1931), 25.
2. This and the preceding quotes from the closing arguments are from "Judge Blake Binds Over Evangelist and Mother," *Los Angeles Times*, November 4, 1926, 20.
3. Edith L. Blumhofer, *Aimee Semple McPherson: Everybody's Sister* (Grand Rapids, MI: William B. Eerdmans Publishing Company, 1993), 297.
4. "Radio Man Indicates Plan to Talk," *San Francisco Examiner*, December 10, 1926, 1.
5. Matthew Avery Sutton, *Aimee Semple McPherson and the Resurrection of Christian America* (Cambridge, MA: Harvard University Press, 2007), 138.
6. Thomas Lately, *Storming Heaven: The Lives and Turmoils of Minnie Kennedy and Aimee Semple McPherson* (New York: William Morrow and Company, 1970), 60.
7. "Evangelist Celebrates Dismissal as Victory," *Los Angeles Times*, January 11, 1927, 1.

30. VINDICATION TOUR

1. *Foursquare Crusader*, March 5, 1927, 2.
2. "Evangelist Celebrates Dismissal as Victory," *Los Angeles Times*, January 11, 1927, 21.
3. Thomas Lately, *Vanishing Evangelist: The Aimee Semple McPherson Kidnapping Affair* (New York: Viking Press, 1959), 323.

4. This and the preceding two quotations are from William Parker, "Mrs. Kennedy's Own Story Bares Row with Aimee," *Los Angeles Evening Herald*, July 16, 1928, 1.
5. Mary Garden, "Why I Bobbed My Hair," *Pictorial Review*, April 1927, 8.
6. Jim Bolger, "Mrs. M'Pherson Plans Movies, *Los Angeles Record*, January 17, 1927, 12.
7. "Aimee Lecture Proves Flop," *The Press Democrat*, January 23, 1927, 1.
8. Jim Bolger, "I'm Happy Says Mrs. McPherson," *Los Angeles Evening Post-Record*, January 27, 1927, 1.
9. Thomas Lately, *Storming Heaven: The Lives and Turmoils of Minnie Kennedy and Aimee Semple McPherson* (New York: William Morrow and Company, 1970), 64.
10. Aimee Semple McPherson, *The Story of My Life* (Waco, TX: Word Books, 1973), 224.
11. Douglas Cameron, "Auburn Haired Evangelist Here Again Tomorrow," *New York Daily News*, February 27, 1927, 2.
12. Daniel Mark Epstein, *Sister Aimee: The Life of Aimee Semple McPherson* (Boston: Mariner Books, 1993), 322.
13. "Iowa Salons Too Busy to Hear Aimee," *Quad City Times*, January 28, 1927, 10.
14. Priscilla Wayne, "You Can't Laugh Aimee McPherson Off—Miss Wayne," *Des Moines Tribune*, January 29, 1927, 1.
15. John D. Goben, *"Aimee": The Gospel Gold Digger* (New York: Peoples Publishing Company, 1932), 3.
16. This and the preceding four quotations are from Goben, *"Aimee,"* 3–4, 36.
17. "Mrs. McPherson in New York to Purge Gotham of Evil," *The Gazette*, Montreal, February 19, 1927, 1; "Aimee McPherson Exhorts Revellers to Turn to God in Tex Guinan's Night Club," *Brooklyn Daily Eagle*, February 19, 1927, 1.
18. "New York Not as 'Tough' as It Thinks, Says Aimee," *The Brooklyn Daily Times*, January 1, 1927, 1.
19. This and the preceding ten quotations from that evening are from "Aimee McPherson Exhorts Revellers to Turn to God in Tex Guinan's Night Club," 1.
20. J. M. Weinstein, "Texas Guinan Sings Hymns as Aimee Pours Out Gospel," *The Brooklyn Daily Times*, February 20, 1027, 1.
21. H. L. Mencken, "Sister Aimee," *The Baltimore Evening Sun*, December 13, 1926, 21.
22. Joseph Henry Steele, "Sister Aimee: Bernhardt of the Sawdust Trail," *Vanity Fair*, March 1933, 42
23. Edith L. Blumhofer, *Aimee Semple McPherson: Everybody's Sister* (Grand Rapids, MI: William B. Eerdmans Publishing Company, 1993), 308.
24. Nancy Barr Mavity, *Sister Aimee* (Garden City, NY: Doubleday, Doran & Company, 1931), 330.
25. "Cleric Gives Her Mother '4 Ways Out,'" *San Francisco Examiner*, July 28, 1927, 1;
26. Mavity, *Sister Aimee*, 332.
27. "Angelus Temple Rebel Suggests Trial by Church," *The Fresno Bee*, July 28, 1927, 1.
28. Mavity, *Sister Aimee*, 332.
29. Epstein, *Sister Aimee*, 334.

31. AFTERMATH

1. Sarah Comstock, "Aimee Semple McPherson: Prima Donna of Revivalism," *Harper's Monthly Magazine*, December 1927, 17–18.
2. This and the preceding four quotations are from "Temple Tribute Triumph," *Foursquare Crusader*, August 15, 1928, 1.
3. "Pure Religion and Undefiled," *The Bridal Call Foursquare*, vol. 12, no. 3, August 1928, 15.
4. Anthony Quinn, *The Original Sin: A Self-Portrait* (New York: Bantam Books, 1974), 127.
5. Daniel Mark Epstein, *Sister Aimee: The Life of Aimee Semple McPherson* (Boston: Mariner Books, 1993), 334.
6. John D. Goben, *"Aimee": The Gospel Gold Digger* (New York: Peoples Publishing Company, 1932), 1.
7. Nancy Barr Mavity, *Sister Aimee* (Garden City, NY: Doubleday, Doran & Company, 1931), 346–47.
8. "Temple Scene of Joyous Occasion," *Foursquare Crusader*, December 11, 1929, 1.
9. "Legs Enter Story," *San Francisco Examiner*, August 23, 1930, 1.
10. Aimee Semple McPherson, *The Story of My Life* (Waco, TX: Word Books, 1973), 227.

32. THE IRON FURNACE

1. Harriet A. Jordan, "Crisis Past as People Pray," *Foursquare Crusader*, September 3, 1930, 1.
2. Daniel Mark Epstein, *Sister Aimee: The Life of Aimee Semple McPherson* (Boston: Mariner Books, 1993), 345.
3. "Mrs. M'Pherson Ills Stir Row," *Los Angeles Times*, November 25, 1930, 1.
4. Rolf McPherson and Roberta Salter, interview by Matthew A. Sutton, New York City, March 16, 2004, transcript.
5. Aimee Semple McPherson, *The Story of My Life* (Waco, TX: Word Books, 1973), 229.
6. Nancy Barr Mavity, *Sister Aimee* (Garden City, NY: Doubleday, Doran & Company, 1931), 356.
7. The preceding quotations between Aimee and Chaplin are from Gerith Von Ulm, *Charlie Chaplin, King of Tragedy* (1940; repr., Bristol, UK: Read & Co. Books, 2007), 331.
8. There are unsubstantiated rumors that this friendship became intimate.
9. "Aimee Cocktail Peeves Her Ma," *The Spokesman-Review*, January 24, 1931, 12.
10. McPherson, *The Story of My Life*, 233.
11. As luck would have it, Guy Edward Hudson, Minnie's second husband, was already married and had secretly hidden this fact. Also, James Kennedy—Aimee's father and Minnie's previous husband—had died in 1921. Probably James's death deserves more than a footnote, but his obituary notes state that reporters couldn't even reach his widow.

12. "M'Pherson Son Wed, Amid Pomp," *Los Angeles Times*, July 22, 1931.
13. Aimee Semple McPherson, "Three Loves; Aimee's Own Story of Life," *San Francisco Examiner*, February 22, 1934, 30.
14. This and the preceding five quotations from Aimee are from her column "Three Loves; Aimee's Own Story of Life," *The San Francisco Examiner*, February 22, 1934, 30.
15. This and the preceding quotation from A. M. Rochlen, "Aimee and Singer Elope by Airplane to Yuma; Wedding Veiled in Secrecy," *San Francisco Examiner*, September 14, 1931, 1.
16. "Aimee Elopes with Singer and Marries in Yuma," *Los Angeles Times*, September 14, 1931, 1.
17. "He Wooed Her Then His Love Turned Cold," *Austin American-Statesman*, September 16, 1931, 1.
18. "Aimee's Mate to Fight Suit," *Los Angeles Times*, September 16, 1931, 19.
19. Aimee Semple McPherson, "Aimee Tells of Grief over Mate's Balm Suit," *San Francisco Examiner*, February 24, 1934, 25.
20. Alma Whitaker, "Sugar and Spice," *Los Angeles Times*, January 31, 1932, 21.
21. McPherson, "Aimee Tells of Grief over Mate's Balm Suit," 25.
22. Roberta Salter Archive, Foursquare Archive, Los Angeles, 44.
23. "Sister Aimee," *The New York Times*, September 23, 1933; "The Theatre: Abbess of Angelus," *Wall Street Journal*, September 25, 1933.
24. Aimee Semple McPherson, "One Hundred and Fifty Days," *Bridal Call Foursquare*, January 1934, 6–7.
25. Matthew Avery Sutton, *Aimee Semple McPherson and the Resurrection of Christian America* (Cambridge, MA: Harvard University Press, 2007), 240–41.
26. Aimee Semple McPherson, "Rich Man and Lazarus 1941," ASM Collection Music, Foursquare Archive, Los Angeles.
27. "Aimee Gives Version of Famous Baby Hoax," *San Francisco Examiner*, February 25, 1934, 59.

33. "WOE UNTO THE ONE WHO BREAKS THE LINK"

1. "Aimee's Son Joins in Row," *Los Angeles Times*, September 27, 1936, 19.
2. "Aimee to Face Court in Battle with Daughter," *The Binghamton Press*, October 5, 1936, 1.
3. Edith L. Blumhofer, *Aimee Semple McPherson: Everybody's Sister* (Grand Rapids, MI: William B. Eerdmans Publishing Company, 1993), 365.
4. Daniel Mark Epstein, *Sister Aimee: The Life of Aimee Semple McPherson* (Boston: Mariner Books, 1993), 410–11.
5. This and the preceding quote are from "Court Rebuke Given Aimee," *Los Angeles Times*, April 15, 1937, 23.
6. "Aimee's Loves; Secret Plot Burden Testimony in Suit," *Spokane Daily Chronicle*, April 22, 1937, 2.
7. "Moratorium Needed," *Los Angeles Times*, April 16, 1937, 4.
8. Aimee Semple McPherson, *The Story of My Life* (Waco, TX: Word Books, 1973), 237.
9. Box 15, Carey McWilliams Papers, UCLA Library Special Collections.

10. Oral History Notes A–Z Focusing on ASM, Foursquare Archive, Los Angeles, 93.
11. Oral History Notes, 8.
12. McPherson, *The Story of My Life*, 251.
13. Aimee Semple McPherson to Giles Knight, January 12, 1944, ASM Collection Personal, pp. 74–75, Foursquare Archive, Los Angeles.
14. Letter from Raymond Cox to Daniel Mark Epstein, April 21, 1993, Foursquare Archive, Los Angeles.
15. "Rolf M'Pherson Takes Over Temple Duties," *Los Angeles Times*, February 2, 1944, 6.
16. Tona J. Hangen, *Redeeming the Dial: Radio, Religion, and Popular Culture in America* (Chapel Hill: The University of North Carolina Press, 2003), 78–79.
17. "Happy Days Are Here Again!" *Foursquare Crusader*, April 1944, 3.
18. "Aimee Semple McPherson Dies Suddenly in Oakland," *Los Angeles Times*, September 28, 1944, 1.
19. McPherson, *The Story of My Life*, 252.

EPILOGUE

1. Matthew Avery Sutton, *Aimee Semple McPherson and the Resurrection of Christian America* (Cambridge, MA: Harvard University Press, 2007), 270.
2. Aimee Semple McPherson, *The Story of My Life* (Waco, TX: Word Books, 1973), 247.
3. This and the preceding four quotes from Minnie are from William Parker, "Mrs. Kennedy's Own Story Bares Row with Aimee," *Los Angeles Evening Herald*, July 16, 1928, 1.
4. Roberta Memoir Notes, Foursquare Archive, Los Angeles, 55.
5. Nancy Barr Mavity, *Sister Aimee* (Garden City, NY: Doubleday, Doran & Company, 1931), 317.
6. "Keyes Turns Philosophers Behind Bars," *Oroville Mercury-Register*, March 14, 1930, 1.
7. "Pomona Widow Regains Half of Oil Property," *Progress-Bulletin* (Pomona, CA), December 18, 1963, 1.
8. Nancy Barr Mavity, "Texas Guinan Talks Over 'Sister Aimee,' New Role, With Biographer," *Oakland Tribune*, October 1, 1933, 2.

BIBLIOGRAPHY

BIOGRAPHIES

Blumhofer, Edith L. *Aimee Semple McPherson: Everybody's Sister.* Grand Rapids, MI: William B. Eerdmans Publishing Company, 1993.

Cox, Raymond. *Aimee: The Life Story of Aimee Semple McPherson.* Los Angeles: Foursquare Publications, 1979.

Epstein, Daniel Mark. *Sister Aimee: The Life of Aimee Semple McPherson.* Boston: Mariner Books, 1993.

Goben, John D. *"Aimee": The Gospel Gold Digger.* New York: Peoples Publishing Company, 1932.

Krist, Gary. *The Mirage Factory: Illusion, Imagination, and the Invention of Los Angeles.* United States: Crown, 2018.

Lately, Thomas. *Storming Heaven: The Lives and Turmoils of Minnie Kennedy and Aimee Semple McPherson.* New York: William Morrow and Company, 1970.

———. *Vanishing Evangelist: The Aimee Semple McPherson Kidnapping Affair.* New York: Viking Press, 1959.

Mavity, Nancy Barr. *Sister Aimee.* Garden City, NY: Doubleday, Doran & Company, 1931.

Sutton, Matthew Avery. *Aimee Semple McPherson and the Resurrection of Christian America.* Cambridge, MA: Harvard University Press, 2007.

AUTOBIOGRAPHIES

Crowley, Aleister. *Confessions of Aleister Crowley.* New York: Penguin Books, 1989.

McPherson, Aimee Semple. *In the Service of the King: The Story of My Life.* New York: Boni and Liveright, 1927.

———. *The Story of My Life.* Waco, TX: Word Books, 1973.

———. *This Is That: Personal Experiences, Sermons and Writings of Aimee Semple McPherson, Evangelist.* Los Angeles: Echo Park Evangelistic Association, 1919.

———. *This Is That: Personal Experiences, Sermons and Writings of Aimee Semple McPherson, Evangelist.* Los Angeles: Echo Park Evangelistic Association, 1923.

INDIRECT HISTORICAL SOURCES

Adamic, Louis. "Los Angeles! There She Blows!" *Outlook,* August 13, 1930.

Ahlstrom, Sydney E. *A Religious History of the American People.* New Haven, CT: Yale University Press, 2004.

Artman, Amy Collier. *The Miracle Lady: Kathryn Kuhlman and the Transformation of*

Charismatic Christianity. Grand Rapids, MI: William. B. Eerdmans Publishing Company, 2019.

Bowler, Kate. *The Preacher's Wife: The Precarious Power of Evangelical Women Celebrities.* Princeton, NJ: Princeton University Press, 2019.

Braude, Ann. *Sisters and Saints: Women in American Religion.* New York: Oxford University Press, 2007.

Brekus, Catherine A. *The Religious History of American Women: Reimagining the Past.* Chapel Hill: The University of North Carolina Press, 2007.

Butler, Anthea. *Women in the Church of God in Christ, Making a Sanctified World.* Chapel Hill: The University of North Carolina Press, 2007.

Davis, Margaret Leslie. *Rivers in the Desert: William Mulholland and the Inventing of Los Angeles.* New York: HarperCollins, 1993.

Davis, Mike. *City of Quartz: Excavating the Future in Los Angeles.* Brooklyn, NY: Verso Books, 2006.

Deverell, William. *Whitewashed Adobe: The Rise of Los Angeles and the Remaking of Its Mexican Past.* Berkeley: University of California Press, 2004.

Duling, Dennis C. *The New Testament: History, Literature, and Social Context.* 4th ed. Boston: Cengage Learning, 2002.

Griffith, R. Marie. *Born Again Bodies: Flesh and Spirit in American Christianity.* Berkeley: University of California Press, 2004.

Halberstam, David. *The Powers That Be.* New York: Open Road Media, 2012.

Hangen, Tona J. *Redeeming the Dial: Radio, Religion and Popular Culture in America.* Chapel Hill: The University of North Carolina Press, 2003.

Hindmarsh, D. Bruce. *The Evangelical Conversion Narrative: Spiritual Autobiography in Early Modern England.* New York: Oxford University Press, 2008.

Klein, Norman M. *The History of Forgetting: Los Angeles and the Erasure of Memory.* New York: Verso, 1997.

Luhrmann, T. M. *When God Talks Back: Understanding the American Evangelical Relationship with God.* New York: Vintage Books, 2012.

McDougal, Dennis. *Privileged Son: Otis Chandler and the Rise and Fall of the L.A. Times Dynasty.* Cambridge, MA: Perseus Books Group, 2001.

McWilliams, Carey. *Southern California: An Island on the Land.* (First published as *Southern California Country*, 1946.) Layton, UT: Gibbs Smith, 2010.

Nelson, Douglas. "For Such a Time as This: The Story of Bishop William J. Seymour and the Azusa Street Revival; A Search for Pentecostal/Charismatic Roots." Thesis, University of Birmingham, 1981.

Ortiz, Paul. *Emancipation Betrayed: The Hidden History of Black Organizing and White Violence in Florida from Reconstruction to the Bloody Election of 1920.* Berkeley: University of California Press, 2006.

Quinn, Anthony. *The Original Sin: A Self Portrait.* Boston: Little, Brown and Co., 1972.

Rayner, Richard. *A Bright and Guilty Place: Murder, Corruption, and L.A.'s Scandalous Coming of Age.* New York: Anchor Books, 2009.

Shirk, Adrian. *And Your Daughters Shall Prophesy: Stories from the Byways of American Women and Religion.* Berkeley, CA: Counterpoint Press, 2017.

Siegel, Barry. *Dreamers and Schemers: How an Improbable Bid for the 1932 Olympics Transformed Los Angeles from Dusty Outpost to Global Metropolis.* Berkeley: University of California Press, 2019.

Sitton, Tom, and William Deverell. *Metropolis in the Making: Los Angeles in the 1920s.* Berkeley: University of California Press, 2001.

Starr, Kevin. *Material Dreams: Southern California Through the 1920s.* New York: Oxford University Press, 1991.

Taves, Ann. *Fits, Trances & Visions: Experiencing Religion and Explaining Experience from Wesley to James.* Princeton, NJ: Princeton University Press, 1999.

Wacker, Grant. *Heaven Below: Early Pentecostals and American Culture.* Cambridge, MA: Harvard University Press, 2003.

Winston, Diane. *Red-Hot and Righteous: The Urban Religion of the Salvation Army.* Cambridge, MA: Harvard University Press, 1999.

ACKNOWLEDGMENTS

This book has been a long time in the making and I'm indebted to so many. I am so grateful to my editor, Jenna Johnson, who inherited this project during the pandemic and who spent several years helping me expand and deepen this into the book it was meant to be. I am deeply appreciative of my agent, Elyse Cheney, and her ongoing support of my work. Danny Hertz in particular immediately recognized the importance of Aimee's story, and he, along with Michelle Kroes, has helped me bring it into the world. Kit Rachlis was fundamental in helping me shape and build this story from the beginning. I had a number of excellent researchers who helped me with this book, so a huge thank-you to Jess Rohan as well as Tom Colligan and Tara Ellenberg. I am also so appreciative of the staff at the Los Angeles Public Library and the team at the UCLA Special Collections who assisted me over the years. Ken Brecher, before he passed away, was a champion of this story.

I have a huge sense of gratitude and appreciation for Steve Zeleny, the amazing and tirelessly cheerful archivist at the Foursquare Church, who has dealt with years upon years of emails from me, asking the most far-reaching and inane questions. His deep knowledge of the Foursquare history and personal faith have helped me understand and care for Aimee on a level that has felt fundamental to telling Aimee's story.

I am deeply grateful to the Leon Levy Center for supporting this project through its transformative biography fellowship program. There, I was lucky enough to have the insight and support of fellow biographers Kai Bird, Thad Ziolkowski, Bill Goldstein, Donald Brown, Julie Phillips, and Michelle Frank.

In my life I have many smart friends and colleagues who have read pages and drafts over the years. In no particular order, they include Amy Wallace, Deirdre Debruyn-Rubio, Joey Fauerso, Dana Goodyear, Reza Aslan, Wendy Heller, Nicholas Lemann, Joel Stein, Lawrence Wright, Eva Payne, Kip Richardson, and Grace Johnson.

Finally, my close friends and family have been so encouraging of this project and so understanding of the amount of time it has taken me. Geoff, William, Yasmine, Kiana, Adriana, Alex, Tara, Catrin, Ortencia, Eva, Davis, Tommy, Tyler, Miles, and the Lisas—all helped me bring this to life in their own way. And my mom, who will always be the person who opened the door for me to the experience of faith and belief. My daughters, Josie and Vivian, did me the favor of having me tell them—many times—Aimee's story as they fell asleep at night. Their interest and fascination in this woman convinced me that Aimee was a figure who deserved to be integrated and elevated into the complex evolving tapestry that is American history. Finally and most importantly, my husband, Ben, has given me Minnie-level support on this project, encouraging me, cheering me on, reading drafts, lining up future readers, and believing always in my abilities.

INDEX

A NOTE ABOUT THE AUTHOR

Claire Hoffman is the author of the memoir *Greetings from Utopia Park* and a journalist reporting for national magazines on culture, religion, celebrity, business, and other subjects. She was a staff reporter for the *Los Angeles Times* and *Rolling Stone*. She is a graduate of UC Santa Cruz and has an MA in religion from the University of Chicago and an MA in journalism from Columbia University. She serves on the boards of the Columbia School of Journalism, ProPublica, and the Brooklyn Public Library.